How to See Europe on 50¢ A Day

THE AUTHOR IN TRAMP ATTIRE.

(From a Photograph taken in St. Petersburg.)

How to See Europe on 50¢ A Day

A Tramp's Trip

Lee Meriwether

Skyhorse Publishing

Skyhorse Publishing books may be purchased in bulk at special
discounts for sales promotion, corporate gifts, fund-raising, or
educational purposes. Special editions can also be created to
specifications. For details, contact the Special Sales Department,
Skyhorse Publishing, 555 Eighth Avenue, Suite 903, New York, NY
10018 or info@skyhorsepublishing.com.

www.skyhorsepublishing.com

10 9 8 7 6 5 4 3 2 1

Library of Congress Cataloging-in-Publication Data

Meriwether, Lee, 1862-1966.
How to see Europe on fifty cents a day : a tramp's trip / Lee
Meriwether.
p. cm.
ISBN 978-1-60239-667-8
1. Europe--Description and travel. 2. Meriwether, Lee,
1862-1966--Travel--Europe. 3. Europe--Social life and customs--19th
century. 4. Americans--Travel--Europe--History--19th century. 5.
Travelers--Europe--Biography. 6. Tramps--Europe--Biography. 7.
Adventure and adventurers--Europe--Biography. 8. Travelers'
writings,
American. I. Title.
D919.M55 2009
914.04'559--dc22
2009001393

Printed in China

TO

THE DEAREST OF MOTHERS AND FATHERS

This Book is Dedicated

BY

AN AFFECTIONATE SON

PREFACE.

The first-class tourist may see the beauties of a country's landscapes and scenery from the window of a palace-car, but his vision goes no further—does not penetrate below the surface. To know a country one must fraternize with its people, must live with them, sympathize with them, win their confidence.

High life in Europe has been paid sufficient attention by travellers and writers. I was desirous of seeing something of low life; I donned the blouse and hobnailed shoes of a workman, and spent a year in a "Tramp Trip" from Gibraltar to the Bosporus. Some of my experiences have been related in letters to the New York *World*, the Philadelphia *Press*, the St. Louis *Republican*, and other American newspapers, and in my official report to the United States Bureau of Labor Statistics, Department of the Interior, Washington, D. C., on the condition of the laboring classes in Europe. While the following pages contain some of those newspaper letters, the greater portion is now in print for the first time.

The reader may possibly not care to make the experiment himself, yet the perusal of how another travelled on fifty cents a day may not prove altogether uninteresting.

LEE MERIWETHER.

St. Louis, *September*, 1886.

PREFACE TO THE FOURTH EDITION.

A FOURTH edition affords opportunity to answer a question put by a number of readers of "A Tramp Trip:"

"Would not bicycling be preferable to tramping?"

Yes—and yet, No.

Generally speaking, the roads in Western Europe are smooth and well paved; if the traveller does not object to occasional steep hills, he will say they are admirably adapted for bicycling. But he who is induced by consideration of good roads to take his wheel must lay aside his ideas of economy. Moreover, he must not expect to gain that intimate acquaintance with the people which it is the fortune of the tramp tourist to obtain. As a tramp, with a modest bag on your back, you will be taken for an itinerant journeyman or peddler, and as such can fraternize and live with the peasants and people. The rider of a bicycle, however, if not mistaken by the simple peasants for some strange sort of animal, will at any rate be looked on as a *tourist*, and will be treated accordingly. Obviously in Switzerland, on account of the mountains, and in some Eastern countries, as Turkey and Bulgaria, on account of the sand, bicycling is out of the question.

It was my custom to arise at five o'clock, drink a pint

of goat's milk, and walk ten miles. At nine o'clock, after breakfast and a short rest, the tramp was resumed. I passed the time from noon until the cool of the afternoon under a tree, reading, writing, or perhaps sleeping. Then, fresh and vigorous, I started again, stopping only at night on finding a suitable lodging-place. In this way, without any feeling of hurry or fatigue, I made twenty-five or thirty miles a day, and saw all of the country that was to be seen.

The bicycler might go faster, but he would see less; so my advice is—leave your wheel at home and walk.

LEE MERIWETHER.

ST. LOUIS, *March*, 1887.

How to See Europe on 50¢ A Day

CONTENTS.

CHAPTER XXVI.

CHAPTER XXVII.

CHAPTER XXVIII.

HOW TO SEE EUROPE ON FIFTY CENTS A DAY.

CHAPTER I.

THE STEERAGE TO NAPLES.

ENTERING the office of the Florio - Rubatino Steamship Line in New York one Saturday morning, I inquired the rate of passage to Naples.

"One hundred and thirty dollars," replied the polite young man behind the desk.

"Have you not a cheaper rate?"

"Second cabin, ninety dollars."

"But your cheapest rate?"   ·

The young man looked at me.

"You do not wish steerage, do you?"

"Certainly."

"Phew!" and the polite young man whistled. "You are aware the steerage is no paradise?"

"At any rate I wish to learn for myself."

"Very well. The cost is twenty-five dollars."

A few moments later I received my ticket—a large piece of yellow paper, with the picture of a ship and a lot of Italian on it—and hurried to my hotel to complete preparations for the departure of the steamer, to take place that same day at noon.

A half hour sufficed to divest myself of the modish raiment

which, taken in connection with a steerage passage, had so surprised the ticket-clerk, and in its place a slouch hat, a coarse flannel shirt, and a heavy sack-coat, warm and compact around the body, was substituted. A knapsack strapped over the back held all the baggage needed; and thus equipped, with scarcely more impedimenta than a lady has in shopping, I sauntered down to the Wall Street ferry, crossed over to Brooklyn, and walked up the gangway of the *Independente* just as the last bells were ringing and the last good-bys were being said.

What a scene was that on the wharf the last half hour before sailing! A crowd of men, women, and children, some staggering under huge bundles of clothing and bedding that they were bringing on board; others collecting skillets and pans and bundles tied in red handkerchiefs — all hurrying and skurrying around like a swarm of disturbed bees.

Some of the passengers were men bearded like the pard, but this did not prevent their fellow-laborers, who had come to see them off, from giving them showers of kisses. One of the ship's scullions—a particularly grimy and greasy looking fellow—stood on the wharf until the last moment, talking with a friend equally grimy and greasy. As the last bell rang, the scullion and his piratical-looking friend affectionately embraced, took a mouthful of farewell kisses, and the last I saw of them they were blowing kisses at each other across the water as the steamer slowly glided from her moorings and started on her long journey across the sea.

The ticket-agent told the truth. The steerage of an Italian steamer is not a paradise. The bunks are in the hold in the forepart of the ship, in rows like shelves, one about three feet above the other. Lanterns hung from the ceiling give just enough light to make visible the rude beds and their dirty, picturesque occupants. Among the crowd of returning emigrants I noted two young girls. Both were handsome—dark olive complexions, sparkling black eyes. Slumbering peacefully, their arms thrown around under the head, supple figures in pretty postures, they seemed out of place in that semi-dark room, with the stalwart forms of men and women of every description around them. They did not seem to mind it, but slept as calmly as if in a grotto of roses. Habit is wellnigh all-powerful. Accustomed to a private chamber, the first night or two in that strange place, those curious characters around me, my eyes closed in sleep less than an hour. The third night an hour's pacing to and fro on deck before retiring overcame such squeamishness, and I slept soundly.

A life on the ocean wave is, all things considered, rather monotonous. The first day out the sea-sick passenger groans and wails, and fears he will die. The next day he fears he *won't* die. After this he is all right, gets his sea legs on, and develops an enormous appetite. At eight in the morning a big bell strikes, and a black-bearded Italian shouts, "Colazione!" which means breakfast of black coffee and bread. At one o'clock there are two bells, the black-bearded Italian cries "Pranzo!" and the emigrant is served with macaroni or potato stew, bread, and red wine. At night the Italian cries "Cena" intead of "Pranzo," and there is more bread and black coffee. This regimen will certainly not produce gout or kindred ailments; it is, however, as good as can be expected, considering that the three weeks' board and lodging, together with five thousand miles transportation, costs only twenty-five dollars.

For the first few days after leaving New York we did not receive any visits from the cabin—first-class passengers get seasick as well as immigrants. After about a week, though, we received a call from a Boston dude, who looked at the steerage in a very supercilious manner, probably with a view to enhance his importance with the young lady he was escorting. They had been studying an Italian phrase-book, and dosed every immigrant they met with "Come State," or "Buon Giorno," or something else equally as original. Passing my bunk, as I lay studying an Italian grammar, the dude said to me in his blandest manner,

"Ah, my good fellow, parlate Inglese?" (Do you speak English?)

I gave him a blank stare, shrugged my shoulders, and replied,

"Non parlo Inglese." (I do not speak English.)

"What a peculiar-looking Italian," murmured the young lady.

"Yes," responded the dude, "he speaks the southern patois. He comes from Sicily;" and the Boston couple went on their way discussing "that peculiar Italian."

On the night of the thirteenth day we entered the Strait of Gibraltar. The moon was shining brightly. Here and there flitted a sail across the water. The sombre coast of Africa lay a few miles to our right, on the left were the hills of Spain, and in front—miles in front—was the rock of Gibraltar, jutting abruptly fifteen hundred feet above the sea—a scene for a poet or a painter! It was midnight before the vessel came to under the frowning English guns, and that enchanting scene gave way to bunks and dreams and sleep. Six o'clock next morning found us on our way for a stroll through the narrow lanes and crooked alleys of Gibraltar. The English soldiers, and their flaming coats and brimless caps that set perched on the back of their skulls, letting the nose burn red as fire; the miles of galleries that honeycomb the prodigious rock; the one-hundred-ton guns; the Arabs with their blankets and naked legs and villanous faces—all were duly admired and stared at, and then at two in the afternoon, the steamer having taken on coal, the voyage into the Mediterranean was begun.

Two days out from Gibraltar a little girl, the child of immigrants returning to their home in sunny Italy, died. They were poor, and there were other children, but the misery in that mother's face spoke to the dullest heart. The little thing was buried in the sea at eleven o'clock at night. The ceremony was short and simple: a few words over the box by the captain, the steerage passengers standing by with solemn faces; the mate counts one—two—three, a splash in the water, and all is over.

There was a man in St. Louis once—Professor Donaldson,

the æronaut—who went up in a balloon and was never heard of afterwards. His body was never found. The last seen of him was near the frontier of Canada, in his balloon, floating towards the icy regions of the north. With the exception of this mode of death, this floating off into space, severing absolutely every tie with mother-earth and leaving not even a corpse to tell the story—with this exception, a burial in the sea seems the most terrible, the most like annihilation. *do not agree*

Mark Twain relates that when he walked into a Marseilles restaurant, and attempted to give his order in French, the waiter laughed at him and began to talk English. Since then everybody else who writes about a European trip gets up something similar. This is all a joke. It reads well enough in a humorous book, but the American who believes it, and who goes to Marseilles expecting to talk English, will have to live on short rations. At the restaurants there are signs like this:

HERE ONE SPEAKS ENGLISH

---

which means simply that when you go there " one " speaks English, and you are that one ; the rest speak French, and you must follow suit or not parlez at all.

Queer things in Marseilles are the vehicles and horses. The horses have their tails cut off, and are either extremely large or extremely small. One moment there passes a lady in a phaeton driving a pony the size of a large goat, the next moment a fellow in a blue blouse comes along with a cart and a troop of horses almost as large as elephants. The cart or dray is an enormous affair, fully forty feet long, and drawn sometimes by eight or ten of these powerful horses, all tandem, and on each horse a lot of bells and a collar surmounted by a curved leather cone a foot or eighteen inches high. These processions look very picturesque and very absurd.

After forty-eight hours in Marseilles, another two days' stop was made in Genoa. The prison of St. Andrea, in that city, interested me. Thirty years ago there was confined within its gloomy walls a Philadelphian, Henry Wikoff, or the " Chevalier Wikoff," as he was dubbed by the American press. The incidents leading to his incarceration in this Genoese prison form a peculiar and, at the same time, a ridiculous story. Wikoff, being left heir when a young man to a considerable property, set out on a jaunt with Forrest the actor. They bought a carriage and rode through Russia in the most romantic style, Forrest occasionally dropping into tragedy, and scaring the wits out of the simple natives. Finally they brought up in London, where Wikoff met a Miss Gamble. Fifteen years later, when again in London, this time a man of thirty-five or forty, he saw Miss Gamble, made her an offer of marriage, was accepted, and the day for the ceremony appointed. The day before the marriage was to have taken place, the expectant bridegroom received a note from his betrothed announcing her intention of going to Italy instead of getting married. Wikoff was astounded, and set out post-haste for Italy. At Genoa he overtook his runaway betrothed, and learning that she was to go to the English consul to have her passport *viséd*, he bribed her coachman to drive to his hotel instead of to the consulate's. She went, was ushered into Wikoff's parlors, and was there confronted by her indignant lover with a demand for an explanation. Her surprise over, Miss Gamble coolly laughed, said it was only a caprice, and repledged herself to go through with the marriage. An hour later, leaving Wikoff's hotel, she lodged a complaint of abduction against him; the unlucky Romeo was waltzed off to jail, and after a long trial and a narrow escape from a ten years' sentence to the galleys, was sentenced to fifteen months in the prison of St. Andrea. In a curious and interesting book called " My Courtship and its Consequences," published in 1855, Wikoff gives an account of his extraordinary love affair. For fifteen months he endured the horrors of an Italian prison, augmented in 1854 by a small-pox epidemic among the prisoners. In the damp, stone-paved room where he spent those weary months is his name, which he scratched on the wall thirty years ago. This is the only relic of the affair left, for in the Sardinian war with Austria, in 1859, the registers and other books of the prison were destroyed. St. Andrea is in the heart of the city, and although on an elevation, is surrounded by such tall buildings that the sunlight never enters the windows of its thick walls.

A very striking feature in Genoa are the policemen—not striking with their clubs, but in their personal appearance. They look more like capitalists or retired bankers than policemen. They wear silk hats, their overcoats are cut in the latest Newmarket style, and the silver-headed walking-canes which they sport would do credit to Broadway millionaires. They are, physically, splendid-looking men, and present a sharp contrast to the soldiers and gendarmes that lounge about Marseilles. The French some years ago were compelled to lower the standard of height in their army. A Frenchman in Marseilles six feet tall is a curiosity; there are scarcely enough of them to whip a small company of Chinese.

A few minutes before pulling out of Genoa there was a great bustle in the cabin. The waiters rushed backward and forward getting easy-chairs, arranging cushions, and spreading awnings. This commotion was on account of Baron Rothschild, of Vienna, who, with his wife, secretary, and a retinue of servants, was on his way to Sicily, thence to Corfu and the Grecian Isles. The famous financier is a cadaverous-looking man, sallow and sickly. The baroness, his first cousin, also his wife, atones for the baron's lack of charms. She has a commanding presence, fine features and form, and a gracious, winning manner.

As an offset to this increase to the cabin passenger list, a company of soldiers and a lot of convicts on their way to some island dungeon were taken into the steerage at Leghorn. They were heavily chained in couples, and again all together by one long chain fastened to their feet. Except at meal-times, when the right hand was freed, they remained in this miserable condition, unable to sleep themselves, and preventing others from sleeping by the horrible clanking of their fetters.

The last week of the voyage in the Mediterranean passes like a dream. The vessel sails along the Spanish coast within full view of old Moorish castles and modern light‑houses, passes near the Château d'If, Monte Cristo's prison, on by Corsica and Elba, places of Napoleon's birth and exile, and at last, on the morning of the twenty-second day, glides into the beautiful bay of Naples.

CHAPTER II.

PEDESTRIANISM creates a tremendous appetite. I became aware of this fact about two hours after I had landed, and set out through the labyrinthian streets of Naples on a search for a lodging-place. Without waiting to lay aside my knapsack, I stepped into one of the numerous cheap eating-shops and ordered five cents' worth of the celebrated Neapolitan "*maccaroni al pomi d'oro*," that is, macaroni cooked with butter and tomatoes.

It was about noon, and the damp, smoky room was filled with laborers and mechanics eating their mid-day meal. My costume and general appearance were quite in keeping with the cheapness and dinginess of the place, but not so, unfortunately, with my Italian. From my broken accent they at once knew I was a foreigner, and the jolly, good-hearted fellows stared at me with curiosity. What was an "Inglese" (Englishman — they do not discriminate between Englishmen and Americans)—what was an Inglese doing in such a garb and in such a restaurant? What did I want? Where was I going? etc. My neighbor at the table, a little bolder or a little more inquisitive than the rest, put these questions, and I answered them, seemingly to his pleasure and satisfaction.

"Il signore non è Inglese ma Americano" (the signore is not English, but American), he said to his companions, "from the country, you know, whither Giuseppe went last year, and where, blessed be our Lady, he sells so much fruit and does so well—è vero—it is true that you come from that distant land?"

I assured him that I did, that in fact I had but just landed, and this seemed to heighten his interest and admiration. He

was foreman-mason on a new building erecting in the neighborhood, and after finishing the macaroni I accepted his invitation to go to the building and look at his men working.
It was interesting.   Instead of having a ton of brick or stones
shot up at once on a steam-elevator as an American would do,
the stones were brought up block by block on the backs of
little boys.   When one block of stone is laid, the mason whis-
tles, or meditates, or looks at the scenery while the boy is gone
for another block.

In Italian cities the higher up the room the higher the rent;
for the streets are very narrow, and only the upper floors receive sunlight.   My friend the foreman, who asked me to stop
with him, had a large family, and he mentioned that fact by
way of apology as he stopped before an open door in one of
the narrow, crooked streets, and showed me that his room was
on the ground-floor.   With his large family he was not able
to rent a room higher up.

In the centre of the room was a pan of smoking embers;
near by sat a little girl knitting, and with her feet rocking a
cradle.   A dog in one corner was suckling a kid—the poor
thing is not allowed to have its mother's milk, that being re-
served for the family or sold in the market.   A piece of salt
pork was hanging from one of the rafters, and as we entered,
the foreman's wife was on the point of cutting a slice to fry
with the artichokes—a dish much relished by those who can
afford it.

"Il signore è un Americano," said the husband, smiling, and
pointing to me, as if showing off a dime museum curiosity;
"he comes from his country to find out what we have and how
we live.   He stays with us to-night."

The wife bustled up to me with a "ben venuto [welcome],
signore," the children crowded around to stare, and another
slice of bacon was cut and two extra artichokes put in the pan.
The foreman went out and returned with a bottle of wine, the
little girl bought two pounds of macaroni with half a franc
that I gave her, and in about an hour the family with their

guest sat down to as jolly a repast as could be found in all Italy.

The Italian laborer usually retires early, but in honor of the visit of a " real live American " late hours were kept, the time being spent in discussing the customs of the country.

What most strikes a stranger is the crowded condition of the masses. A whole family, consisting of parents and sometimes five to ten children, live in one room—a room stone paved, damp, and, even if looking on a street, surrounded by such high walls that the sunlight scarcely ever enters its portals. During the day, the beds that at night, perhaps, cover every inch of the floor, are rolled up and piled in one corner, leaving the bedroom to serve as a workshop for the father and the family.

A marvellous degree of economy is practised even in the smallest details. Coffee-grounds from the wealthy man's kitchen are dried and resold to the poor. In a similar way oil is twice and sometimes three times used, the drippings after each successive frying being gathered from the pan and sold to the poor. Old shoes, hats, clothes, candle - ends, dried coffee-grounds, " second-hand " oil, and a hundred other articles are spread out upon the broad stones of the Piazza, or square of a town, and it is here to a great extent that the Italian workman procures his supplies. A laborer's suit, consisting of breeches, jacket, vest, shirt, socks, necktie, and shoes, costs anywhere from $4.45 up. His food is as simple as his clothing and his habitation. In the morning a great loaf of black bread is passed around; each member of the family gouges out a piece of the inside, until finally only the hard crust is left. At noon this crust is eaten, softened by a little wine. A plate of macaroni costing two or three cents finishes the bill of fare. At night more macaroni, then the beds or pallets are spread and the family goes to sleep, to get up and go through the same routine on the morrow.

The rent of one of these rooms is from ten to twelve dollars per year; the cost of the macaroni, wine, and bread is about ten cents per day for each person; but even at this cheap rate of living the workman who has a family often finds it difficult to make both ends meet. A skilled bricklayer averages only two lire and a half (fifty cents) a day.

All this and much more my host told me, and then unrolling a straw mattress on the floor, we said good-night and retired. The next morning, as we had all slept in one room together, so we jumped into our clothes together. The foreman's wife and eldest daughter, a comely lass of thirteen or fourteen, did not have much toilet to make, simply slipping their light-colored gowns over their heads and lacing the corset they wear around the waist, on the outside of the dress; this little they did without minding in the slightest the presence of a masculine stranger.

Nothing is so apt to confirm our belief in republican institutions as a view, first of the palaces, then of the hovels, of Italy. The king's palace in Naples is magnificent; its art collections and decorations and furnishings are the finest that human ingenuity and skill can provide; but as I walked through its gilded saloons and softly carpeted galleries, I could not help thinking of the hovel of my friend the foreman. What privations and squalor do the masses endure that kings and nobles may revel in ease and luxury.

CHAPTER III.

THE Bay of Naples forms a crescent. Naples is at one horn, at the other, nine miles to the south, is Mount Vesuvius.

The ascent of the mountain is very easy if one have a pocketful of money. For five dollars a carriage takes the traveller to the inclined railway-station, seven miles from Naples; for another five dollars the railroad takes him to the summit of the old cone; he is then passed on to guides and "strap-bearers" and "chair-carriers" and "stick-renters," and so forth, and so on, who carry him to the crater without the slightest personal inconvenience. The stick-renter charges for the use of his stick, the strap-bearer for his strap, the chair-carrier for his muscle and chair, and altogether, one hundred and sixty lire will hardly more than cover the trip. With such figures how is a poor man to ascend Vesuvius?

The problem was a difficult one, but I attempted its solution. Relieving my knapsack early one morning of its few changes of underclothing, its one or two books, and the pads of writing-paper that constitute a pedestrian's outfit, I substituted a bottle of wine, several pones of bread, some cheese and figs, and accompanied by a chance travelling companion picked up in Naples, set out on foot for the famous volcano.

For six miles the way lies along the bay, on easy, level ground; then a gradual ascent begins, and after another six miles the tourist finds himself at the foot of the cone, three thousand feet above his starting-point. After the village of Resina is passed, all vegetation is left behind, and the tramp is through a vast field of lava, the picture of barrenness and desolation — no verdure, no fertility, not even a twig, only lava and ashes, a forerunner of the cone which still remains to be scaled, a steep mountain of soft ashes.

It rises at an angle of thirty degrees—it seems ninety. The ashes, soft and penetrating, permeate the clothing, get down the boot-legs, are blown in the face, ears, and eyes. Hour after hour I toiled up that steep ascent, sinking to my knees in the loose ashes, taking two steps up and sliding down one, until I began to think that our task of climbing Vesuvius greater than Hercules's twelve labors combined. When about half the way up we entered a rain-storm, and for the rest of the journey were enveloped in mist and cloud. By the time we had achieved the summit night had set in, and the rain had given place to snow. I was cold and miserable. After all this effort and fatigue was there to be no view? no glimpse at the crater? I determined to investigate the possibility of getting quarters for the night with the man who stays in the little shanty built at the base of the crater, attending the upper end of the railroad.

"Do you sleep here?" I inquired.

"Yes," answered the man, after a pause; "but why do you ask?"

"Oh, nothing, only I was thinking it must be rather lonely. I will stay with you to-night, though, if you like. I am in no hurry to return to town before to-morrow."

A younger bird might have been caught by such chaff. This Italian, however, had been too long in the business.

"Young fellow," he said, "if you want to stay up here you can, but not until you have paid me ten lire."

Ten lire—two dollars! I saw at once that he mistook me for a duke, and to undeceive him I offered "una mezza lira"—ten cents—for his accommodations. There was considerable haggling; I was compelled to raise on my ten cent offer, but the Italian came down from his two dollar demand, and at last we struck a compromise on one lira—twenty cents. Immediately on striking this bargain I spread on the floor the quilt which my host gave me, and after leaving directions to be called in case the storm should abate, lay down for a little rest and sleep. It was midnight before I was awakened from my dreams. The Italian was tapping me on the shoulder.

" Wake, signore; the snow stopped, you get fine view. You go to crater, you see lava and fire."

It was a starless night, inky black, our hands scarcely visible before our faces, but there was no difficulty in finding the way. The roaring and rumbling of the volcano, and the lurid glare that shot forth every few seconds from the summit, beckoned on far better than any guide. When at last the brink of the crater was reached, its working was visible to perfection.

The thousands who use the simile, " standing over a volcano," can never appreciate its full meaning unless they have actually stood over a volcano as we stood that dark night, looking down into the huge caldron of boiling lava, watching the fiery mass as it seethed and steamed and came hissing through the fissures in the mountain's sides. Until far in the night we watched that terrible sight, and listened to the rumbling and roaring that seemed to come from the very bowels of the earth. The scene, standing at midnight on that volcanic peak, a world of blackness around us, was awe-inspiring. I took no note of time, and was only called to myself by an event that nearly proved my quietus. While gazing into the fiery sea of lava, there was a terrific rumbling, followed by a shower of red-hot stones which flew in every direction, missing us, as it seemed, only by a miracle. The second eruption followed after an interval of less than a minute, but even in that short time we had descended, rolling and leaping, at least three hundred feet down the side of the cone. The situation was big with danger. On the one side was an impenetrable mist; a mountain of fire was on the other. The eruptions continued, and the sky was still illumined by the showers of burning stones, some of which fell dangerously near. My companion was struck on the arm by one of the smaller missiles—perhaps one of the smallest— and although not seriously injured, received a very bad burn.

Even when out of reach of the fiery hail our course was by

no means easy. The whole summit of Vesuvius is composed of recent eruptions of lava, much of it scarcely cooled. To pick a way across this at mid-day is no easy matter; at midnight, covered by clouds, the chances of stepping on a place not sufficiently hardened, and of breaking through into some sulphurous pit, are dangerously great. It was not until after an hour's slow and painful walking that we found our way back to the low room and sank exhausted upon the floor.

The Italian government has taken possession of the excavated city of Pompeii. A law recently enacted strictly forbids strangers entering or remaining after sunset. I was anxious to see the ruins by moonlight, and resolved to spend a night in that resurrected city of the Romans, the law to the contrary notwithstanding. The preceding night had been spent on Mount Vesuvius, and early in the morning I arose from my lofty couch and descended the side of the mountain towards Pompeii along the same route that the lava and ashes took eighteen hundred years ago, when the unfortunate city was buried. The earth excavated from Pompeii has been thrown around the city, making a wall twenty or twenty-five feet high. The only entrance is through a gate with a revolving stile, where the visitor pays forty cents admission.

Pompeii is a wonderful place. The old inhabitants, subjects of the Emperor Titus, are still there—there in glass cases, in the very postures in which they died eighteen centuries ago. In the court-yard of one house is still standing a pedestal bearing a bust of the owner of the house—Cornelius Rufus. It has been there two thousand years, and is as good as new except for a little piece of the nose which has been chipped off. Even with this defective nose one can see what manner of man Cornelius was—a rather handsome fellow, with benevolent aspect. I dare say, when he came in in a hurry, he used often to throw his toga or hat over this very bust.

Towards set of sun, worn out with wandering among the curious ruins and relics of the dead past, I sought a place wherein to rest and wait the rising of the moon. In the Temple of Isis still stands the altar where the Pompeiian priests once delivered oracles to the credulous people. The statue head, whence issued the oracles, stands now, as it then stood, on a pedestal, under which the cunning priests had hidden themselves. Into this silent and secret place I crawled, refreshed myself with a luncheon from my knapsack, and lay down to rest. The descent from Vesuvius and the day's sightseeing proved too much for me. I sank into a sleep, not deep, but disturbed by dreams of things long dead and gone. I saw old pagan priests talking through the sculptured head to humbug the ignorant worshippers. I saw the gaping crowd of women and men, with faces of awe and reverence, receiving the lying oracles; then suddenly, as it seemed, a man of grave and reverend aspect, with long, flowing beard and long hair, confronted the deceiving priests, and with commanding gestures ordered them away and overturned the oracle head, which fell with a crash amid the pagans' cries and shouts.

I started up wildly, so vivid was the scene. I found myself in darkness, the sound of rough voices were shouting near by; I could not at first realize where I was.

"Ahime — diavolo — lui è qui!" (The d—l, here he is!), shouted the rough voices. Then a man with a lantern poked his head into the place and threw a sudden light upon me. I was blinded and dazed. The man began talking Italian at me so rapidly that I became still more bewildered. Was I dead and in Hades? The brigandish-looking fellow with the lantern seized me fiercely, jerked me up and out of my hiding-place, and dragged me along to the gate of the city. Once in the open air, my dazed senses cleared and I began to take in the situation. A fierce-looking fellow with a bristling mustache and showy uniform went through my pockets and knapsack, and then I was escorted down the high-road to Portici, a village about seven miles distant, in the direction of Naples. There I was lodged in jail, and the next morning brought before an officer of justice, charged with the heinous crime of sleeping in the dead city of Pompeii. Putting on an innocent

air, I said in my best Italian that my intentions were not fe-
lonious, that I had taken nothing, that I had fallen asleep from
over-fatigue—Vesuvius, sight-seeing, and all that; and finally,
as no purloined relics were found upon me, I was let off with
a reprimand, and a warning not to do so again.

I discovered on a second visit that the stile through which
the visitor enters Pompeii registers each person passing in.
At sunset another stile registers the exits; exits and entrances
must tally.   On this eventful eve they did *not* tally, and so the
silent streets and houses of the dead were searched with the
result described.

CHAPTER IV.

THE little island of Capri is noted for its women, who possess a peculiar kind of beauty. They are as straight as arrows, have regular features, magnificent eyes, perfect teeth, dark, olive complexions, and straight, coal-black hair. Not a few English artists who go to Capri to paint, end by marrying their models and settling on the island for life. An American artist has been there twenty years. He has a wife and grown children who do not speak a word of English. I asked an artist who had been on the island only a few months, whether or not such marriages proved happy.

"As happy as any marriages," was the reply. "The artist comes with the intention of painting a few views and leaving with the summer. But there are so many views, and his model is so lovely, he concludes to finish out the year. By that time he has become enervated by the soft climate; he is no longer the pushing, energetic man of the North. His ambition has abated, he is content to paint just enough for a living. His sketches find a ready sale in London, he settles down, marries his model, and forgets, and is forgotten by, the world. There have been a dozen such cases, and will probably be a dozen more."

"Are you not afraid of drifting into it yourself?"

"I may—who knows? I have been here three months. I already feel myself weakening."

"Why do you stay, then?"

"Well, the views are fine—and the women."

A year afterwards I learned that he had married his model and settled in Capri for life.

The rocks of Capri jut abruptly from the sea to a height of two thousand feet. On one of these cliffs is still standing the villa and grotto where Tiberius performed those inhuman and atrocious deeds that startled the Roman world and live to this day in the pages of Tacitus. From this very rock the despot caused his victims to be cast one thousand nine hundred feet into the sea, where their dead bodies were mangled by the boatmen stationed there for that purpose. The salons that once witnessed the orgies of the Roman monster are now used as cow stables, only one room being left for human habitation—that on the extreme summit, occupied by a solitary hermit, a kindly-faced, simple-hearted man who spends the greater part of his life before an altar in the room where, perhaps, were worshipped in olden times the heathen gods of Rome. From the hermit's cell a charming view is obtained, not only of the whole island of Capri, but of the Ponza Islands, of Surrentum, of Naples, and of Vesuvius, smoking in the distance, seven or eight miles away.

As I stood watching the famous old volcano, the hermit entertained me with an account of the great eruption of 1872, which he had witnessed from his cell.

"The flames shot up for three days and nights," he said. "The rumbling and roaring was awful. A fiery stream of lava poured down the mountain. I fell on my knees and prayed for the safety of those below."

The good man's prayers were not altogether effectual; some forty persons were overtaken by the river of fiery lava and suffered a cruel death.

Looking down on Capri from this villa of Tiberius, the island presents the appearance of a vast natural amphitheatre. The steep mountain sides have been terraced, and every inch is under cultivation. These terraces are ten, fifteen, and twenty feet high, but from the lofty altitude of Tiberius's villa they seem scarcely a foot in height, and give one the idea of a great circular stair-way carpeted in green, leading from the bay to the top of the mountain. It is only when you descend, and are compelled to follow a stony, winding path, that you realize how high those terraces really are.   In coming down I tried to use them as steps, but after scrambling over the wall of one of the lowest, and nearly breaking my neck, I was glad to get back to the winding path again.

In Capri, streets of ten feet width are considered wide.   The usual width is about five feet.   Both sides are walled up in the town by high houses, and in the country by high garden walls.   Strolling through these narrow lanes made between the tall houses, you catch glimpses here and there of peasant life, of the women as they sit in their door-ways spinning, weaving, or combing the children's heads, and of the men as they puff their pipes, or lie sprawling on the ground snoring and sleeping the sleep of the lazy.

The streets are as steep as they are narrow ; they form so many troughs down which, even with an ordinary rain, the water rushes in torrents.   I was caught one afternoon in the upper part of the town by a sharp rain, and in a few minutes the road leading to my hotel, about a quarter of a mile off in a part of the town five hundred feet lower down, was converted into a rapid stream that would have run a good-sized mill. For an hour I waited hoping the rain would cease ; it did not, and I at length accepted the offer of a stalwart fellow to carry me down on his back.   I was thus brought into the hotel like a bag of potatoes or turnips.   I weigh a full hundred and fifty pounds, but that is no load for the stalwart men of Capri, accustomed all their lives to hills and precipitous rocks.

Women carry on their heads one-hundred-pound sacks of flour, and with this burden can skip up the path from the sea to the Piazza—an elevation of six hundred feet—with as much rapidity as can a stranger with no encumbrances at all other than his own weight and clothing.   I have seen numbers of young girls in the western part of the island climbing up what seemed almost perpendicular bluffs with great stacks of grass on their heads.   They cut this grass at the foot and at the sides of the mountain, and carry it up for their goats and cows.   A goat gives a quart of milk a day which sells for four cents. To cut grass for only half a dozen goats is a hard day's work. It is plain, therefore, the Capri peasants cannot often become rich. Fortunately, living is cheap. The peasant builds his hut for himself out of loose stones; thus lodging he gets gratis. His black bread, macaroni, and occasional portion of cheese or pork, costs on an average eight cents a day.

One of the delights of Capri is its comparative freedom from tourists and beggars. Of the two it is hard to say which are the greater pests. The beggars you can get rid of, but the tourist is always there, opera-glass strapped over his shoulder and red-covered Baedeker* in hand. In my laborer's garb I was more than once mistaken for an Italian by the opera-glass, red-book people. One day on the Via Koma, in Naples, a man with a guide-book in his hand stopped me and addressed me in a peculiar kind of Italian that he had doubtless himself invented. He said, "Sono io sulla via alla stazione?"

I saw at once that he was English, that he did not understand ten words of Italian.

"Una, due, tre, quattro" (one, two, three, four), I began, rapidly counting in Italian.

"The d—l!" exclaimed the tourist, "what is this thick-headed fellow talking about? Stazione, signore, stazione—I want to go to the stazione."

"Cinque, sei, sette, otto" (five, six, seven, eight), I continued, and the Englishman, thinking I was complying with his request to direct him to the railway-station, got out a dictionary and asked me to speak more slowly. I said, "Wouldn't it be better to talk English?"

The man with the Baedeker and opera-glass wilted.

One day in Pompeii I saw a Dutchman standing out in the rain, an umbrella in one hand, the ever-present Baedeker in the other. For every glance he gave the ruins he gave two to his guide-book.

---

* A guide-book.

In Capri there is nothing of this. The light-hearted pedestrian can wander from one end of that little island to the other and see not a single beggar nor a single unpicturesque, landscape-marring, guide-book tourist.

During my stay in Naples I was not an early riser. A day's sight-seeing in that crooked place is not a little fatiguing, and one can easily lie abed mornings until eight or nine o'clock. On one particular Monday morning, however, five o'clock found me up and dressed, and on my way to the northern gate of the city, which leads into the Appian Way and to Rome. As I reached the gate the sun was just peeping above the hills that lie a few miles back of the city; the green gardens glistened with dew; all nature was bright with beauty and verdure.

I was told an acre of this land rents for thirty dollars a year. For an artist the scenery is worth a hundred times that sum; but it is not easy to see how the peasants, even with their thrift and economy, are able to clear thirty dollars net every year on each acre of ground. It is true their climate enables them to make two, and sometimes even three crops where we make only one; they, moreover, utilize every inch. I have seen peasants carrying earth in sacks to put on rocks and make fertile what before was barren. At distances of twenty-five or thirty feet trees are planted. The limbs of the trees serve as fuel, the trunks are used as supports for the grape-vines. These vines run on wires, ten or fifteen feet above the ground, from tree to tree. On the earth underneath is grown a crop of finnochio,* or asparagus, or berries. But with all this—with this double crop—one on terra firma, one in the air—thirty dollars still seems a high rent per year for an acre of ground.

Ordinarily it should not require more than eight days to walk from Naples to Rome. I would have made it in that time but for an adventure that befell me on the sixth day out from Naples.

It was about three o'clock one afternoon, in the heat of the

---

* A kind of coarse celery.

day. I had stopped under a tree on the roadside to rest and await the cool of the evening before continuing my journey. The heat, as also the fatigue of the long walk, produced a drowsy effect. Without further ceremony I whipped out my sleeping-bag, crawled into it, and drawing the mouth close around my neck, I laid my head on my knapsack and was soon fast asleep. My slumbers, however, were not to be undisturbed. I had slept hardly half an hour when there was a tugging at the bag, and I felt my feet seized by a stout hand and lifted from the ground.

"What in the mischief do you want?" I yelled in English, forgetting for the moment that I was in a foreign land.

There was a loud laugh, and my feet dropped to the earth again.

"Ah, un' uomo—it is then a man, not a devil," said a big, jolly-looking fellow, who did not seem to think it at all impudent to disturb one's sleep. He stood off a few paces, arms akimbo, grinning and staring at me.

"No, I am not a devil," I said, crawling out of my bag, "but it is enough to make one as mad as the devil, jerking one's ankles in that manner."

"No offence, signore," grinning and bowing, "no offence. I was just a bit curious; I couldn't make out what you were; I picked you up to see. Lei dorme in questo — you sleep in this?"

"Yes," I replied, recovering my temper — his good-nature was infectious—"I sleep in this bag to keep out the ants and bugs. But what are *you* doing here? Where are you going?"

It was on one of the loneliest parts of the Appian Way, near the beginning of the Pontine Marshes, where for a stretch of many miles there is not a single town or inn. The Italian's jolly face sobered. He hesitated before answering.

"Going?" he repeated; "oh, si, capisco—yes, signore, I am going to Tuscany. And you?"

"To Rome."

By this time I had folded my bag and put it in the knapsack, and we started off together. He was a sociable fellow. With the little English he happened to know (he said he had been a sailor and touched in English ports) and the bad Italian of which I was master, we managed nicely. I told the usual yarns foreigners like to hear about America—the large sums laborers receive, the wonderful size of the country, the four thousand miles of land between Maine and California; then the conversation came down to Italy and the Appian Way, and the business that brought me, solitary and alone, on that now unfrequented road.

"You no afraid of brigands?" he asked, in his broken English.

"Brigands? Of course not; there is no more of that sort of thing in Italy, is there?"

"I not know, but may be. Where you stay to-night?"

I had not thought about that. The Appian Way, where it runs through the Pontine Marshes, is very beautiful; the branches of a long line of tall trees planted on each side meet overhead and form a delightfully shaded arch; but there are no villages, no inns. To go back to the last town to sleep was out of the question.

"What are you going to do?"

"Ah, I show you. Come with me; I take you nice place."

I agreed, and we tramped forward. For several miles we continued on the main road, then, suddenly stopping short and looking up and down the Way, the Italian, with a brief gesture to follow, struck off rapidly through the forest. In ten minutes he had so wound around, and traced and retraced his course, that I was completely lost. To my question as to whither he was leading me, he only gave grins and grunts, and strode rapidly on. I had come so far, had lost myself, that there remained no choice but to follow him to the end. After two hours' tramping up and down through the trees and lowlands of the Marshes, he suddenly stopped, and turning around, said, abruptly,

"Signore, ho perduta la strada.—I am lost. I cannot find the way. We sleep here."

I was greatly disgusted, and a little alarmed. Was I not trusting too much to my dusty and travel-stained appearance? What if the fellow, despite my travelling on foot and my shabby looks, should imagine I had money? The loneliness of the place—almost in the centre of the Pontine Marshes, several miles from the road—gave me some uneasiness. I endeavored to console myself by looking at the Italian's jolly, good-natured face.

"At any rate," I thought, "there is no help for it now. I must make the best of it."

So, spreading my rubber coat on the ground, and getting into my bag, I lay down and endeavored to dispel thoughts of malaria, robbers, and brigands by dreams of home and loved faces thousands of miles across the sea, in far-off America. Thus musing, with an occasional word of reassurance from my companion, who had wrapped himself in his cloak and was lying a few yards away, I fell into a doze, and finally into a sound sleep.

I do not know how long I slept—perhaps only an hour, perhaps it may have been four or five hours—but it was still pitch dark when I heard voices and tramping of feet, and awoke to find a file of soldiers around me. My companion of the evening before was nowhere to be seen. The officer in command of the gendarmes spoke to me very rapidly, in a dialect I but imperfectly understood. I made no reply, whereupon two of the soldiers stepped to my side and took each an arm. Two others went in front as *avant couriers;* the rest followed in the rear.

Since the affair in the Portici jail, my taste for adventure in strange lands had given place to practical ideas of common-sense. I was deeply disgusted as I was marched along in the middle of the night by those soldiers, who could not explain whether they wanted to shoot or to hang me. We reached the Appian Way in about three-quarters of an hour. It was daybreak before a halt was called. To my vexation and disgust, I found I was in the very town I had left the preceding afternoon on beginning the journey through the Pontine Marshes. I was taken to the station, kept waiting an hour, and then conducted into a room where a very sour-looking individual scanned my face critically, and compared it with some photographs he held in his hand. The result was apparently not satisfactory. He frowned, handed the photographs to another official, pointed at me, and shook his head. The result of all which was, they gave me a breakfast and told me to go, which I was not slow in doing.

Later in the day I learned how the adventure came about. That jolly, good-natured Italian was no other than Luigi Cordonna, a brigand for whom the government had been looking for six or eight weeks. Two months before he had robbed a farmer in Sicily, near Messina, and then fled as far as Capua on the Via Appia. As I have related, he came near being nabbed in the Pontine Marshes. Getting me to sleep in that out-of-the-way place was an excellent scheme to throw suspicion on me and give him time to escape. It was doubtless my dilapidated appearance that saved me from his nimble fingers.

Having enough of the Appian Way, at least of that portion in the Pontine Marshes, I decided to finish the journey by rail. There was a station twelve miles across the country. I was fortunate enough to arrive there in time for the afternoon train. This time there were no brigands or gendarmes to delay the journey. I arrived in the Eternal City safe and sound.*

---

* In France the following winter a case occurred which would seem to indicate that to travellers leaving the beaten route such experiences as mine at Portici and on the Appian Way are by no means so uncommon as may be supposed. Mr. Stanley J. Weyman, a London barrister, was making a tour with his brother among the Pyrenees. On the way from Oloron to Pardeto they occupied an interior seat in the diligence, in the company of a sub-official of gendarmes. The officer chatted pleasantly with his fellow-travellers until Aramitz, a village seven miles from Oloron, was reached; there he suddenly dropped the rôle of fellow-passenger, donned his official dignity, and demanded the Englishmen's names and papers of identity. Mr. Weyman in his report says:

"Notwithstanding we at once gave our names, and that I on my part handed to him a passport issued by the Foreign Office, London, as well as a banker's letter of recommendation, he arrested us. It was in vain that I showed him we carried a considerable sum of money, and had besides a receipt for a large quantity of luggage then on its way to Biarritz; in vain, also, that we repeatedly stated to him we were British subjects. After being allowed to send a telegram to the vice-consul at Pau, we were taken—it being then 6 P.M.—to two cells which formed a wretched out-house adjoining the gendarmerie. These cells were mean in the extreme, with dirty, rough-cast walls, a stone floor, and no windows, but merely an unglazed aperture above the door. They were such places as would scarcely be used in England for dogs. Nevertheless, in these two cells we were severally locked up for thirteen hours (during which the doors were not opened), without light, fire, or any warming apparatus. It was freezing cold, and the night air entered by many apertures beside the large one over the door. Our knapsacks, as well as money, watches, and papers, having been taken from us, I had no protection against the excessive cold except two thin and frowsy coverings which formed the bedclothes. I suffered so greatly that I was compelled to spend the last three or four hours before daybreak in walking up and down the cell. During the whole night I was not able to obtain ten minutes' sleep. My brother, although he was in some degree protected by a railway rug, of which he had not been deprived, also suffered greatly from cold. We had offered to pay for accommodation at the hotel, but that was refused. Soon after 8 A.M. on the 15th (December, 1885), a telegram vouching for our respectability was received from the vice-consul at Pau, Mr. Musgrave Clay. Unfortunately, I then stated to the officer who had originally arrested us that we intended to complain of his conduct; he forthwith took us back to one of the cells, in which we again remained locked up for three hours. About noon we were permitted to eat some lunch outside in the sun.

"Between 1 and 2 P.M. we were taken on foot to Oloron, and during the greater part of the journey had to carry our baggage, the gendarmes threatening that if we did not do so they would handcuff us, and compel us to perform the journey in that fashion. This threat they enforced by preparing the chains and handcuffs. They had before in our presence ostentatiously loaded their revolvers. In this way we were conducted, a gendarme on either side of us, through several villages and a great part of the town of Oloron, in the presence of some hundreds of people.

"At Oloron we were charged before the Procureur with being without the necessary papers of identity, and as lying under the suspicion of being German spies. The Procureur, at sight of the vice-consul's telegram and our own papers, liberated us, but refused to grant us redress on the ground that neither my passport (not being *viséd* for France) nor my banker's letter (being printed instead of written) were sufficient evidence of identity to fulfil the law.   We were released at ten minutes to 6 P.M., after being twenty-five hours in custody, nine of which were subsequent to the receipt of the vice-consul's telegram."

The London *Times*, in its issues for December 21 and 22, 1885, contains all the details connected with this case, together with lengthy editorial comments.

CHAPTER V.

FROM my note-book I copy the following *Rules for Tramp Tourists:*

First : Look as shabby as possible.

I met one day among the ruins of Pompeii five Danes, students, men of educated families. They said they had not been approached by a single commissionaire since the day they had left Copenhagen. Why ? Because they looked shabby. They had walked all the way from the northern frontier of Germany, and were as tough a looking set as one could imagine. Worn boots, tattered garments, uncut hair, huge clubs in their hands—no wonder guides and hotel-runners avoided them. They were on their way to Palermo, Sicily, whence they intended returning home by steamer through the Mediterranean, the Strait of Gibraltar, and the North Sea.

Second : No matter whether or not you speak the language, to commissionaires, guides, cabmen, etc., feign absolute ignorance. It is the only method of ridding yourself of their importunities. Sometimes I put my finger to my ear and intimated by signs that I was deaf and dumb—it insured against further annoyance.

Third : If English or English-speaking, never let the fact be known. If possible pass for a German. German students have the very pleasant reputation of being extremely impecunious. If lucky enough to be taken for a German, you may be sure of bottom-rock prices. Englishmen, on the other hand, have the reputation of being rich, and given to all kinds of absurd freaks. You may dress in rags, and walk yourself into a condition of dilapidation worse than that of any professional tramp in America, but as soon as your nationality becomes known the game is up.

"Ah, Inglese!" exclaims the landlord or shopkeeper, and placidly proceeds to add thirty or forty per cent. to his charges. A marked diminution in prices is noticeable the greater the distance from England. Beginning with Sicily and the southern part of Italy, where first-class hotels only charge thirty to forty cents for rooms, the price increases little by little until in Belgium and Holland, countries immediately across the channel from England, sixty to eighty cents is charged by a second or third rate inn. In Italy and Switzerland servants do not expect fees of more than two or three cents. In Belgium and Holland, "Sixpence, if you please, sir," and the donation of a less amount produces a look of withering contempt from the haughty menial.

These rules, it must be observed, are given only with reference to shopkeepers, hotel padrones, and the like; they do not apply to the laborers and peasants. This class, unspoiled by pecuniary dealings with travellers, are hospitality and kindness itself. With laborers and peasants no careful bargaining is necessary; with the other classes mentioned it decidedly is necessary. Baedeker, the great guide-book man, advises his readers to give one-third of the price demanded. This would be good advice if it went far enough. The hotels and shopkeepers have learned of the advice given by Baedeker, and now ask *four* times as much as the article is worth, and as much as they will finally accept if pushed to the point. It would hardly be exaggeration to say that the man at the post-office who sells stamps is about the only man who does not expect a fee and does not have two prices for his goods. The stamp-man, for a wonder, asks always the same price for stamps— five cents for stamps (Italian, "franco-bolli") for foreign postage, four cents for letters within the kingdom, Sicily, and the other islands included. Does any one think this an overstatement of the case? Let us see. Take the railroads for an instance.

The fare from A to B will be advertised as, say, one dollar. You buy a ticket with the figures $1.00 stamped thereon. Do you pay only one dollar for your ticket? Not a bit of it. Hand the agent the exact amount the ticket on its face calls for, and he will calmly keep both money and ticket until there is forthcoming the few cents extra that is always charged by the railroad to help pay their taxes.

How is it with express and carrying companies? I had occasion when in Rome to send a package to Berlin.

"What is the charge?" I asked the express agent.

"Three lire" (sixty cents).

It so happened that an acquaintance, an Italian, had sent a similar package to the same destination, and I knew that he had paid but forty cents—two lire—so I said,

"Troppo caro—too dear, signore. I will give two lire."

"Ah, signore, impossible; two and a half?"

"No, two, not a centesime more."

"Due, solo due—only two? Ah, well, let me have it. It is little, but I will send it."

Imagine a customer haggling with the Adams Express Company about the tariff on a package from New York to Chicago!

This system is annoying, but with experience comes wisdom. And then the tricks of roguish shopkeepers are rather amusing than otherwise. I stepped up one day to one of the numerous lemonade stands that adorn the Piazzas of Italian cities, and said to the vendor,

"How much for lemonade?"

I knew very well the regular price was one cent per glass, but I wanted to play with the fellow. He looked at me sharply, calculating how green I was and how much I could stand.

"Cinque soldi" (five cents), he said.

"Five soldi," I repeated, as if almost of a mind to buy; then, drawing back: "No, signore, too dear, I cannot pay it."

"Too dear? No, very cheap. It is fine lemonade. Come, cinque soldi."

"No; too dear."

"Ah, sainted Maria, what do you wish? Four soldi?"

"Still too dear."

"Three?"

"No, one. I will give you one soldo."

"What, one soldo? one soldo? My God in heaven! it is nothing; but take it, signore, take it. I lose, but you can take it," and he proceeded to pour out the lemonade.

In this the reader has a picture of bargaining in Italy.

Hotels frequented by English and Americans charge English and American prices, that is, two or three dollars a day. Hotels of the same class frequented by Italians charge from eighty cents to one dollar a day. Private lodgings of a respectable character may be had for from fifteen to thirty cents a night.

About six in the evening I reached Rome. Without removing my knapsack or laying aside my staff, I began a search for quarters.

To succeed in this may seem no difficult matter, but investigation proves the contrary. A great many houses bear a sign announcing rooms for rent, yet many of these houses have no rooms to rent. The reason is this: signs are taxed. This tax once paid, the landlord naturally wishes it to last as long as possible. If he were to take the sign down on renting the rooms, and when they became vacant again put back his sign, there would be another tax to pay. The consequence is he lets it stay, rented or not rented, and nine times out of ten when you inquire at a house bearing the legend " casa locanda " (rooms to let), you have only your trouble for your pains.

After considerable search I at length stumbled across a man who had a small room on the fourth floor, for which he asked two lire, but took fifteen cents per night. There was nothing magnificent about the room, but it was neat and clean, white curtains at the window, fresh, clean sheets, a few pictures on the walls—on the whole, such a room as in America would cost half a dollar a night, even when taken by the month.

Very much cheaper are beds in workmen's lodging-houses, which are not over-nice. I did not try them after leaving Naples. Twenty or thirty men sleep in a single room, the beds arranged like bunks one above the other, and, though only two feet wide, two occupants to the bed, the sleepers " spooning " to each other, packed like sardines. I always paid an extra cent for the privilege of enjoying my bed alone. I then ensconced myself in my sleeping-bag, and, thus armored, reclined on my four-cent couch and talked myself to sleep questioning and answering the ragged, unwashed, but good-hearted Italians.

In the interior of Italy are numerous inns—osteria they are called—but I preferred to stop overnight with the peasants, who, as a rule, are most hospitable and kind. Few if any travellers go into these out-of-the-way places. The stranger as he enters the gates of an interior town creates a commotion similar to that occasioned in American towns by the arrival of a circus. The children at the first glimpse of the strange-looking man with the slouch hat, dirty boots, and knapsack, rush into the house to tell their mother. I draw near, the good woman comes to the door to investigate matters.

" Buon giorno " (good-day), I begin, add something about " La bella lingua Italiana " (the beautiful Italian language), tell her that I am an American, and the way is smoothed at once. The Italians have two weak points—pride of their language and interest in America. Praise the Italian and say you are American; no more need be said, you are friends.

When you have stopped with these people you have stopped with the hewers of wood, the drawers of water—with the *workers* of the land; and no other method of travel will afford so clear and accurate a conception of the condition of a country's masses, of the millions who produce the wealth which the few enjoy.

I have seen little creatures, six, seven, and eight years old, picking leaves along the roadside to feed silk-worms. I saw a little girl, apparently about five years old, over a tub washing clothes. Old men, lame and weak, hobble along with brooms and baskets, sweeping up the fertilizing material found along the roads. Little children and old people gather up twigs and splinters for fuel, and use them with such close economy as astonishes an American. There is no coal nor large wood; the fire-places in some of the houses, however, are immensely large, as if expected to accommodate the huge back-logs of western America. The hearths are raised two feet above the floor. On each side is a bench where, when not at work, the peasant sits and smokes. I saw a woman one cold day fill a small bucket with hot ashes and put it under her stool to keep herself warm; it made me think of Sellers and his candle in the stove.

The item of lodging for a poor man is small—four cents if you are willing to room with others, and only fifteen cents where you have a bed and curtained room all to yourself. Let us see what his food costs.

For three cents, a pound of excellent black bread may be obtained; a large bowl of milk costs two cents; macaroni costs two or three cents a plate; figs four cents a pound; so-called wine, the last squeezings of the grape, not intoxicating, little more than sour water, costs eight to twelve cents a quart.

My daily expenditures for food in Naples averaged seventeen cents, divided about thus:

Bread, one pound	3	cents.
Macaroni	3	"
Half pound of figs	2	"
Finocchio, a kind of coarse celery, wholesome and good	2	"
Wine	3	"
Milk	4	"
Total cost of food per day	17	cents.
Lodging	4	"
Total daily cost of living in Naples	21	cents.

This diet was varied occasionally by an egg omelette cooked with oil (this in place of macaroni), or by artichokes, pomegranates, chestnuts, etc. The total cost, however, remained the same.

This bill of fare will probably recommend itself to very few, yet it is better than that of the average Italian mechanic;

and, for my own part, I must add that I found it both palatable and wholesome. My health improved; my weight increased. A daily walk of twenty or twenty-five miles gives one such an appetite, everything tastes good, and proves good for the human system.

In Naples there are no dairies, no milkman to waken you at 6 A.M. with a big bell, and sell you a quart of milk-and-water for nine cents. Instead, men walk from street to street leading cows by strings, and when a customer comes the cow-man stops and milks the desired quantity. I purchased a small tin bucket, and every morning and evening took a short stroll until I saw a man with a cow, from whom I got a quart of milk, and on this, with bread and figs, made an economical and nutritious meal. One would imagine this method would absolutely preclude surreptitious watering of the milk. I thought so, but soon found my mistake.

I noticed the milk I drank was peculiarly thin, yet, as I had stood by while it was milked I was at a loss to understand the cause. Could it be that the cows drank too much water? One day the mystery was explained. It happened that when I came across my cow-man he was milking for an Italian. I was surprised when I saw the Italian suddenly step up and squeeze the cow-man's arm, and still more surprised when, as a result thereof, I saw a stream of water spurt from the cow-man's sleeve.

I mentioned this incident to the American consul, who told me it was a very common trick. Cow-men keep a bag of water under their coats, letting it down into the milk through a rubber tube concealed in the sleeve. When detected, a shrug of the shoulders, a "Santa Maria, what difference?" is the cool reply; when not detected, the Neapolitan cow-man silently laughs as he squirts water through his sleeve and sells it to you at six cents a quart.

CHAPTER VI.

A GALLERY OF SKULLS AND BONES.—IL SANTO BAMBINO.—A NEW
ENGLAND LADY IN ST. PETER'S.

APPEARANCES in Rome are often deceptive. The most cost-
ly galleries and magnificent palaces may on the outside look
like dilapidated rookeries. Treasures of curiosities are concealed in the same way. One day when strolling down a very
narrow and crooked street, I happened to glance through the
iron grating of a window of a house which looked like the
rest of the houses in Rome—solid, and a thousand years old.
There was nothing extraordinary about the window; there was,
though, something very extraordinary about what I saw through
the window. I saw a ghastly array of grinning skeletons,
some propped up on sticks, others reclining on couches, others
in a kneeling posture, a rosary and a prayer-book clutched in
their fleshless fingers.

That dingy-looking house so like its neighbors, right in the
heart of Rome, passed daily by dozens of unsuspecting tourists
—that house is the home of the Capuchin order of monks. My
knock at the door was answered by one of the monks, a gray-
headed man clad in coarse sack and cowl, with beads and rope
—in fact, he was a walking St. Jacob; that is, if the St. Jacob's
Oil Company have not been giving the American public spuri-
ous likenesses of their pious patron.

This St. Jacob very willingly showed me through the establishment, and seemed to take a delight in tapping the skulls of
deceased saints.

"This," he said, picking up a skull still covered with skin,
and with the ears attached—"this was Fra Guillaume of Modena, the city I came from. I knew him when he was a boy.
He has been here sixteen years."

" Where ?   In the monastery or on this shelf ?"

" Oh, on the shelf.   He has been in the monastery thirty
years.   This niche was the one intended for my head," he
continued, pointing to a place adjoining the shelf where re-
posed the skull of Fra Guillaume of Modena.   " I liked the
place because it is near my friend ; but we must submit to the
will of the Lord."

" Why, what is the matter ?   If you wish, what is to prevent
your skull from decorating the niche, and keeping company
with your friend ?"

" Ah, the government," with a profound sigh.   " Since 1872
we are forbidden to place any more skeletons in our vaults, and
when we die now we are taken to the cemeteries.   Poor Guillaume, he will miss me," picking up the skull and fondling it,
" he will miss me.   It was all arranged, and he expected me to
fill the niche next to him."

This gallery of skulls and skeletons has been in progress of for-
mation upward of one hundred and fifty years.   In one niche,
standing upright, clothed in cowl and gown just as in life, is
the skeleton of " Fra Benedetto da Riete, morto 21 Febbrajo,
1728 " (Brother Benedetto, of Riete, died 21 February, 1728).
The same cross and string of beads which he used one hundred
and fifty-seven years ago are in his hands now, and his fingers
are in the act of telling those beads just as they told them
in the days when America was a small British province, half a
century before Washington and Napoleon were born.   Gazing
at Brother Benedetto, one thinks of the changes that have
taken place since he was first stood up there in that nook of the
Capuchin monastery.   The world has moved since that time.
How much more must it move before men will cease repining
because they are not permitted to ornament the walls of their
rooms with human bones and skulls !

This skeleton gallery is eighty or one hundred feet long.
The ceiling is lined with finger-bones ; from the centre of the
vaulted arches depend flower-baskets, scales and weights,
scythes, lyres, hour-glasses, all made out of the different

bones of the human skeleton. Pinned on a skull are a couple of verses in Italian. The first verse, in English, runs about thus:

> "This form, bereft of every grace,
>   Which thou beholdest with wondering eye,
> Was, whilst alive, as fair of face
>   As thou art now, oh, passer-by."

The monk who conducted me around said their object was to make familiar the idea of death, so that when the final hour comes the grim monster may be greeted with equanimity. If all the monks are like the old fellow I saw, the gallery of skulls is a success—a large success. Not even a grave-digger could appear less concerned at the thought of departing this world than the gray-haired friend of Guillaume of Modena. When on a second visit to Rome during the following winter, I went again to the Capuchin monastery. It chanced to be All Souls' Day, and the gallery of dead men's bones was illuminated with hundreds of candles and lamps. Guillaume of Modena had not been forgotten. When I looked for his skull I found it lighted up by two tapers, which were spluttering and dripping wax down into the eye-holes and ears.

Returning from a trip to the Catacombs of St. Calixtus, I had scarcely entered the Appian gate when I espied a church where I thought it would be well to stop and rest before walking into the city. Externally it was a dingy, poor-looking edifice, but internally it was more interesting than St. Peter's. On entering the door I beheld a crowd of men, women, and children climbing up a steep staircase on their hands and knees. They kissed every step with resounding smacks, and accompanied this osculatory process with what were intended for pious ejaculations, but what seemed to me like grunts arising from indigestion.

This staircase, the "Scala Santa," was brought from Jerusalem in 326 by the mother of Constantine. It is supposed Christ ascended it once, so those Catholics weighted down by unusually heavy sins, crawl up these steps and drop money in the box of the priest who awaits them at the top, then walk off with easy consciences.

One man who was going up as I entered had done too much sitting down. There were two large holes in the rear of his breeches. The position he occupied—on hands and knees—stretched that garment, and rendered glaringly apparent the two windows in the rear. This comical sight, added to the colicky groans with which he punctuated his kisses, was too much for my gravity. I smiled and would have laughed outright had not a pious priest frozen me with an indignant look. I rushed away lest my risible propensities should prove too much, and I should shock pious souls by peals of laughter.

There is a very cosey and tidy little restaurant on the Piazza of the Pantheon. It was my custom when anywhere in that vicinity to dine there, and pass half an hour or so after dinner gazing at the Pantheon and deciphering its inscriptions. In the little street to the rear of the Pantheon, where it is joined by the Thermæ of Agrippa, lives a jolly, fat-faced Italian, a hat presser or ironer. He was born in the room where he presses hats, has lived there ever since, and will probably die there.

"Yes, signore," he said, after I had stopped before his shop every day for a week or more, to gaze at the venerable walls of that Roman building—"yes, signore, it seems strange to me. People come from every land. They stop before my shop. They stare, they talk, they write in little books. Sometimes two or three years go by, then I see the same people again. They look and stare just the same. Ah, I know them—I remember *you* when you come back, maybe ten years from now. I see so many — they waste so much time. The wall is old? Santa Maria! it is old, very old—what then? I not understand —seem to me American, Inglese, wrong here," and the mystified Italian tapped his forehead and resumed his ironing.

There was one American whom my friend the hat-presser should have seen. I met him in the vestibule of the Pantheon, and attempted to awaken in him some enthusiasm over those massive bronze doors—those doors which have withstood the ravages of Time and Man, and remain to-day as solid and sound as the day they were first swung on their hinges nineteen centuries ago.

"Pshaw," said the American, "they ain't much—ain't anything to compare with the doors of the Capitol at Washington."

The Capitol at Washington was his criterion for all that was grand or beautiful in the way of architecture. When he saw St. Peter's he smiled contemptuously.

"Brag about *that* dome?" he said, "why, it can't hold a candle to the dome at Washington."

One of the celebrities of Rome is "Il Santo Bambino"— the Holy Child. It is kept in the church of St. Maria in Aracoeli, on the Capitoline Hill, and may be visited only by conforming to a number of peculiar ceremonies. After conducting me into a mysterious-looking chapel, the monk got on his knees and unburdened himself of a long Latin prayer. Then proceeding to the altar, he took out a large iron key, turned it in the lock, the iron door over the altar flew open. Pressing a spring caused a box to slowly roll out from the recess behind the iron doors. In this box, swathed in the costliest satins and silks, covered with diamonds and rubies and pearls, lay Il Santo Bambino — a wooden doll made of cedar from Mount Lebanon. It is many centuries old, and is believed by all good Catholics to possess the power of healing the sick. When it is carried through the streets of Rome on its way to the houses of the sick, passers-by kneel on its approach, and mutter prayers for the success of its mission.

Meeting a New England lady in St. Peter's one day, I mentioned the Holy Bambino, and told her she should not fail to see it.

"What!" exclaimed the lady from New England, "Holy Child? I will not countenance such superstition by going to see it."

She added that she thought it a sin to come to see St.

Peter's. She had committed that sin, but wished now she hadn't; at any rate, she would not commit another sin by going to see the Holy Bambino.

" Why, then, are you in Rome, madame ?"

" Certainly not to visit the Catholic churches and other works of superstition," she replied. " I am spending the winter here to study the old ruins, the Forum, the Colosseum—"

" But are you not aware that these also are the results of superstition ?"

" Yes," was the answer; " but, you know, Pagans had no light. There is not that excuse for Christians."

I met this New England lady a few days afterwards in the Vatican. Did she think that grand edifice the result of " no light ?" or was she growing charitable to darkness?

St. Peter's, on Sunday mornings, is filled with priests and peasants. The priests officiate first at one altar, then, followed by a gay and picturesque crowd, they proceed to another altar in another part of the vast edifice, and swing their censers and chant again their solemn masses. The eleven confessional boxes, for as many different languages, are all occupied by father confessors. A long, slim rod sticks out of the door of each confessional. The penitent kneels in front of the box, the priest taps him on the head with his rod, and he arises with a light heart and clear conscience to kiss St. Peter's toe near by. Kisses have worn the toe smooth; enough, however, still remains for many future generations to enjoy the pious pleasure of pressing their lips on its shiny surface.

Among the most ancient statues in the Vatican are the two sitting figures, " Possidippus " and " Menander," by the sculptor Cephisodotus, son of Praxiteles (B.C. 364). Almost as old is the celebrated " Laocoön," chiselled in the time of Alexander the Great, and which once occupied a position in the palace of the Emperor Titus. The

" Tomb of the Scipios contains no ashes now,"

but the tomb still exists. The inscription, as legible almost as if made yesterday instead of two hundred and sixty years before Christ, relates that Scipio was "a brave and a wise man" (*fortis vir sapiensque*) ; that he was virtuous, was a consul, a censor, an ædile.*

In the Capitoline Museum is the bronze wolf which Cicero mentions as having been struck by lightning B.C. 65. Near by, in a cage, are kept, and have been kept for ages, two live wolves —"lineal descendants" of the wolves that suckled Romulus and Remus. One of the principal theatres in Rome—the Amfiteatro Umberto—is constructed in what was once the tomb of Augustus Cæsar. The enormous mausoleum which Hadrian had erected to hold his ashes is now a soldiers' barrack. The one emperor's tomb converted into a barrack, the other into an opera-house !

These are a few of the things of ancient Rome. They are fully described in the guide-books, but as all travellers write about them, I ring in a few merely not to be out of the fashion.

---

* The full inscription runs thus : " Cornelius Lucius, Scipio–Barbatus–Cnainod–Patre–Proc-natus–Fortis vir sapiensque–Quojus Forma Virtutei–Parisuma–Fuit–Consul–Censor–Aidilis Quei (j) Fuit–Apud vos–Taurasia–Cisauna–Samnio Cepit subicit–Omne Loucana Opsidesque Abdoucit."

CHAPTER VII.

THERE were not many people astir the morning I left Rome. The hour was early, a drenching rain was falling. When I reached the Piazza del Populo I paused to take my last look at the Eternal City. The hills of the Pincio were on my right, the domes of three churches were to the left; beyond, a little without the gate, were the beautiful gardens of the Villa Borghese. The sight of a stranger standing in that hard rain at the base of the Egyptian obelisk, now staring down the Corso, now gazing at the Pincio, the ancient garden of Lucullus, the scene of Messalina's orgies—this sight excited the surprise of the passers-by, who stopped and eyed me curiously.

Summoning my blandest manner and purest Italian, I said, "Pardon, signore, but can you tell me what city this is?"

The man stared at me in amazement.

"This—this—signore—why, this is *Rome*."

"Ah, Rome?"

"Si, signore, si, si, si. Surely you do not pass through Rome without stopping?"

"Rome?" I repeated. "Ah yes, I have heard of Rome. Fine town. But I am going to Florence. How far have I to walk to Florence?"

This was the finishing stroke. Thinking me an escaped lunatic, they retired to a safer distance from the heavy club I held in my hand. There they stood and stared and talked.

The rain was not so bad. An ample rubber coat protected my body; the broad-brimmed sombrero which I had had made to order in Rome served admirably to protect my head. Only my feet got wet—soaked, and after ten miles I took off my heavy, soggy shoes and went barefoot. This proved a happy

experiment, for the broad stones of an Italian road do not cut
the feet; with shoes strapped to my knapsack instead of where
they are usually worn, I made a mile more per hour.

Thus prepared for a storm, there is a certain feeling of pleasure in braving it, breasting the gusts of wind and rain; a feeling of independence, of power to meet and overcome surrounding circumstances. I went on enjoying this feeling: it was
about all I had to enjoy, for the country surrounding Rome is
singularly devoid of interest. The broad, rolling fields carpeted in green, all the brighter and richer for the recent rains,
form beautiful landscape scenes. They scarcely compensate,
however, for the almost total absence of human life—for the
absence of villages and peasant huts. I walked fully twenty
miles before I saw a single human being. He was a shepherd,
standing leaning backward on his staff, both hands busily engaged in knitting. He wore a coarse shirt and breeches of goatskin. With my blandest manner I approached him.

"Buona sera, signore" (good-evening, sir).

A grunt and increased rapidity in the knitting.

"Ah, bel tempo oggi" (fine weather to-day).

"H'm — non lo credo" (I don't believe it), the knitting-needles fairly flying, and the knitter still propped on his stick.

"Where do you live?"

Removing the prop and standing on his own legs, he slowly
turned.

"Here," he said, staring at me. "Where do *you* live?"

"In America," I politely replied. "I come thousands of
miles to see Italy, to know Italian people. You say you live
here. Where, on the ground?"

He began to thaw.

"Come, I will show you," he said, glancing at the sun, which
in setting was making one last effort to break through the
clouds. Whistling to his dogs, we started off across the hills
and fields, the shepherd driving his sheep before him.

For the last ten miles of my walk I had noticed what seemed
to be antiquated hay-stacks; and not observing any farms or

peasants in the region, I wondered how they came there. The answer to these speculations was close at hand. After going about a mile we came to one of these ancient-looking hay-stacks. I was surprised to see smoke issuing from the top and from crevices in the side. In tropical countries grass is some-times set on fire by the rays of the sun, but how had this hay become ignited in Italy, in winter, and in a drenching rain?

The hay-stack was not only a hay-stack, it was also the resi-dence of my new friend, the Roman shepherd. When in the Indian country I saw no more rude or primitive dwelling. A small aperture in the side served as an entrance; the inte-rior was dingy and full of smoke. A hole in the ground in the centre of the apartment was the fireplace, where burned a few twigs and sticks, giving forth much smoke and little warmth. A pile of straw in one corner served as the shep-herd's bed; a three-legged stool was his furniture. This he offered me, but I preferred to squat on the floor; the smoke that was arising made it less unpleasant to breathe near the ground.

Our supper that night consisted of bread and oil—nothing more. The sheep he so carefully tends sell for three dollars each. Two months' salary of this miserable man would hardly more than suffice to buy one sheep. The Roman shepherd re-ceives seven cents a day, and out of that sum he clothes and feeds himself. His hay-stack hut is his world, the sheep his people. Living within twenty miles of Rome, he said he had not been there since he was a boy. He herds sheep during the day, and at night, after a supper of black bread sopped in oil, washed down by bad water, he lays himself on his bundle of straw and sleeps: thus he passes his life of unvarying sameness and drudgery.

When the sun rose next morning in a clear sky, he went on with his herding and knitting, while I continued my walk to Florence.

To an American of practical proclivities it seems strange to see the towns and villages perched upon high hills or the al-most inaccessible sides of mountains, as they always are in his-

toric Italy. The reason is doubtless owing to the fact that the
villages and towns began in the savage age when war was the
general business of life, when people had to prepare to defend
themselves against attacks.   Narrow streets were advantageous;
it was cheaper to wall in small towns than large; compactness
was an economic measure.

Another noticeable thing is the difference in the religious
ceremonies of Catholics under the eye of the supreme pontiff,
and in America four thousand miles from the supreme pontiff.
The curious sight witnessed as I climbed up one thousand
two hundred feet to the village of Montefiascone made me
note this difference.   First came a procession of about one
thousand men and boys, all wearing long sacks which covered
them from the tops of their heads to their heels.   In the sacks
were two holes cut for the eyes and one for the nose.   Some
of these sacks were of a sombre color, others were bright red,
others yellow and blue.   Next came a little army of men, also
fantastically dressed, some swinging lamps, others bearing large
crosses, while some held Bibles or skulls in their hands.

This priestly army was followed by about five thousand peasants, men, women, and children, in gay holiday attire.   They
marched into a large church which stood on the summit of a
hill overlooking the beautiful lake of Bolsena.   As many as
could crowded into the church; the others stood outside.   Some
fell on their knees and told their beads as the priests chanted
within.   This performance commemorated the cessation of a
plague that long years ago had afflicted the people.

Modern machinery is yet a novelty in the interior of Italy.
Old-fashioned farming implements are still used.   Women still
spin and weave after the manner of our ancestors.   Weaving
is carried on in dark rooms and damp cellars.   A rapid weaver
can make nine yards of cloth a day.   He is paid three cents a
yard.   By working late the women can make thirty cents a day.

In my report to the United States Bureau of Labor Statistics
upon labor and the cost of living in Europe, I prepared a number of tables showing in detail the expenditures of families with

whom I had stopped and made myself acquainted. The following, quoted from that report, describes a family of Italian woollen weavers :*

" *Condition.*—Family of five : parents, two children five and six years of age, and mother of the father. Parents work at hand-looms ; the grandmother spins (at home), attends to the children and to two goats, the milk of the goats being sold at four cents per quart. Occupy a room with earth floor on a level with the ground ; room divided into two compartments. Weaving-room on same street, up a steep hill ; only six looms, level of room three feet below level of street ; no windows, lighted by the door. Each weaver has a small bucket or jug of hot ashes or coals. This the women put under their dresses ; the men place them at their feet. In unusually cold weather a large pan of coals is set in the middle of the room. The weavers quit their work occasionally to sit for a few minutes around this pan and warm their hands and feet.

"The fuel for this primitive heating arrangement consists to some extent of brushwood, clippings from old grape-vines, etc. Coal is imported from England. Price per ton at West Mediterranean ports, $5 to $6 ; price in interior, $7 to $10.

" *Diet.*—Breakfast : bread, coffee or wine. Dinner : macaroni or cheese, funnochio, bread, sometimes tripe, wine. Supper : bread, wine or coffee.

Amount earned by Family :

Earnings of father		$126 00
" " mother		97 50
" " grandmother (spinning)		48 75
" " " (sale of milk)		43 80
Total		$316 05

Cost of Living :

Rent	$14 40
Bread	53 00
Macaroni	69 40
Groceries, finnochio, olives, eggs, oil, etc.	72 50
Wine	51 00
Coffee and milk	17 25
Wooden clogs and leather shoes	7 50
Clothing	19 65
Iron bedstead, chairs, etc.	8 70
Total expenditures	$313 40

* Report of the Commissioner of Labor, 1886, p. 413.

Talking with a weaver one day, I told her of our country, our big forests, abundant fuel, good wages.

"Thirty cents a day is not bad," she replied. "I put by ten cents every day."

"But think, signora, in America your husband can get one or two dollars a day—meat, vegetables, a room with a plank floor, and a window."

"Ah, signore! can that be true for poor people? But it is so far—so far away," and she went on throwing her swift shuttle to earn thirty cents a day.

In the interior places the peasants are so little accustomed to the visits of strangers they cannot understand why a young man should stroll over the land, poking his way into the cottages and spying out the customs of the people. The only possible reason that presents itself is that the traveller is hunting for a wife. When the Italian peasant wishes to marry he sets about it in a practical way, as a man does when he wishes to own a horse. While talking to the weaving or spinning women they almost invariably questioned me on the subject.

"Married, signore?"

"No; no wife."

"Is she dead?"

"No; she never lived."

"Ah, il signore is looking around to find a wife?"

I was asked this question frequently. On one occasion I departed from the truth in my reply—that is, perpetrated a ridiculous joke which caused me more annoyance than I had expected. It happened thus: one evening as I sat on the ruins of the town wall watching the sun set, a bright little girl of twelve or thirteen stopped and stared at me. As I did not exhibit any dangerous proclivities, she shyly drew nearer, and we soon fell into a friendly chat.

After a while came the inevitable query:

"Married, signore?"

"Unhappily, no, signorina," I replied, in a melancholy tone, as if my soul were pining to be mated.

"Ah, il signore vuole una moglie?" (the signore wants a wife?).

"Five, signorina. I am looking for them now. In my country we all have five wives."

"Cinque moglie!" (five women!), and her big eyes growing bigger, she turned and fled as from a monster. From the way she met that polygamous idea, I imagine Mormonism would not prosper in Italy.

That little girl spread the news through the village, and wherever I appeared on the streets a mob of boys and girls followed and stared at me, and now and then one would cry out,

"Cinque moglie—lei vuole cinque moglie!" (brutal — five women! he wants five women; he is brutal!).

I took care after that to talk no more nonsense to the little peasant girls.

CHAPTER VIII.

ITALIAN HIGH LIFE.—A CALL ON OUIDA.—TAKEN FOR A THIEF ON
THE LEANING TOWER OF PISA.

A FRIEND of mine lived in Florence, an American lady. She had married a nobleman and lived in considerable style. It was out of the question to call upon her in my workman's garb; so, going to a fashionable tailor on the Via Calzaioli, I left my measure, and for the modest sum of six dollars obtained a very good and stylish-looking suit.

I learned from my friend a good deal about the upper classes. Their lack of energy and willingness to drift surprises an American. An American, no matter how great his wealth, works. It is the work he likes. He would be unhappy with nothing to do. Not so with the Italian. His ideal life is where there is nothing to be done. An Italian of wealth lies in bed until ten or eleven in the morning, alternately sipping coffee and dozing. From eleven until two he amuses himself with his toilet, with papers, correspondence; then luncheon. At three or four he goes out for a drive upon the Cascine; at six or seven he dines. The evening is passed at balls, operas, or private salons. In this idle round he passes away his existence. The Cascine, a beautiful drive along the Arno, is the scene of the Florentine's match-making. Mothers with marriageable daughters drive out here in the afternoon. The carriage stops for madame to sip an ice or to gaze at the sluggish flowing of the Arno's waters. The gay gallants pass by, cast soft glances at la bella signorina with the dark eyes; the next day signor papa is visited, the next week or month they are married. That is the Italian style. The young people never know each other until after the wedding-day; then they know each other sometimes too well.

An officer of the army cannot marry unless possessed of at least forty thousand lire ($8000), which he must deposit with the War Department, drawing therefrom four per cent. interest for the benefit of his family. The pay of a captain is one dollar a day, which might suffice did he not have to bear out of his own pocket the expenses of servant, horse, rent, rations, and uniform.

The Italian villa is usually square in shape, containing two halls intersecting each other at right angles. The lower floor is used for the sleeping and dining rooms; the living-rooms, parlors, reception-rooms are up-stairs. A handsome villa, with garden, furniture, and everything ready for immediate occupancy, may be rented in the suburbs of Florence for two hundred and fifty lire (fifty dollars) per month. A landau, two horses, and man in livery to drive, costs three hundred and fifty lire; or if only one horse, three hundred lire per month. A woman cook is paid thirty lire, a man cook fifty lire per month. Supplies are bought from day to day in small quantities—five cents' worth of rice at a time, eggs by the half-dozen. Apples, strawberries, cherries, potatoes, etc., are bought by the pound, bread by the yard, pins by the ounce. Sweet potatoes come from Africa, and are bought by the pound.

"For sixty lire per month," said my friend, "I get a man cook, a regular *chef de cuisine*. I have literally no responsibility. Every evening he sends me a bill of fare for the next day. I approve or make alterations as the case may be. The next day we dine as arranged, *à la carte*. It is usual to make a certain allowance for the table, and you tell your cook to furnish the best bill of fare possible within that sum. Ten lire (two dollars) a day is a very liberal estimate for a family of five."

The cost of high life in Italy appears to be considerably less than in America. For a family of five the figures would stand thus:

Rent of furnished villa..........................	$50 00	per month.
Rent of landau, driver and horses.	60 00	"
Lady's-maid...................................	4 00	"
Cook	10 00	"
Food, at two dollars per day	60 00	"
Total........................	$184 00	per month.

One hundred and eighty-four dollars a month for a fashion-able home, carriage and horses, three servants, and a liberal table—the same living in America would cost treble that sum.

Ouida, the well-known novelist, lives in a charming villa in the suburbs of Florence, just without the Porta San Frediano. I sent her a letter from the American consul, accompanied by this note of my own:

"FLORENCE, *May* 10, 1885.

"As one of the many Americans who read your works and admire your genius, I am desirous of calling and paying my respects. May I not hope to be accorded this honor?

"With respect,
"LEE MERIWETHER.

"To Mme. DE LA RAME,
Villa Farinola, Via di Scandicci."

"Of course she will see you," said my friend, when I showed her a copy of this note. "Ouida is very vain, and would see anybody who wrote like this—'her works and genius.' But what is this?" getting down to the address—"*Madame* De la Rame? That settles *it.*"

"Settles it! How?" I queried.

"Settles it that you will never see Ouida. You have wound-ed her in her most sensitive part. 'Madame'—why, she will never forgive you."

"But is she not 'madame?' not married?"

"Certainly not. But I will tell you all about it;" and resum-ing my seat, I listened to the story of Madame, or Mademoi-selle, De la Rame, a story as romantic as any of her novels.

A number of years ago, when she first came to Florence, before her peculiar views and eccentricities were known, she was received into Florentine society, and a certain marquis paid her attentions. The affair had made considerable progress. Even the trousseau, it is said, was prepared. By this time the eccentricity of Ouida's character had begun to dawn upon the noble marquis. When questioned one day by his Dulcinea, he determined once for all to end the romance.

"Did you think I was in earnest?" he said, and turned away.

Ouida gave him one of those stony stares so often described in her novels, and forthwith bought a pistol and announced her intention of shooting the marquis on sight. The better and the sooner to get a sight—she had a presentiment that the marquis would not call again—she secured the villa adjoining the residence of her ex-suitor, and for six months kept a strict vigil, pistol in hand, with the gory purpose of putting a period to her ex-lover's days. The ex-lover, however, did not wish a period, nor even a comma, put to his days, and believing in the adage, "Discretion is the better part of valor," he started on a trip for his health.

Unable to revenge herself on the marquis, Ouida revenged herself on the Florentines. She wrote "A Winter City," in which the frivolity, the insincerity, the ignoble qualities of the inhabitants of the gay Tuscan capital, are depicted without mercy.

It is astonishing how soon one becomes—if the expression is permissible—educated to antiquities. For instance, there is Bradly, a young Philadelphian. When I first met Bradly in New York he was overflowing with the usual Philadelphia reverence for Independence Hall and for the relics of Washington, the antiquities of which his home boasts. After Pompeii and Rome and the Pantheon, Washington and Independence Hall seemed things of yesterday.

"Oh, bother!" exclaimed Bradly, when I pointed out the resting-place of a saint of the eleventh century, "I don't care to see these modern tombs."

In comparison with Scipio's tomb, the tomb of the eleventh

century saint is modern. Scipio's tomb is modern compared with the tombs in the Egyptian Museum of Florence. Here are coffins that date back 3000 years B. C., and one nice mummy is said to precede even this early period by a thousand years. It is the mummy of a boy. The hair is combed in quite a modern style. There are other mummies finely preserved, but none so well as this boy, this contemporary of Adam, this boy older by five thousand years than any other boy in the world.

To come down to modern times—that is, to about the year 1500—there are in the Buonorotti Gallery some very interesting sketches by Michael Angelo. One sketch, a small off-hand affair in pencil, has this line scribbled in one corner:

" Send this to Bologna, 1597."

Seeing these pencillings so fresh and so clear, brings the six teenth century very near to us.

No city in Italy is more charmingly situated than Florence. Heading from the Porta Romana, and winding around and up the neighboring hills, is a broad and magnificent avenue shaded on both sides by a line of stately cypress-trees—a drive that possibly has its equal in Paris and the other great European capitals, but has not its like in Italy. There is nothing in the vicinity of Rome to be compared with it, and when the king wishes a really first-class drive he must needs come to Florence.

I went over to Pisa from Florence, and saw something there considerably more astonishing than the Leaning Tower. Just as I was entering the door of the tower for the purpose of ascending, a smirking little fellow, with a thick shock of well-greased hair, stepped up and said, in Italian,

" Good-day, signore. Do you wish me to go up in the tower with you ?"

" Why should I wish your company ?"

" Oh, pardon !" said the Italian, " I thought you were going up the tower."

" So I am."

"Ah, then, signore, you will need me. I will go with you for half a lira, and another man, a friend of mine, I can get to go also for half a lira."

I set the man down as either witless or possessed of unlimited impudence. Neither assumption was correct. When I entered the tower, the custodian informed me that permission to ascend was given only to parties of three.

"Why?" said I.

The custodian shrugged his shoulders.

"Read this," he said, pointing to some printed regulations hanging on the wall. I read, and found such was the fact. Less than three persons are not permitted to ascend the Leaning Tower of Pisa. The reason? I can only imitate the custodian, and shrug my shoulders.

The steps leading to the summit of the tower are much worn. Two ruts have been made in each step by the many feet that have trod them during the last seven hundred years.

While gazing from the summit of the tower upon the quaint old Italian city below, upon the sinuous Arno and the blue Mediterranean, a party came up, consisting of four blooming young girls and an elderly lady of rather stern and disdainful aspect. The young ladies made a break for the railing and the view, but the elderly lady cast a furtive glance at me, then deposited her luncheon-basket, parasol, and other etceteras on the floor, and plumped herself down beside them.

"Why, auntie, what's the matter?" exclaimed one of the girls. "Come to the railing for the view."

"Never mind me, girls," was the grim response.

"Good gracious, aunt, why climb up this dreadful tower if you don't intend to see the view?"

"Hush!" said the old lady, with a grim glance at me. "Do you not see that villanous-looking Italian? I must stay by the things."

"Madam," I said, in my best English, "as I have seen the view, I am happy to afford you relief by descending."

The old lady wilted, and the young ones stared.

CHAPTER IX.

NEARLY a year later I again visited Florence. I came direct from the muggy, drizzly fogs of England, and on that account, perhaps, found the sparkling clear atmosphere that surrounded the old city particularly pleasant and agreeable. I hastened to enjoy myself while the opportunity lasted.

The very afternoon of my arrival, after depositing my goods and chattels in the room at the hotel, I donned a spring suit and sallied forth for a stroll through the famous Boboli Gardens.

There was not the slightest sign of rain, there was not even a cloud; nevertheless, I took my umbrella from habit acquired in foggy England. Ordinarily the act of carrying an umbrella is not attended by any serious or unusual result. It was so attended in this case, however, and that is why I am particular to mention the fact; indeed, had it not been for the umbrella there would not be this tale to tell.

But to proceed.

The sky was cloudless, the air balmy. I went along swinging my umbrella and whistling a tune for joy at seeing the sun once more. For an hour I strolled through the shaded walks of the garden, then as evening drew nigh, I ascended to the heights which overlook the Arno and afford such an excellent view of Florence. Alas! the sunset was a failure. Before I had climbed half-way a breeze sprang up; when I reached the summit there were clouds; when I stood near the statue of David, and gazed to see the sunset, there was rain. And this was sunny Italy!

I was about to give vent to an expression more forcible than elegant, apropos of the villanous weather that pursued me, when my eye was caught by a fair young creature, crouching on the lee side of the monument, in an effort to secure some slight shelter from the rain. I felt sheepish and ashamed. Here I was with a big umbrella complaining, while that lovely girl was being drenched. I resolved to play the Good Samaritan at once.

"Scusatemi, signorina," I said, mustering my best Italian as I approached her—"scusatemi, signorina, ma cê una pioggia terrible. Volete stare con me sotto l'ombrello?" (Excuse me, signorina, but it is a fearful rain. Will you not stand under my umbrella?)

She gave me a shy glance, then blushed and looked down. I knew that Italian etiquette was very severe, but, certainly, if there was ever a time for dispensing with ceremony it was on an occasion like this.

I repeated my offer, and without awaiting her consent stepped to her side and sheltered her as best I could. For some moments there was constraint between us. I used the interval in observing the beautiful complexion and silken tresses of my companion. Singularly enough, she was a pronounced blonde. Her hair was of that lovely golden shade known as "Titian," from being the favorite color of that great master, though I do not know where Titian saw any golden-haired women. There seem to be few in Italy to-day. My fair companion was growing restless.

"Io credo—io credo che bisogna partire" (I think—I think I must be going), she said, presently, in the softest Italian.

"Con piacere ma sotto il mio ombrello" (with pleasure, but under my umbrella).

"Che'—what, I keep dry and let you get wet? Never," and she smiled and displayed her pretty teeth.

I was delighted. I saw she was thawing.

"Then we will both keep under the umbrella," I said. "Tell me where you live, and I will take you home."

"Gia', ma e' lontano" (but it is far).

"Ma, io insisto" (nevertheless, signorina, I insist).

She hesitated, I remained firm; she yielded—we started off together.

The rain did not seem half so unpleasant now as it had before. Indeed, I should have felt badly had it ceased. Fortunately it continued, and with vigor, so that not only did my lovely companion have no excuse to dispense with me, but to keep at all dry she was obliged to stick close to my side. I am bound to confess that after the first shyness had worn away she stuck well. The space between us was scarcely appreciable, and I felt a proportionate amount of bliss and ecstasy. There was one drawback—I had forgotten most of my Italian. I could ask and answer simple questions, but that was all. As the conversation grew more general, I got into deeper and deeper water.

"The d—l!" I exclaimed, at length, in English. "What a pity I can't talk Italian!"

"Oh! are you English?" she exclaimed, in excellent English, and broke into a little peal of laughter.

I was covered with confusion. She had heard and understood my impolite ejaculation.

"Your pardon, signorina, but truly I had no idea you understood English."

"You did not?" She laughed. "What a notion. I am almost English myself, and papa is English. I was born and brought up in Italy, but papa always talks English to me. I understand everything, though," modestly, "when I speak it is with an accent."

She did have an accent, but it was a delightful one, and I told her so. This girl was becoming more charming every moment, and now that our talk was in a language we both understood, progress became rapid.

"Ah, you are a tourist?" she said, presently.

Now, in Italy tourists are looked upon with a kind of contempt—are looked upon as simpletons, with nothing to do but stalk around with red guide-books, and poke about old ruins.

I could not bear to have this fair creature look upon me in that light.   I answered, boldly,

"No, not at all.   It is not your ruins but your fruit that attracts me."

"Our fruit?"

"Yes.   I am a fruit-merchant.   I am buying fruit for our New York house."

She looked at me beamingly.

"Well, if that isn't a coincidence.   Why, papa is a fruit-merchant.   He sends a great deal of fruit to England.   How nice if you could meet him!"

I confessed it would be nice, but as I did so I began inwardly to marvel at the ease with which our acquaintanceship progressed.   It came about that I told her my name.   She told me hers—Bettola Brown; she liked Italy, but was anxious to see her father's native land.   No, her mother was not living, she lived alone with her father; and thus we chatted until suddenly she paused before a house and a garden surrounded by a high wall.

"This is papa's villa.   We must ring here."

A moment and the heavy door swung open.   A handsomely dressed, elderly man appeared with hat and umbrella, as if on the point of going out.   The lovely Bettola relinquished my arm and flew to that of the elderly gentleman who opened the gate.

"Oh, papa!   how glad I am to find you at home."

"Yes, dear," replied the old gentleman, "you just did find me.   I was about to start out to look for you.   Are you not drenched?"

"No, indeed, and that is why I am glad to find you.   I want you to thank this gentleman.   It was he who protected me," and she forthwith introduced me.

Mr. Brown was a cordial man.   When, after passing a few commonplace phrases, I lifted my hat to say good-day, he took my arm and with a hearty laugh led me into the house.

"My dear sir," he said, "pray do not be so ceremonious.

You have brought my daughter out of the wet, and now you must accept a seat by my fire until the rain holds up."

"That's right," chimed in the daughter. "Besides, papa, I know you will like to talk to Mr. Meriwether. He is a New York fruit-merchant."

"Indeed !" exclaimed Mr. Brown; "well, that settles it. I cannot let you go until we have had a good chat;" and so saying, he led me through the hall of his villa into a spacious and handsomely-fitted drawing-room. It was not cold, but the damp was penetrating, and the cheerful glow that came from the grate was anything but unwelcome.

"The couch of the wicked is not of down." I soon found cause to regret that little romance about being a fruit-merchant. Mr. Brown asked more questions about fruit than I had ever heard before. I was sadly ignorant of the subject. and gave what must have been astonishing replies, though Mr. Brown, from politeness, doubtless, made no comment.

"How is the Sicilian orange regarded in America?" he continued. I knew nothing of the Sicilian orange. I don't think I had so much as ever seen one. How was I to answer such questions?

"Not so favorably as the Florida orange," I answered, at a venture.

"Ah, its flavor is perhaps inferior to that of the Florida orange, but do you not think it preserves better?"

"Well, no—that is—er—yes—I mean I am not sure about it," and so the conversation continued, to my great inconvenience and discomfort.

Signorina Bettola had changed her dress and was now sitting opposite me, warming her feet by the fire. She looked lovely, bewitching, but her father's fruit conversation was so depressing that I arose to leave. Mr. Brown accompanied me into the hall; he opened the door to afford me exit. The wind and rain blew in in a gust, almost extinguishing the lamp in the hall.

"You may as well lay aside your hat and umbrella, Mr.

Meriwether," said Mr. Brown, closing the door. "I cannot think of turning you out in such a storm as this."

"But," I remonstrated, "I am a stranger to you—I have an umbrella—I cannot impose—"

"Say no more, say no more," he replied, bluffly, but cordially. "You have shown a kindness to my daughter, and must accept my hospitality for the night," and without further ado he took my arm and led me back to the drawing-room.

I was in mortal fear lest he should resume his queries as to the fruit trade. Fortunately the conversation turned upon other topics. What was still better luck, in a few minutes Mr. Brown excused himself and left his daughter to entertain me. And how delightfully she succeeded! It was a joy even to look at her—when she spoke with her charming Italian accent, I felt myself becoming dangerously romantic.

"Do you not play?" I asked, seeing the open piano at the end of the room.

"No; or at least only accompaniments. I sing a little."

"You will sing for me then?"

"Yes, if you like songs."

If I liked songs! Of course I liked them. I would have liked anything from her lips. She took her seat at the piano, and, first running her fingers idly over the keys, began a soft Italian ballad. I am aware that what I am now about to confess was not proper. I will even admit that it was very improper; but there certainly were extenuating circumstances. It was in Italy, the land of romance and beautiful women, the land of Romeo and Juliet. If a body is not to become romantic in Italy, pray, where *is* a body to become so?

I became romantic.

As the soft vowels floated to my ears my right arm somehow got itself around Bettola's waist. I bent over, my cheek touched her silken hair, my soul rose to heaven — a clap of thunder brought it to earth again. Mr. Brown's heavy hand was on my shoulder. His voice rang in my ears.

"What!" he exclaimed, "your arm around my daughter?
You *are* affectionate upon first acquaintance!"

I was surprised—and relieved. He had seen all, yet did not
mean to kick me out of the house. I admitted that I had
permitted my absent-mindedness to carry me too far, and Mr.
Brown generously permitted the subject to drop. Not the
least surprising part about this business was the fact that
Bettola had remained perfectly unconcerned when her father
discovered my arm around her.

"She looks as if she were quite used to it," I thought.

"I was only singing Mr. Meriwether a song," she said, with
a light laugh, and neither she nor her father referred to the
subject again.

Despite this generous treatment I felt a little embarrassed,
and was only too glad when at last my host, remarking that I
must be tired, rang for a lamp, and himself conducted me to
my room.

"Before you retire," he said, placing the lamp on the table
and drawing from his pocket a leather case, "I wish you to
try one of these cigars. The tobacco is Turkish. I think you
will relish the flavor."

I accepted one and bade him good-night.

The room—not a large one—was immediately over the hall,
its one window looking out on the garden. The bed was
placed at the window end of the room. The head of the bed
partly obstructed the view from the window. I made these
observations after I had closed the door and lighted my cigar.
I had not before felt particularly drowsy; all of a sudden, however, my eyes seemed to grow heavy — I could scarce get in
bed fast enough.

Putting my watch and pistol under the pillow, I hastily di-
vested myself of my clothing, threw aside the half-smoked
cigar, and tumbled into bed as fast as I could. I seemed almost instantly to sleep. How long the sleep lasted I cannot
say; but it was not a peaceful slumber. A dream that was
almost a nightmare played through my brain, and at length

became so vivid that, chilled and trembling, I awoke. Where was I ? My eyes grew accustomed to the darkness. I looked. Yes, there was my door standing wide open. What did it mean ? Had that cigar been drugged ? Who was this Brown ? How reckless to sleep in a strange house! These and a hundred similar thoughts rushed through my mind. I drew myself slowly up, I endeavored to pierce the thick darkness. There at the foot of my bed lay the crouching figure of a man !

The suddenness of the discovery quite took away my breath. Recovering myself, I reached slowly for my pistol, then springing from the bed and backing against the wall, to be safe from attack behind, I demanded,

" What do you want ?"

There was no answer.

" Who are you ?"

Again no answer.

" If you do not speak I will shoot," I cried, and at the same time sprang forward and dealt the man a stunning blow with the butt of my pistol. He rolled over. I seized him by the throat. It was cold — the man was dead — I had struck a corpse !

The discovery froze my blood. That there had been foul play in the house I did not for a moment doubt. The body had evidently been placed in my room to direct suspicion upon me. It was a delicate situation. Without an instant's delay I resolved to beat a retreat. Dressing and pocketing my valuables, I stole softly out of the room, down the steps, and to the hall door. Horror ! It was locked, and the key was gone!

What was to be done next? It did not require a moment to decide. Cautiously feeling my way to the farther end of the hall, I tried the door there. It was unlocked. I opened it, and found myself in a room literally strewed with tables, chairs, and débris. There had evidently been a desperate struggle, and the murdered man, whoever he was, had died hard. I struck a match, and by its faint light discerned the cards, counters, and other appliances of gambling. Suddenly the sounds of footsteps reached me. Extinguishing the match, I drew behind the door. The next moment Mr. Brown entered, holding a candle in one hand and with the other stanching a flesh wound on his cheek. I waited until he was fairly in the room, then making a rush, I—

I awoke. It was simply a case of Italian nightmare.

CHAPTER X.

CURIOUS CARS.—THE ITALIAN RAILROAD SYSTEM.—A FUNERAL IN VENICE.—HOW GLASS EYES ARE MADE.

THE country north-east of Bologna is dull and uninteresting. Nearer Venice it is not only disheartening, it is impassable. There are nothing but marshes, lagoons, and bogs. A tramp in that district is like a tramp in the Mississippi bottoms directly after an overflow. Therefore I repressed my pedestrian proclivities, invested $1.81 in a third-class ticket, and boarded the train for Venice.

When one buys a ticket at an Italian station there is a choice of three kinds—first, second, and third. The first entitles the holder to a seat in a car almost, though not quite, as luxurious as a Pullman ; the second class entitles the holder to a seat as comfortable as the first class, but not as elegant or as fine, that is, the plush is not quite so new or so red. Almost all well-to-do travellers ride in the second class. "Foreigners and fools," as the Italians say, ride in the first. The third class is patronized by peasants and the poorer classes generally, and occasionally—only occasionally—by an economical tourist.

After buying your ticket you are allowed to enter the station and the train. As a rule you are not bothered or noticed again until at your destination, where your ticket has to be shown and given up before you can pass out through the gate. As no conductors go through the train, I wondered what there was to prevent one buying a third-class ticket and getting into a first-class car.

" If you dress well," said an Italian fellow-passenger, " no notice may be taken of your being in a first or second class car."

"But should a guard happen to ask to see your ticket, what then?"

"Oh, I tell you, I would rather sit on a board bench for a few hours, than possibly have to peck rock in a stone jail for several months."

Pecking rock is not a pleasant pastime, and as the fraud in question is a penal offence, I no longer wonder that it is seldom attempted. Four out of five might pass undetected, but then as each thinks he will be the fifth, the absence of conductors is no security.

Some Italian cars are two stories high. The lower floor is divided into three sections, the two at the ends being second class, that in the middle first class. The upper floor, reached by a spiral staircase at the end of the car, is one large compartment used altogether by third-class passengers. The third class has harder seats than the other two, but the superior view makes up for that. The advocates of the European style of car claim that it secures exclusiveness. It is to be hoped the exclusiveness is satisfactory; there is nothing else to brag of. There are no water-coolers, no closets; you cannot stand up and stretch your cramped legs, or walk about when wearied with sitting. The passenger is locked up like so much freight, and shipped to his destination. Somewhere about half-way from Bologna I became tired of sitting still, and thought I would get out and stretch a little. By climbing half way out of the window, and nearly falling out and breaking my neck, I at length managed to reach the bolt and unfasten the door. Then I stepped out with a feeling of relief. In a very short minute I had to step back again, and this time with a feeling of anything but relief, for the guard, who came running up, fairly hustled me in. He seemed outraged at what he called my "rashness."

"The train may start at any moment; you endanger your life in trying to jump on."

I meekly replied that I merely wanted a stretch and a drink of water.

"You can have the water, but you can't have the stretch," said the injured official. Then he whistled for the water-man. A glass of it was brought to my window, for which I paid one cent.

The pedestrian can stretch and drink water *ad libitum*, but when he enters a town of only a thousand or two inhabitants he is waylaid at the gate and required to give a history of himself—whence he comes, how long he means to stop in the town, what is his age, his profession, what the profession of his father. These questions answered, the officer at the gate begins a personal examination. If you have a piece of cheese and bread, a bottle of wine, or other article of food, you are taxed from twenty to one hundred per cent. on the value of your luncheon. One day I was entering a town with a bottle of wine and a little bread and cheese. An officer stopped me and demanded seven cents tax.

"Tax for what?" I asked.

"On those provisions."

"But I do not mean to sell this luncheon. It is for my own use."

"Can't help it—seven cents."

"Oh, *you* can't help it, eh? Well, *I'll* help it." So going to a grassy plot near by, I ate my luncheon then and there. When, a few minutes later, I passed through the gate on the outside of the luncheon, instead of the luncheon on the outside of me, the officer grumbled and looked indignant at being "done" out of his seven cents.

As the train was entering Venice I noticed two peasant women stuffing chickens under their dresses. The scheme seemed likely to succeed. They had delivered their tickets up to the gate-man, and were passing on out of the depot when, in an evil moment, the half-smothered fowls set up a loud cackling. The poor peasant women were hauled back, and their hens confiscated, for attempting to smuggle.

Venice is one of the few places in Italy that fully comes up to one's previous ideas, which does not suffer from being seen in reality instead of through poet's dreams. From the very nature of her surroundings change is impossible. In Rome whole streets have been, and are now being, levelled and widened and modernized. Even in Pompeii, which it would seem ought to retain undiminished all its ancient interest—even Pompeii loses much because of the nineteenth century modernisms that environ it. To hear the engines whistle and the cars rattle and the guards cry, "Pompeii—all out for Pompeii!" is necessarily disillusioning to the romantic tourist, who wishes in fancy to go back two thousand years and live in the past.

In Venice the streets of water cannot be straightened, cannot be widened, cannot be changed. The city cannot expand. As was Venice three hundred years ago, so she is to-day. The gondolas are as black, are as graceful as in ye olden time. The palaces with their steps leading down into the water are as quaint and as curious. The people with their lazy, indolent habits are as proud now as I imagine were the ancient Venetians in the days of their city's greatest glory.

When I first read about Venice, as a school-boy, in school geographies, I had the idea that the only way to get about there was by the gondola. That is not so. The one hundred and seventeen islands upon which the city is built are islands by reason of the one hundred and forty-seven canals that wind in and around and about them. Along the sides of these canals you cannot walk; the houses and palaces are built to the water's edge, but in the rear of the houses are streets, the strangest and most curious imaginable. Some of them are not above three feet wide, "fat men's misery" streets, as it were. Three hundred and ninety-eight bridges connect the little streets, and one who is good at threading labyrinthian ways may go all over Venice without looking at a gondola.

"If there is any place," I thought, "where I shall have to abandon cheap living, that place is Venice. Here I cannot tramp about in search of cheap lodging and eating places."

This was a mistake. Depositing my knapsack at the station, paying therefor a two-cent fee, I set out through the crooked little streets, seeing the city, and at the same time keeping my eye open for signs of furnished rooms and inns, of which I found any number for fifteen cents a day. I got a very nice apartment on the Riva degli Schiavoni, looking out on the sea and commanding a charming view of the Grand Canal with its gondolas and gondoliers. The Lido, which I could see from my window, is the Coney Island of Venice. The gay Italians go there to sport in the Adriatic's waves. I went and sported also. It is a fine place. The bathing-houses are comfortable and spacious; the long gallery overlooking the sea is usually, of summer afternoons, crowded with ladies, who watch and applaud the skilful swimmers. The bright black and dark dreamy eyes of the fair Venetians are no doubt a magnetic stimulation. The bathers under their influence were wonderfully expert.

I have taken swims in almost all the great bodies of water on the globe — in the Pacific on the western, in the Atlantic on the eastern coast of America; in the Gulf of Mexico, in the great lakes of the North, in the Mediterranean Sea at Capri, the Adriatic at Lido, the Black Sea at Varna. For a swim of the most novel and delightful sort, however, I would recommend none of these, but rather the waters of the Great Salt Lake. The ocean in comparison with that body is almost fresh. You cannot sink in Salt Lake. It is like lying on a feather-bed. You can recline easily on your back, stick your feet out of the water, and perform other experiments that in ordinary water would insure drowning in two minutes. The day I went in that remarkable lake a big Mormon came floating by me; in his wake was a procession of his wives. It is not every day you see a man bathing with four or five of his wives.

Nothing is more fascinating than "gondoliering." The very atmosphere makes one lazy. In Venice not more than a day is necessary to attune the most restless soul to the slow, luxurious movement of the gondola. The gondolier stands at the extreme rear of his shell-like boat; you do not see him, the monotonous stroke of his oar is all the sound you hear; the boat you loll in seems a thing of life, moving of its own accord.

At night the charm and romance is heightened. The moon lights with a pale and silvery hue the old palaces that rise up direct out of the water; other gondolas glide by, some silently, some sending forth the music of the guitar, or the songs of youth and love—all this makes even the most practical fellow from America feel as if he had at last found a fairy world.

Gondoliering appears to be easy. I thought I would try it.

"Voi siete stanci" (you are tired), I said one night to my gondolier. "If you like you may rest, and I will row for you."

"You, signore? Why, you cannot learn to stand up here in less than two months."

I smiled scornfully, and resolved to show this ignorant Venetian what an American can do when he chooses.

"I have rowed boats on the Hudson, on the Mississippi. These smooth waters are nothing to our big rivers."

"Ah, buono—good, signore, I take you where you have nice swim. Signore, you take clothes off."

Although I did not in the least accept the idea that there was the slightest necessity to take off my clothes in order to be ready for a ducking, still, as he slowly paddled over to the lagoon between the cemetery and Murano, I pulled off my clothes to take a plunge after my first lesson in the Venetian art of gondoliering. As said, nothing seems easier. The oar rests in an oar-lock a foot or eighteen inches high. There is nothing to hold the oar in the lock, but this I did not notice until I tried it myself. It stayed there so quietly and pleasantly as long as the Italian was at the stern, that it never occurred to me but that the oar belonged there, and stayed of its own accord—another mistake!

Scarcely had I taken position at the stern of the boat and made the first stroke, when the oar flew out of that lock, and I flew out of the boat into the water. I thanked the gondolier for his friendly warning. My clothes were saved a wetting. After swimming around to my heart's content, I climbed into the gondola and tried it over again, with the same result. A third and fourth attempt proving no more successful, I came to the conclusion that gondoliering is not so easy as it seems.

Going back to my room, I saw a number of people swimming about the streets. In Venice people go swimming in their back yards or along the streets and avenues.

Gondoliering is cheap—twenty cents for the first hour, ten cents for each hour thereafter. The price is the same for one or four persons, so if you have three companions, you may gondolier around the hundred-isled city at the low rate of two and a half cents an hour.

Everywhere in Italy funeral ceremonies differ from those in America. In no place is the difference so great as in Venice. Strolling in the neighborhood of the Grand Canal, I heard a chant in a church near by. Entering, I found myself with several hundred others at a Venetian funeral. The corpse lay on a pyramid in the centre of the church, surrounded by huge candles, each candle five or six inches in diameter. Priests were saying prayers, hired mourners were groaning and grieving at so much per hour, and a number of boys were swinging vessels of incense, which, though doubtless inoffensive to the deceased, were fairly stifling to the by-standers.

After an hour of praying, chanting, swinging of incense, etc., some men climbed up on the pyramid, got the coffin down, and carried it out. Other men shouldered the huge candles and walked along-side the coffin, half a dozen on each side. Scarcely was the coffin without the door when a lot of ragged men fell upon their knees, and began scraping from the marble floor into their caps the drippings of the large candles. So keen was their rivalry, it seemed for a moment as if their respective claims to the candle drippings was to be settled by force.

Without the church a procession was formed, first of girls in white dresses, each bearing a candle three or four feet long; then the coffin with a line of men on each side, with candles six feet long; then the family and hired mourners; then a brass band. The undertaker wore white gloves and a white hat, and the gondola hearse was gaudy with gold and silver trappings. All other gondolas in Venice, by an old law of the

Middle Ages, are painted a dead black; only those boats intended for the dead are white and gay.

After the family had embarked in their gondola, the hearse
was launched, and soon a long procession was gliding along
the smooth waters of the canal, under the bridge of the Rialto,
on to the cemetery. The cemetery is an island three-quarters
of a mile from the city. There the burial ceremony was concluded; the body was laid away, there was a loud flourish of
trumpets, the brass band played some lively airs, and then everybody went home—the mourners probably to a dance, the
family of the deceased probably to a theatre. For that is the
way in Italy; they are a gay-hearted people, and don't let a
little thing like a funeral disturb their equanimity.

As I was about re-embarking for the city, I saw another
burial, not so imposing as that just described, but equally as
interesting. The deceased was a poor soldier, a private in the
Italian army, who was being laid away to his last rest. The
gaudy plume and coat of the dead soldier were spread on the
plain deal box. His comrades bore him to the long trench
that lay open, already half full, and looking as if yawning for
more. This poor man—one of the half million men that Italy
takes from their homes to die of disease, bad food, and hardships in her standing army—this man was buried with scant
respect. The priests hurried with their prayers, as if grudging
them to a common soldier; then his coat and plume were removed—they belonged to the State, and will serve for another
soldier; the box was covered with earth, and all was over.
The priests hurried back to the walls of their cool monasteries,
the soldiers re-entered their gondolas with smiles and rude jests
on their lips.

How fortunate that man has not the gift of foresight! What
would not the mother of that soldier-boy have suffered when
nursing her innocent babe on her knee, had she foreseen the
day when a crowd of rough and careless men were to lay him
away — lay him away in a trench along with paupers and
thieves in an island in the sea!

While on the subject of funerals I will mention another method of disposing of the dead which I witnessed among the Indians of the wild West. There it is the custom to bury the dead in trees. A tree with spreading boughs is selected, and the body, wrapped in sheets and blankets, is placed on a kind of platform built among the limbs, where it is left free and high in the air. Eight miles from Fort Reno is a cemetery of these tree-graves, where, during my stay in the encampment, a squaw was consigned to her last resting-place. For several days afterwards the friends of the departed yelled and wailed around that tree as if demented; then they picked themselves up and went back to their tepees. A singular thing about Indian grief is its periodicity; that is, it comes and goes—ebbs like a fever. A bereaved widow or mother may be in an agony of grief to-day, to-morrow it is over, and may remain over for perhaps several years; then suddenly the long pent-up sorrow bursts forth again and there is more howling and wailing. The day the burial above referred to took place, there were some mourners under the tree crying over—or, more correctly, under, for the corpse was up in the tree—the body of the chief, Stone Calf, then dead for upward of seven years. Exposed to the dry air and sweeping winds of the broad prairies, the body soon crumbles away, leaving only a skeleton loosely wrapped in sheets and bandages. It is hard to conceive how emotion can be aroused over (or under) such remains.

Venetian glass is famous the world over, not a little of which reputation is owing to the family Rubbi. The knack of making artificial eyes seems in particular to be an hereditary gift in this family; they have been making glassware and glass eyes for three hundred and eighty-six years. I watched Signore Rubbi make a glass eye. Two small glass tubes, one held in each hand, are turned and twisted in a very hot flame. When at the proper temperature the operator blows into one of the tubes and forms a ball at the end the size of a plum, which ball is ultimately to be the eye. The other tube, which is of colored glass, is used in making the colored part of the eye.

It is heated to the correct temperature and incorporated in the ball of white glass at the spot where the pupil is to be. This done, and the white of the eye having assumed the proper creamy color, the delicate feat of making the veins is performed. In doing this, heated tubes of red streaked glass are drawn very deftly over the white surface, leaving tiny reddish streaks behind—the veins.

"It is difficult to say how long it takes to make an eye," said Signore Rubbi. "That depends on what kind of an eye you are making. This lot of eyes here, for a hospital in Australia, is made in a short time. It need hardly be said that making a hospital eye is different from making an eye for a fashionable young lady. The one customer, so long as he has any resemblance at all to an eye in his head, is satisfied. His eye costs about two dollars. The fashionable young lady, however, will probably have half a dozen eyes made before she is satisfied. Now it is the veins that are a little too red, now the pupil a trifle too small or too large. And," continued the signor, "it is odd that these fastidious people are more particular with their night than with their day eyes."

"Night and day eyes? What do you mean?"

"Were you not aware that a different eye is worn for night? Certainly; the pupil is much smaller in daytime than at night, and your fashionable woman would not think of entering a ballroom with the pupils of her eyes of different sizes. When I receive orders from this class, I have to study the eye at all hours of the day and night. Very distant customers sometimes have an artist paint a portrait of the eye, but that method is not altogether satisfactory, and the rich customer generally comes to have his eye personally examined."

On the completion of an eye, before being wrapped in its soft bed of cotton, it is laid on a platter to cool. The first glimpse of a platter of eyes is startling. They seem so natural, look so like they had just jumped out of their owners' heads, that they cause an involuntary start of surprise.

The only horses in Venice are those in bronze over St.

Mark's.   They were originally in Alexandria, whence they were brought to Rome by Augustus.   Constantine transferred them to Constantinople, where for many centuries they ornamented St. Sophia.   The Doges drove them over to Venice.   Several centuries afterwards, when Napoleon began his celebrated feat of whipping all Europe, the French drove them over to Paris.   There they remained until Napoleon went to St. Helena, then they came back to Venice again.   Other trips these bronze horses have made, but they somehow always managed to trot or gallop or fly or swim back to Venice, where they are at the present day, perched upon St. Mark's—a standing curiosity to people unaccustomed to regard horses in the light of church ornaments.

The largest piece of land to be found in Venice is the Piazza of St. Mark, probably large enough to hold the Fifth Avenue Hotel.   It is thronged every evening by thousands of people. A citizen may live several miles away, but when evening comes he jumps into his gondola and goes to St. Mark's Piazza to stare and to be stared at.   Certainly many of the strollers one sees there are worth staring at; specimens of so many nationalities are not often seen elsewhere.   Eastern races are well represented.   I saw a Turk promenade every evening up and down the Piazza, smoking long cigarettes.   His dress was of the brightest colors, his silk trousers were very baggy: they came only a little below the knee.   His jacket of silk was so scanty it hardly sufficed to cover his back.   There were tassels on his shoes and on his turban.   He was always alone, seemed to be objectless.   I wondered what had brought him westward.

Westward?   Venice west!   That sounds odd to American ears, yet relative to Stamboul or Damascus, Venice is in the "far west."   The first time I was in San Francisco I overheard a conversation in the hotel dining-room.

"Well, Bill, good-by," said one man to another.   "I shall not be East again for some time."

It was my first trip west of the Rockies, and I naturally thought I was at the western limits.

"Excuse me," said I to the stranger, "but did you remark that you were not coming East again?"

"I did. What of it?"

"Why, I wanted to know when were you East?"

"When was I East? By the horned spoon, man, where do you call me now?"

The gentleman was from Honolulu.

Before leaving Venice I visited the arsenal and looked at the mediæval relics. The armor worn at Lepanto in 1571 by Sebastiano, Captain-general of the Venetian Republic, is there, as is also his sword, with which he doubtless thumped many a hard-headed Turk. More interesting than Sebastiano's armor is that of Henry IV. of Navarre. Near by is his sword and the identical white plume which he bade his soldiers watch and follow into the thickest of the fight. The plume, discolored and torn by time and rough usage, was presented to Venice in 1603.

CHAPTER XI.

THE STORY OF A RESTLESS TRAVELLER.—A PICKWICKIAN INCIDENT
IN MILAN.—THE ROYAL FAMILY.—FAREWELL TO ITALY.

EN ROUTE from Venice to Milan I stopped in Padua. There is not much to see in Padua—only a few churches and a university—but I was interested in the place from its association with a very singular gentleman whose acquaintance I made several years ago when an attaché in the office of a western newspaper.

It was during the dull season, and I was lolling in an easy-chair, running over the morning issue of the paper, when there entered a gray-haired gentleman, spare and lean in figure, and his deep-set eyes nervous, restless, glancing quickly here and there, as if on the watch for some hidden enemy.

"I wish to subscribe," he said.

"Certainly," said I, arising. "What name, sir?"

"W. Keane King."

"And the address?"

"The address — the address?" repeated the man, with deep-set eyes, nervously — "the address? Well, send it to — to Padua."

"To where?"

"To Pad— No, after all you may as well send it to Paris."

"Paris, Tennessee, or Paris, Kentucky?"

"Paris what?" exclaimed the gray-haired gentleman. "Why, Paris, France. That is my address—Rue St. Honore."

It was not every day that we had subscribers from Padua and Paris, so I endeavored to draw the old gentleman into conversation. At first he was shy and cautious; by degrees, however, he relaxed, and finally related something of his strange life.

"My wife died many years ago," he said, "and since her death I have wandered from place to place, never pausing, never resting. My headquarters are in Paris. There I keep my books and paintings and papers. Once a year I go there and, burying myself in my chambers, read in the papers that have accumulated the world's history for the past year. Then I resume my travels. I have apartments in every capital in Europe —in all I feel equally at home. I had expected to spend the winter in Padua, but now that I think of it, I shall go instead to Paris and Madrid. I start on my forty-ninth voyage across the Atlantic next Saturday."

We sent the paper to the Rue St. Honore, Paris, as directed, and from time to time our singular subscriber sent me foreign journals, now from Spain, now from Russia, the next week perhaps from Turkey or Persia. A year or two passed, when one morning who should enter but Mr. W. Keane King, and as quietly and sedately as if he had been absent but a moment to step across the street. He renewed his subscription to the paper, this time directing it to be sent to Moscow, and was about to leave without further remark, when my brother, who, as it happened, had only returned that morning from a trip to Australia, came into the office. I introduced him and mentioned the fact of his recent trip.

"What, from Australia?" exclaimed Mr. King. "Tell me something of that country. Singular," he added, musingly— "singular I never thought of going there."

My brother's account interested him.

"You may send the paper to Sydney," he said. "I shall not go to Moscow."

That was the last I ever saw of him. Our telegraph editor, who knew the old gentleman—as did, indeed, every one in the office—showed me a few days later a despatch announcing his sudden death in Memphis, Tennessee. So far as I could learn, he died without heirs, and his books, art collections, etc., in the various States of Europe escheated to the respective governments in which they were located.

I was surprised on arriving in Milan to observe that that city had sidewalks. Most Italian cities—Rome and Naples, for instance—scarcely know what sidewalks are. Sometimes there is a miserable apology for a sidewalk, as that on the Corso, the chief street of Rome, but these are worse than none at all. They are so narrow that after falling off every yard or two the pedestrian finally quits in disgust and takes to the street, where there is a good chance of being run over, for vehicles are permitted to drive faster on streets with sidewalks than on streets without them.

Another thing that lends to Milan an appearance of the nineteenth century is the fact that the people are in a hurry. I don't mean, of course, in an American hurry, but in an Italian hurry. They move about rather briskly, not as in Venice and Naples, at the rate of an Alpine glacier, six thousand feet in forty-two years, but possibly at the rate of a mile an hour. They have also in Milan big shops with large windows, and goods tastefully exhibited therein—a thing unknown in the southern Italian cities, where the smallness of most of the business shops is astonishing. In Rome, for instance, the Fratelli Bocconi, the only firm that seem to have caught the modern style, have by far the largest dry-goods establishment in the city; yet their whole business occupies no more space than in America is sometimes occupied by the window displays of a dry-goods house.

There is a great arch at the north-west gate of Milan commemorating the completion of the Simplon road in 1806. An inscription records the fact that " the grand armies of Victor Emmanuel II. and Napoleon III. passed through this arch on the occasion of Italian Independence." On another side is, " Napoleon I., dedicated under his auspices, 1807." The arch is in the Roman style of architecture. Its statuary and reliefs resemble the arches of Severus and Constantine in Rome. On the summit is a bronze chariot, drawn by six gigantic horses. In the chariot is an heroic figure, in bronze, curbing the steeds with one hand, and holding aloft a crown of laurel with the other. This great arch, magnificent in design and execution, is a fit terminus for the splendid road across the Simplon. The rugged Alpine heights and precipices have been left behind, a short strip of the Lombardian plain has been traversed, and when the road reaches this arch it enters Milan, not as a winding mountain-way, but as a broad and shaded avenue.

The morning I returned from visiting this arch I had an adventure not unlike that experienced by the celebrated Mr. Pickwick. My route back into the city lay across a large field half a mile square. The hour was nine in the morning, the place of my adventure was in the centre of that field. While strolling leisurely along, the martial blasts of bugles suddenly broke upon my ears, and in a few minutes a line of about five thousand men appeared in sight marching towards me.

"One man's convenience must give way to that of five thousand," said I to myself, and turned to retrace my steps and give them the right of way. To my surprise, I saw another body of five thousand men armed and marching upon me with a flourish of trumpets. Mr. Pickwick's adventure flashed upon my mind. I did not wish to be the target of ten thousand marksmen, even though blank cartridges were the ammunition; so without losing a moment, I ran as fast as I could parallel with the two lines of soldiers, and in the direction of the other side of the square. I had a narrow escape. By the time I reached a place of safety, the two armies met in the shock of mimic battle. I congratulated myself that I was not flattened lifeless in the collision.

That field is the manœuvring ground of a corps of the Italian army. After the companies had well whipped each other in the sham battle, there was a grand review by a general from Rome. The columns passed by the cathedral, and as far as the eye could reach either way down the broad avenue there was a glittering array of bayonets, swords, and guns. The cannon, officers, and infantry were all there. They were several hours passing a given point. This great military force is the force in one city only; Rome, Naples, Genoa, etc., have their army divisions also. The support of this great army of non-producing men is the chief cause of the great poverty of the masses. For the good of the people, there are two hundred thousand too many soldiers in Italy.

King Victor Emmanuel kept a stable of eight hundred blooded horses, and when he died he left debts to the amount of twenty-eight million lire. It was his playful custom to fall in love with other men's wives, pension the husbands, send them off on foreign missions, and make the wives his mistresses. These pensions and debts he left for his beloved people to pay. In token of their gratitude and appreciation, the aforesaid beloved people have given him a tomb in the Pantheon, and named half the squares and corsos in Italy in his honor. The present king is retrenching expenses. Humbert is called economical. He draws a salary of only three million dollars a year, and lives within its limits. The royal stables have been reduced to one hundred and fifty horses, and the harem of mistresses has been abolished altogether.

King Humbert is a great improvement on his father. His personnel shows him to be a less coarse, less sensual man. His father had thick lips, and a nose that only escaped flatness by being snubbed and turned up in the last degree. King Humbert wears his hair combed back, stiff and erect—a singularly unbecoming style. His mustache is very heavy, and stands out on each side straight and fierce like a stage pirate's. The prince of Naples is a small edition of his father—the same stiff, quill-looking hair, and a promise of the same piratical mustache.

Queen Margherita—I fell in love with this truly royal woman; royal, yet so amiable, so gracious. She looks the ideal queen. Tall, slender, graceful, lustrous black eyes, a pretty nose, beautiful hair, Queen Margherita is a splendid specimen of Italian beauty. I saw her and the Prince of Naples out driving one day in Rome. The admiring homage she received from her subjects as they doffed their hats and bowed and smiled, seemed paid more to the woman than to the queen.

In Bergamo I paid a visit to the palace and art collection of

Signore R———. The gallery, composed of upward of forty halls and salons, possesses, besides many modern paintings, a large number of antique works by Vandyke, Rubens, and others. A Raphael representing the sacred family is the gem of the collection. The Virgin's expression is remarkably sweet, and the red of her lips and the delicate flesh colors are as beautiful as though painted yesterday.

This painting has quite a history. During the Napoleonic wars, when the French were overrunning all Europe, and particularly Lombardy, it was a difficult matter to keep valuable paintings. Napoleon took the best and sent them to Paris. When Milan was captured Bergamo fell also, and to prevent the seizure of this work, another picture was painted over the divine faces Raphael had pictured. Of course such a daub was scorned and left by Napoleon's agents. The device was good, but it had a drawback; in the painter's haste, no mark was left for the recognition of the work, and the result was, that upon the final expulsion of the French all the works of the gallery came to the owner again, but there was no means of knowing the Raphael. Not until 1868 did an accident reveal its identity. In that year the outer painting began to scale off, and thus the long-lost treasure was brought to light again.

Petrarch's picture is more comical than poetical. His head is swathed in a red cloth; only the face is visible; on his chin grows a scanty beard of ten or twelve hairs, the longest about an inch in length. Laura's portrait seems like that of a lackadaisical school-girl. I could not see in her face either beauty or intellect.

I left the cool halls of this fifteenth-century palace to stroll through the hilly and winding streets of Bergamo. The town is situated on the side and summit of a hill, and from the castle on the top a fine view is obtained of the Alps on the one hand and the far-stretching plains of Lombardy on the other. On a clear day the spires of the Milan Cathedral, thirty-nine miles away, can be distinguished. I stopped to inquire the way of a middle-aged lady. My inquiry led to a chat.

"You wish to get a view?" she asked, with true Italian politeness. "Come with me. I will show you."

I followed her through a garden — her own — to a point whence the view was indeed of unexampled loveliness. Below was the peaceful green valley, which looked as if only content and happiness should abide in it. Silently admiring the scene, I forgot my guide, and was reminded of her presence by a deep sigh. Turning to her quickly, I was struck by the appealing wistfulness in the sad eyes which were fixed upon me. Without stopping to think of the impropriety of familiarity to this lady, a total stranger to me, I asked if I could serve her in any way.

"You are an American, you say?"

"Yes—an American."

"Well, I want you to tell me, have you seen my son? He is in America. He went there ten years ago. I have not seen him since."

This was pitiful. How few the chances that I had seen this poor mother's son among all the millions of America; yet I had not the heart to rudely tell her this.

"What is your son's name?" I asked, as gently as if I thought I might satisfy her yearning.

"Luigi Mazonni. He is in Paraguay."

Paraguay! I disliked to explain to her how great the distance between Paraguay and the land of my birth. I thought it would only increase her vague ideas of the dangers of her son's whereabouts. I merely told her I was sorry I had not seen her son—sorry that I could give no good news of him.

And now I bid adieu to Italy, the land of romance, the land of beautiful women—Italy the land of—macaroni! Her art stores, her palaces, her antiquities, all afford the traveller interest and instruction, but nothing, not even the treasures of Pompeii, the ruins of ancient Rome, nor the romance of Venice, gave me so much enjoyment as did the study of the peasants and the people. Amid the greatest hardships and poverty, I found the Italian people ever gay and happy. Neither the hovels of Naples, nor the malaria of the marshes, nor the cold winds of the Apennines, seem able to repress the irrepressible gayety of this happy race. Their country, a land hoary with age and antiquities, is an ever-present reminder of the shortness of human life, of the vanity of all things human.

Accustomed to seeing the Forum where Julius Cæsar expired, or wagon ruts made in Pompeii twenty centuries ago, the Italian looks upon Time with different eyes and different feelings from the American who thinks of Washington as almost as remote in the past as Cæsar; and of the discovery of his country as a thing almost prehistoric.

The longest period of life—one hundred years—seems very short in Italy. The Italian deems it wise to make the best of his little day while it lasts, leaving the future to take care of itself. To him, perhaps, as well as to the stranger viewing this land of past peoples, do the lines of the poet* recur:

> "From cradle to coffin we struggle and seek,
>   Till the fugitive years of our lives are past,
> But whether our lots be blessed or bleak,
>   We are tossed like dogs to the worms at last.
>
> "What is the use of it, then, I say?
>   Why are we brought from the blank unknown,
> To weep and dance through a little day
>   That drifts us under a burial stone?"

---

* Will H. Kernan.

CHAPTER XII.

NOT the least enjoyable feature about travel is the opportunity afforded of observing odd and interesting characters. On the *Independente* one evening, while standing on deck watching the setting sun, a black-mustached, dark-skinned Italian, who knew I was an American, and who was filled with patriotic desire to show up the superior attractions of his own hemisphere, pulled me by the sleeve.

"Dio mio!" he cried, with enthusiasm. "What you see in America like that? What you think? What you want? Where you see sunset like that?"

"Nowhere, signore," I gravely replied. "There is nothing in America like that."

"What! you like that?" he burst out, exultantly, shaking his finger at me. "Ah, you wait; that is *no*-thing. Wait till the Mediterranean; *there* I show you *some*-thing!"

In Genoa this patriotic Italian went with me to the Church of San Lorenzo.

"Dio mio! what you think? what you want?" he exclaimed, as we gazed at the gilded columns. "What you see in America like that—eh?—eh?"

"Nothing, signore. We have no church like that."

"Ah!" with a sigh of extreme satisfaction—"ah, you wait; this is *no*-thing. I bring you to Naples; *there* I show you *some*-thing."

In Naples my Italian went through a similar performance. Whatever I saw to admire, although far excelling anything

I had left behind, was nothing to the glories I would see at some other Italian place.

There sat opposite me one day in a Milan milkery a young man who, like myself, was making a frugal breakfast of bread and milk. From his appearance I judged he was an American. He had an amiable, kind face, so I ventured to open a conversation.

"Fine weather," was my original and brilliant remark. Slowly turning his eyes upon me—they had an abstracted, far-away look—he gravely asked if I had given much thought as to the ultimate end of man? I confessed I had not.

"Man's end is only a question of time. You must know," he went on, after gulping down the last drop of milk in his glass—"you must know his end is only a question of time. I have been turning over in my mind what it is that will end him. What do you think of freezing?"

"A very good way, if it must be done; but I hope it may be put off as long as possible."

"It won't be done in our time."

"I am glad to hear it. I like warmth."

"Oh, it will come on so slowly we will hardly know what it is that is killing us. Scientists predict a return of the glacial period."

This young man was not at all a lunatic, although at that first meeting I took him to be one. He was only a little eccentric. That meeting was the beginning of a companionship I found very pleasant. I dubbed him "Professor." We travelled together through Switzerland on foot.

Rivo is a small hamlet one thousand feet above Lake Como. The Professor and I climbed up to Rivo, there to pass the night, and in the morning begin with fresh strength the ascent of Mount Generoso, some four thousand feet above Rivo. Few travellers pass this way. We were objects of curiosity; the women in Rivo stood in their doors and stared at us. Going up to an elderly dame, we asked if she could lodge us.

"Wait; I will ask my mother," said the old lady.

Her mother! She looked like a grandmother herself. Back she trotted, and behind her trotted a still older woman, who peered at us keenly from under her shaggy old eyebrows, and agreed to lodge us and give us a supper of bread and milk—all she had. The younger woman had never married, and still maintained the habit of filial obedience, although she looked sixty or seventy years old.

We began the climb next morning at daybreak, in a mist of fog and cloud. When at an elevation of some three thousand feet, we heard a voice shouting from the other side of the deep ravine. We dimly discerned through the mist a man gesticulating violently.

"We must be on the wrong track," I said to the Professor; "that man thinks we are in danger."

Not the least discomposed, the Professor coolly took out his guide-books and maps. But I was afraid to trust a dreamer as guide on the top of a mist-covered mountain with deep ravines and precipices, where one might stumble without a minute's warning. I had more faith in the peasant, who continued to shout and wave his hands warningly. Without more ado, I called the Professor to follow, and began to jump from stone to stone along the sides of the ravine. Fifteen minutes brought us to the peasant, who, as I expected, said we were following the wrong path, and pointed out the right. I gave him a few cents for his kindness, and we walked on. The Professor smiled on me with grave pity.

"My friend," he said, "you think that innocent peasant wanted to show you the right way? All he wanted was a fee, in return for which he has shown you the wrong way. The Swiss peasant resents a tourist's mountaineering without a guide. He feels at liberty to humbug travellers if he can."

Refusing to believe that simple-hearted man capable of such a trick, I pursued the path he pointed out, in full confidence that the Professor was mistaken.

"I don't mind the extra walk," said the Professor. "It is a delightful morning, and we have plenty of time." And so we kept on, until the path wound around the ravine and began a plain and rapid descent.

"Now," said the Professor, "you see this path leads to the base, not to the summit of the mountain."

I saw.

"There is nothing left but to retrace our steps, or to pitch out through the woods and find the summit for ourselves."

It was my turn to follow, so we plunged into the wet brush-wood and pushed on. Emerging from the wood, with some consternation we saw ourselves confronted by a great green wall nine hundred feet high. It seemed hardly possible that we could climb this grassy, slippery ascent.

"At the worst, we can slide down if we fail to climb," said the Professor.

The grass was wet, but fortunately was strong. When our foothold gave way, we wound our hands in the long blades of grass, and lay flat on our faces to rest and recover exhausted strength. The Professor had spoken cheerfully of sliding down, but I did not fancy the idea; a nine hundred foot slide down a steep, almost perpendicular, mountain-slope is no light matter. My hair almost stood on end whenever, as several times happened, the grass came up by the roots, and I felt myself slipping down. When at length we reached the end of the slope, we were covered from head to foot with a greenish slime. And what was the reward of this fatigue and peril? A view about ten yards in diameter!—ten yards and no more; for the mist in which we had been enveloped for the last two hours still remained, cutting off the magnificent panorama of the Alps and the Italian plains that is to be seen from this lofty height on a clear, sunshiny day.

Stuffing his guide-books in his capacious pockets, the Professor produced a bottle of ink, a pen, and a diary, and began to write. Looking over his shoulder, I read:

"June 1st, 11.31 A.M. I write this in a cloud on the summit of Mount Generoso, 6531½ feet above the sea."

That was the Professor, exact to the half inch. If you

mention Tiberius, the monster who nineteen centuries ago horrified mankind by his atrocious deeds, the Professor will correct you and say that it is not nineteen centuries, but eighteen centuries and sixty-five years. He is unhappy unless exact. When I pointed out a rock affording a slight pre-eminence above the spot upon which he was writing, he stuffed his ink-bottle and diary back in his pocket and resumed his writing only after he had scaled the rock, and was literally and exactly on the very summit of the mountain, $6531\frac{1}{2}$ feet above the level of the sea.

When we passed through Morragio that afternoon after descending Mount Generoso, I stopped at the village shoemaker's to have repaired a slight rent in my knapsack. From sad experience, I had learned to be cautious in all pecuniary dealings; so, before letting him have the sack, I asked, "Quanto" (how much?).

"Oh," replied the shoemaker, smiling, "meno di cento lire" (less than a hundred lire).

"But how much less?"

"Think not, signore, that I cheat you. Meno di cento lire."

"True," I thought, "in so small a matter there is no room for extortion," and so handed him the sack. In twenty minutes the rent was repaired.

"Quanto?" (how much?), I asked.

The shoemaker, no longer the smiling, obsequious man of half an hour before, but now an arrogant, insolent churl, demanded four lire—eighty cents. In those parts a shoemaker's wages for a whole day amount to less than half that sum.

"Let me see if it is all right," I said, taking the knapsack and looking it over. Then, in a casual way, I put it over my shoulder. After strapping it securely, I took out of my pocket one lira, three times as much as he deserved.

"This," said I, "is all I shall pay you. Will you take it?"

Refusing, I flung the coin on his bench. The shoemaker boiled with rage, and made as if he meant to come at me.

" Stand back!" I cried, flourishing my heavy mountain staff
—" stand back! If you touch me I will club you."

As I backed out of his alley, still flourishing my club, the
friendly shoemaker informed me that I was a thief, a murderer,
and, worst of all, a brute and an anti-Christ.

To reach the Simplon road we struck across the country
from Mount Generoso, and there took the boat for Pallanza. It
is very pleasant on the Swiss and Italian lakes. The scenery is
sublime, the waters of the lakes look cool and inviting. The
situation would be perfect but for one thing—the impertinent
interference of man. The lakes are on the frontier; the land-
ings are now in Italy, now in Switzerland; and just as the traveller begins to fairly appreciate the beauties of nature that surround him, he is tapped on the shoulder by a man brilliant
with gold braiding and brass buttons and sword. It matters
not whether you mean to land or remain on the boat, this gorgeous individual in brass buttons is the customs officer, and he
goes through your knapsack as if expecting to find stolen diamonds. These frequent examinations are annoying. I was
glad when Pallanza was reached, and the foot trip over the
Simplon begun.

As night drew on we met the peasants returning from the
fields loaded with hay. The women, harnessed to wagons like
mules or oxen, drew great loads that in New York Bergh would
not allow a horse to draw. It was a relief to turn the gaze
from these poor, overworked creatures to the beauties of nature—to the crystal stream that flowed by the side of the road,
to the walls of the ravine that come nearer and nearer together
as the road winds upward, to the bonfires that blazed on a doz-
en cliffs and peaks lighted by woodsmen, who, although the
month was June, had in their lofty huts the cold of December.

It was ten o'clock at night when we climbed into the village
of Vogogno, where a strange scene met our gaze. The Piazza
of the town was dimly lighted with oil lamps, a rude trapeze
and turning pole was erected in the centre, and a man and his
wife and two sons were giving an acrobatic performance. The

whole village was there *en masse*, and the simple feats of the acrobats were applauded with a gusto that the professionals of Barnum's shows rarely receive, or at any rate rarely merit. This circle of happy but dirty faces seen by the flickering light was pleasant and picturesque. I listened to the usual conundrums, dressed up in Italian, which the wife, who played ringmaster, propounded to her husband, the clown. Then when the drums ceased beating, and the lights were put out, and the people gone, I followed the mountebanks to their wagon, and drew them into a short chat.

"We don't get rich," laughed the wife, "but it is a free and easy life, and we like it. We have always enough to eat. Everybody gives his soldo. The villages are not far apart. We exhibit every night. By five o'clock in the morning we will be on the road, and early in the afternoon at our destination. We get there early that we may rest before the performance."

An American circus, with its "aggregation of conglomerated wonders," takes in thousands of dollars a day. This modest Swiss-Italian affair is content with fifteen lire—not quite three dollars. Often it does not make that.

Five o'clock next morning found me up. I was rewarded for my early rising by seeing the stage from Brieg drive up with a grand flourish. The only passengers were an Englishman and his daughter. The Englishman remained sitting, but the young lady descended and entered the hotel to get a cup of coffee. She was the first English-speaking maiden I had seen for some time; moreover, she was very pretty, and when, on her return, she experienced a slight difficulty in climbing the stage steps, I sprang gallantly forward and assisted her. I forgot that I was a "tramp"—a working-man, not a gentleman.

"Thank you, my good man," she said, in tolerable Italian, handing me a copper coin; then to her father, in English, "I suppose one must give money if one is only looked at by these poor Italians."

There was a genuine lout of a peasant lounging at the door,

who of course did not understand a word of English; nevertheless, I addressed him in my best mother tongue, at the same time tossing him two coppers.

"The signorina wishes you to drink her health, and you may also drink mine."

The face of that young girl was a study. It turned pale, then red. I bowed and walked off, leaving both father and daughter in a curious state of perplexity.

Many articles which in America are made of wood, in Italy are made of stone. Benches, roofs, floors, tables are often of stone; not, however, until I tramped over the Simplon did I see telegraph-poles of stone! Wood in this particular region is comparatively abundant. Perhaps stone is used on account of its superior durability. A stone telegraph-pole certainly has excellent lasting properties.

After leaving Vogogno the scenery grows grander and wilder. The road winds along on the side of a foaming mountain torrent called the Tosa; the pretty town of Domo d'Osola, the last Italian town, is passed. At Crevola the valley abruptly ends, and the ascent of the Simplon begins through tunnels and ledges that have been blasted in the solid rock. At noon, under the shadows of the overhanging precipices, we ate our bread-and-cheese luncheon; wild strawberries that grew in abundance along the steep mountain's sides made our dessert. How we enjoyed that frugal meal! Stretched on our backs, our heads resting on our knapsacks, we feasted on the beautiful red berries, and our eyes feasted on the scenery. There were the giant pines of the forest, and the great gray cliffs that hemmed us in, thousands of feet high, on every side. In contrast to all this was the huge wall of an avalanche a few hundred yards up the road from our resting-place. A tunnel was cut through the huge mass of snow for the passage of vehicles and pedestrians; but fired with the true mountaineer spirit, the Professor and I determined to climb *over* the avalanche. Some distance up men were digging out a buried hut. When about half way to them the Professor slipped, and came near sliding down over the tunnel into the gorge below. This seemed to dispirit him, and I sought to cheer him with stories of *real* Alpine disasters.

"There is Lord Douglass," I said, " who slipped down a high avalanche and fell three thousand feet. If you were to fall and slide down this avalanche you would at most go only five hundred or a thousand feet—a mere bagatelle compared with Lord Douglass's fall."

The Professor's perceptions were quick. Seeing the truth of my remark, he resumed his staff and continued the climb. Afterwards we walked through the tunnel. The Professor brought out his note-book again.

"I write this," he wrote, "June 3d, at 12.31 P.M., on the Simplon road, under a tunnel of snow."

Having thus recorded his original ideas, we proceeded on our way. As we went, an alarming change came over the Professor's face. First I observed a black spot under his right eye, then another black spot appeared on the end of his nose, then the spots seemed to break out thickly all over the visible parts of his person. Every time I looked at him there was a new spot. A dreadful suspicion of congestion or plague darted on my mind. I asked the Professor if he felt ill?

"Ill? Not at all; never felt better in my life."

"Then why are you breaking out as if you had the black plague?"

The Professor turned pale. Hastily pulling out his pocket-mirror he surveyed himself anxiously.

"What in the d—l is the matter?" he exclaimed; then, suddenly, a flood of inspiration breaking upon him, " I know. It is my ink!"

So, indeed, it was. He had fastened his bottle insecurely, and the ink had been steadily dripping out. Every time he put his hand in his pocket it became smirched, and every time he put his hand to his face that became smirched. Thus it was he looked so black and plague-stricken. At the first stream the Professor undressed and took a bath. His underclothing was dripping with ink, and the stain on his body and face made him look like a kind of two-legged zebra.

Many English and American tourists see all the sights in a perfunctory way, as if sent by a task-master and bound to get through in a certain time. I saw an Englishman in Santa Croce, Florence, who almost ran through the galleries and halls. In the quarter of an hour I spent examining a single fresco—it was worth more time—he had stuck his nose into the cell of every monk, glanced at Savonarola's cowl and beads, and hurried out to "do" some other show-place of the city, probably so as to see Rome the next day, and leave for London the day after. Conversing with one of these lightning travellers, he said,

"Oh yes, I was in Florence a day. Saw all the sights—Santa Croce, and all the rest."

These tourists, however, are a blessing to the countries they rush through. They pay hotel bills and guides, and buy views, but it is difficult to see wherein they benefit themselves. The German tourist is at the other extreme. Precise, methodical, the German marks off the sights in his guide-book as he would check off a consignment of goods. He feels no emotion, no sentiment, no romance; he looks on the antiquities of Naples and Rome as he would look on the ruins of a house of yesterday. He is only careful to check off what he sees, that he may not mistake and waste time over the same sight again. The Frenchman flies rapidly from one point to another, obtains a superficial knowledge of everything, and in after-conversation makes a better and more brilliant display than the German, who is slow, yet really knows twice as much of the subject.

To an American accustomed in his own country to one language through an extent of four thousand miles, the variety of languages in Europe is a matter of curious interest. It is doubly so to the pedestrian, who is able to note the minutest changes. The traveller who is whisked by train from Milan to Paris or Vienna only knows that whereas yesterday it was Italian, to-day it is French or German. The pedestrian crossing the frontier can note the gradual change, the dovetailing, so to speak, of one tongue with another. In a three days' walk I encountered all shades of the three languages, French, German, and Italian.

At Simplon, the last town before reaching the Pass, we got a luncheon of milk and honey and black bread, and then pushed rapidly on. The wind was biting, the air was thin and keen. We kept warm only by the most vigorous walking. For twenty minutes the road runs through the Pass, neither descending nor ascending; then this level stretch passed, I noticed the drippings from the snow-banks had changed their course; a little more and we passed through a tunnel, over the roof of which a foaming torrent leaped, precipitating itself into the valley; then the long and winding descent began. The distance to Brieg, measured in miles, is a full day's journey, but it is all down hill; we made it in four hours.

We did it by running two-thirds of the way.

CHAPTER XIII.

GENEVA is very appropriately called *le petit* Paris—the little Paris. It is full of Parisians, and French is the language spoken. It is, in fact, a kind of lounging-place for Parisians, who jump on the cars and go there to rest and enjoy the cool breezes of Leman Lake. In the evening the Rue de Rhone is brilliant with a long line of lights. Almost every shop is a café, where bands of music—usually women musicians—play, attracting large crowds, who sit on the pavement and sip vermouth and listen to the music, the effect of which is not a little heightened by the surroundings—the rippling waters of the Rhone a few yards away, and beyond the clear waters of the lake shining like a silver mirror in the light of the moon. The music at one café no sooner ceases than the fiddles and harps of the next one take up the strain; the music sways from one end of the line to the other, and then back again. Fashionable people dash up in their carriages, newly married couples ride up on their "sociable" tricycles, and nine o'clock in the evening finds this brilliant avenue almost blocked with a crowd composed of all nationalities. One-third of the seventy-five thousand people in Geneva are foreigners.

I was interested in the Geneva Art Gallery, not on account of the paintings, but from the fact that the floor was of wood. It was the first wood floor I had seen in Europe. In art galleries it is forbidden to carry a cane or umbrella. Those articles must be deposited with the custodian, who, of course, expects a fee for his trouble. In Geneva I saw a man who avoided this regulation in an odd way. While I was looking at a statue of Rousseau, the custodian came running in after a man who had entered without depositing his cane.

"Don't you see I am lame?" said the man, in a reproachful tone.

The custodian looked. Sure enough, the gentleman was limping—badly too. Of course a lame man could not be deprived of his staff, and the custodian left without the cane and without his fee. Then there was a transformation. The "lame" man winked at me, his limping ceased, and he walked as straight as a major! That was a small trick to save a two-cent fee. In America we do not know how to save two cents. The average American is not up to two-cent economy. In Europe it is a matter of importance with the great body of the people. Housewives in Geneva buy ham, beefsteak, chickens, bread, soup, vegetables—everything ready cooked. In Italy the house-keeper buys the raw material, and carries it to a public "cookery," where a beefsteak or roast is cooked in the shortest possible time for a mere trifle of money. An European with an income of five thousand dollars does not live in a house detached from others, with lawn around it and plenty of fresh air. He lives in a flat, with stores underneath him, and above him a shoemaker or tailor shop, or perhaps even worse—revelling students and their mistresses. In Geneva I heard of several instances of this kind, the first floors of a flat being occupied by respectable, well-to-do merchants, and the top flat by carousing students. One can image the rencontres to which, under such circumstances, the pretty daughter of the merchant, or lawyer, or doctor on the first floor may be subjected.

Geneva is a great centre for music-boxes. Their manufacture is the chief industry of the place, affording employment to thousands of men, women, and children. I visited one of the largest factories.

"Take a seat," said the polite attendant. I did so. Instantly there were strains of delightful music. The chair was a music-box.

"And now," continued the attendant, "if you will leave your cane and hat here, I will take you through the workrooms."

I hung my hat on the rack and put my staff in the stand. Music began to issue from the hat and from the stand. Afterwards, in writing my name in the visitor's register, I dipped the pen in the ink. Music burst forth from the inkstand. If you sat down, the chair made music. I thought myself transported to fairy-land.

"Music-box making," said Mr. Conchon, of the "Star Works," "is a business that requires the utmost patience and nicety. The different parts are made by men, who become experts in those parts, and in those parts only. After the rough cylinder is made, the music is marked thereon by a man who has served years of apprenticeship. In every mark made by this man a peg is put by another man. That is the sole business of one set of men—putting pegs in their places. A fourth set of men file the pegs to a uniform length. The comb or set of teeth which strikes the pegs and makes the sound is now arranged, and the cylinder revolved to see that every peg produces a proper tone. Then comes the most delicate work of all. Each peg is revised by a workman whose ear for music must be good, and who must see that each note is in its proper place, and that each peg is bent at the proper angle. The parts polished, the springs arranged, and the instrument in its case, all is then finally examined by an expert, to see that the movement is good and the time perfect. The music-box is then complete, ready for sale."

I inquired of Mr. Conchon how much his men received.

"Oh, very good wages indeed," was the reply. "Many of the men average five francs ($1.00) a day."

Observing that I evinced no surprise at the vastness of the sum, he added,

"But there are some who earn eight and even nine francs a day. Those who mark the cylinders and adjust the pegs have to serve an apprenticeship of ten or twelve years, and they make fully nine francs a day."

An average of one dollar a day for the nicest, the most delicate mechanical work known? My protectionist friends had
told me that tariffs make wages high. Wages were *not* high
in Switzerland. I began to think I had stumbled on a free-
trade country. I was mistaken. Investigation revealed the
fact that almost everything worth mentioning is subject to an
import duty at the Swiss frontier. True, ice is excepted. Switzerland, with its glaciers, its mountains of eternal snow, has a
corner in the ice market. She generously permits her citizens to
keep cool without being taxed for the privilege. Glass, clothing, perfumery, ironware, farming utensils are all heavily " protected." The tax on locomotives is one dollar and ninety-three
cents for every two hundred and twenty pounds' weight. Estimating the weight of a locomotive at thirty tons, the tax on one
locomotive would amount to about six hundred dollars. The
tariff on asses is low, only nineteen cents per ass, big or little.
The protectionists were evidently afraid to impose too high a
duty on asses; without " asses " it would be impossible to pass
a tariff bill for protective purposes.

When I went by steamer to Lausanne, I put up for the first
time in Europe at a first-class hotel. I did this for two reasons: first, I was curious to know how a fashionable European
hotel is conducted; second, at this place in Lausanne Gibbon
wrote the concluding chapters of his great history.

"On a table in the garden in the rear of the hotel," says
Baedeker, " he finished the last lines of the last chapter one
night at eleven o'clock one hundred years ago."

I like and admire Gibbon; so on reading those lines in the
guide-book I made up my mind to stop at that hotel and write
a letter on the very table that Gibbon wrote upon, and at which,
as he tells us in his autobiography, he sat sadly until after midnight reflecting that, his history done, like Othello his occupation was gone; he saw nothing in the future to do. I wrote
a letter from " the table in the garden," and am bound to say
I received no inspiration. The fact is, the " table in the garden " is a fraud, so is the Hotel Gibbon. The house in which

Gibbon lived was torn down eighty years ago, and the present building was not erected until 1825. As for the table, it is comparatively new. The very garden is new, having been filled up to a depth of twelve feet since the time of Gibbon. The flashy waiters, and formal table-d'hote dinners, and bogus Gibbon relics were too much for me. I left the Hotel Gibbon and walked down to the Castle of Chillon. There I looked at some more bogus historical relics: the names of Byron, Hugo, Eugene Sue, and other celebrated men carved on the pillars of the dungeon. There were also the names of Tom Jones, John Smith, and others of those families. *Their* genuineness I did not doubt. In the dungeons of the Doges at Venice a cell is shown where Byron had himself shut up for twenty-six hours. I can believe this. In a prison the great poet no doubt was able more vividly to feel as a prisoner would; but to stand on a stool and carve one's name on a stone wall could bring no inspiration. It is not probable that Byron, or Victor Hugo, or men of that stamp, would commit such petty folly.

Trees line the edge of the lake at Chillon. Under their friendly shade, and the shade of the old castle's walls, we took a plunge in the cool waters, and then set out for a pedestrian trip to the mountain passes of the interior. On the walk from Martigny to Chamounix I made this note:

"Peasant girl offers flowers — we run — she runs — being swiftest footed, we escape."

The first time a bright, pretty girl comes at a fellow and offers him flowers, he accepts with pleasure and pays willingly. But after the fortieth, or four hundred and fortieth time, it becomes monotonous, and he dodges or runs. Unless he is a Vanderbilt, he thinks of his purse, and if the bright-eyed girl persists in following him a mile or two, arms out-stretched, all the while offering flowers, it rather makes a fellow feel that life is a burden. It always hurts one's heart to refuse beauty a few coins. The moment the Professor and I saw a girl a little ahead of us with flowers we broke into a run and shot by her like a flash, leaving the poor girl to suppose we were escaped lunatics or hunted brigands, or anything her imagination might suggest; but our coppers were saved and we went our way rejoicing. In Italy there was no necessity for this artifice. Walking in Italy is so unusual that a man on foot is supposed to be too poor to indulge in wild flowers. In Switzerland pedestrianism is the fashion with rich and poor. The foot-traveller with knapsack and dusty garb is as often the subject of importunities of beggars, guides, and flower-girls as the tourists in carriages. We spent the night in a small chalet in the Tete Noir, and early next morning set out for Chamounix, not *around* the mountains by the broad road, as less ambitious (and less foolhardy) travellers would have done, but *over* the mountains by way of the Pass of the Col de Balme. In other words, though there is a perfectly plain road from the valley of the Tête Noir to Chamounix, we went by an unfrequented way over a mountain half as high as Mont Blanc, and that seemed to be covered with as much snow as the monarch of mountains itself.

The peasant with whom we stayed said a guide was necessary; but as guides in those regions charge twenty or twenty-five dollars, we set out alone. The snow covered the steep side of the mountain in vast drifts. There were places where to have lost our holds would have sent us sliding down the slippery inclined plane thousands of feet. Indeed, at several points the frozen crust did give way, or rather became dislodged from the general mass, but by thrusting our poles deep in the snow, and remaining perfectly quiet, serious results were avoided, and the sliding confined to at most thirty or forty feet. Especially was this danger present in crossing the glacier of the Tête Noir. The ice of the glacier is far more solid and slippery than the crust of an avalanche. A slip on a glacier almost always means death. There are great fathomless chasms in the ice; his footing once lost, the unfortunate traveller slides down with increasing velocity until he enters one of those dreadful chasms and disappears from sight forever.

The ascent occupied the greater part of the day. From the summit we saw Mont Blanc's snow-covered cliffs and peaks towering up into the clouds; thousands of feet below was the smiling valley of Chamounix. The sun was on his downward course. The prospect of a nocturnal tramp over that vast expanse of snow and icy marsh was anything but cheering. The Professor proposed that we should follow the snow-drippings.

"Water," he wisely remarked, "always pursues the most direct route. If we attempt to cross those snow-fields we will freeze stiff before we reach Chamounix."

The latter part of his proposition I could readily believe, the former I received with some doubt.

"Water can go where we cannot—over a precipice, for instance, or under a rock."

With the confidence of a scientist the Professor overbore my objections, and we began to descend the ravine following the watercourse. This ravine is formed by the steep sloping mountains, towering on each side, from two to three thousand feet high. The two sides come together at a sharp angle. The water that rushes down between them fills the entire space, leaving only the rocks and bowlders upon which to pick a way. This impetuous torrent that leaps and bounds from bowlder to bowlder in the deep ravine of the Col de Balme is the beginning of the river Arve, which at Geneva, where it empties into the lake, seems so placid and still.

For an hour no absolutely insurmountable obstacle was encountered; the Professor was about to congratulate himself on the success of his "direct water-route," when a bend in the gulch revealed a fall, a sudden descent where the water leaped not less than thirty feet. We had descended fully one thousand five hundred feet; to retrace our steps the Professor declared out of the question.

"To go back to the summit and cross the avalanches in the night will be fatal," he said.

"But what is there to do?"

The Professor critically surveyed the situation.

"*I* am going down right here," he said.

It looked like madness; nevertheless, he actually began to

climb down that water-fall! I held my breath as I watched the feat. The walls of the ravine or gorge at this point are almost perpendicular, and not more than three feet apart. Stretching his legs between the walls, the Professor began letting himself down a foot or two beyond the dash of the water, as a skilful workman goes down a well, supporting the weight of his body by the pressure of the hands and feet on each side of the wall. For some distance beyond the actual dash of the water the walls were wet with spray. The sides were slippery; the slightest mistake, the slightest relaxation of the strong and steady pressure of hands and feet, would have tumbled the Professor on the sharp rocks below. I breathed easier after he safely reached the bottom. Could I also succeed? I did not choose to run the risk, preferring the rather forlorn hope of finding a way around the water-fall. Cautiously stepping from bowlder to bowlder, I critically surveyed the situation. The steep sides of the ravine environed me; a pair of wings would have been more prized at that moment than millions of money. Selecting a place that seemed slightly less perpendicular than the rest, I began that terrible climb, aided by my trusty pike. The slope which from a distance had seemed composed of rough ledges of stone, proved to be a mass of crumbling shale. It slipped and slid beneath my step. Great masses that looked as solid as the rock of Gibraltar crumbled at a touch and rolled away. In vain I diverged, now to the right, now to the left, allured by the hope of finding solidity, each time disappointed, each time the same deceptive, crumbling material.

Painfully pursuing this zigzag course for an hour or more I looked about to take my bearings. Cold horrors seized me as I saw I was within a few yards of a precipice. Were my strength to fail me one moment I would slide down that precipice with the shaly soil that continually crumbled beneath my weight. I knew at a glance that slide would be into eternity. I lay flat on my face, holding my breath and thrusting my pike deep into the soil. During the ten or fifteen minutes that I lay there I thought of my happy home in far-off America. It seemed millions of miles distant, as distant as if I had left the earth and was lost in some foreign world. I saw the grief-stricken face of my father and the anguish of my mother, and fresh strength and energy came to me and fresh hope. Before budging, I coolly considered how I should proceed. I began slowly, cautiously, to crawl upward, stopping still when I dis-lodged blocks of the soft shale. After more than an hour of this terrible climb, almost exhausted, almost despairing as I saw the darkness coming upon me, I heard the faint sound of voices in the distance. Lifting up my own, I gave such a yell as the rebels of the South in their palmiest days would have envied. On a ledge of rock far above me I dimly discovered the forms of men. One was the Professor, the other two were peasants. They had ropes and lanterns. The rope was let down, I made it fast under my arms, and was soon drawn up to a place of safety.

The Professor had waited for me at the first shepherd's hut; my prolonged absence had alarmed him, and he set out with the two shepherds on the search, following a goat's path that wound along the side of the ravine some eight hundred feet from the bottom. After a few minutes' rest we set out for Argentiere, where we arrived about midnight, too nervous and exhausted to continue the trip to Chamounix.

My tramps into the interior of Switzerland afforded interest-ing glimpses of peasant life. Many of the peasants own the hut and land on which they live, although the cow and farming implements are often rented. A cow is treated with as much care as a baby. A man or woman generally sits near by, knit-ting, and taking care that the cow does not fall off the side of the farm. Then the milk, how carefully each drop is saved to make the big cheeses! Merchants from Geneva and Berne and other cities ride in the fall from one house to another and buy the cheeses, which ultimately go to all parts of the world. Be-fore winter sets in the Swiss peasant has a little money snug in hand, the rented cow goes back to her owner, and during the winter, when the deep snow and mountain storms keep him at home, he and his wife and children sit around the pine fire and carve little wooden figures, human faces, all kinds of animals, deer, bears, etc.   These they sell in the spring, when the cheese-making begins again.   Such is the life of the Swiss peasantry, simple and happy.   They are economical and temperate, save in the matter of tobacco.   Big pipes are filled to the top, and the peasant puffs steadily as he knits and watches his cow.   Around each chalet, as their cottages are styled, is a small patch of flax or hemp.   They have also a few sheep, and in the winter when not carving, they spin flax and make cloth from the wool of their sheep.

One day in a small interior hamlet a travelling shoemaker came by.   He takes old cowhides, makes them into rough shoes and leggings, and for this receives at the peasant's châlet his lodging, meals, and about fifteen cents a day in money.

"Yes," he said, " I always have work enough.   I go from place to place, and there is always some one needing shoes or wanting a cowhide dressed.   They save up the hides until I come and make them into boots and shoes."

The following table shows his income and cost of living:

Table of the Swiss Shoemaker.

Income—estimating board and lodging at fifteen cents per day.$54 60
Fifteen cents per day in money, averaging two hundred and ninety
days per year.. 42 50

                    Total yearly income........................ $97 10

Diet.—Breakfast: rye-bread, whey or milk.   Dinner: rye-bread, potatoes,
milk, sometimes cheese.   Supper: rye-bread, whey or milk.   Cost of
food per day:

Bread.................................. 4 cents.
Potatoes or cabbage.................... 3   "
Milk................................... 4   "
Cheese, etc............................ 2   "

                    Total per day........... 13 cents ; per year..$47 45
Lodging ....   "   7 30
Clothing, including hats and shoes.....................   "   17 26
Tobacco and wine, or beer..............................   "   19 90
Incidentals..   "   6 66

                    Total cost of living................   " $98 57

In Berne I knew that I was at last in German Switzerland by the long words that greeted me at every turn. The names over the shops and on the lamp-posts are so long they go around once or twice, and even then sometimes the end is left hanging over. Such a word, for instance, as *brennmaterialienhandlung* is entirely too long to get over one door, so part of it is hung over the door of the neighboring shop. I met this noble word frequently in Berne; it commanded my awe and respect. I thought none the less of it when I found it meant simply " coal dealer." On the contrary, my respect increased for a language able to use such big words for such little things.

CHAPTER XIV.

On my way to the Grimsel Pass I stopped at Interlaken, and there visited the celebrated Milk-cure. A German milk-cure is a curious thing. They are not so numerous as the "beer cures," but they are interesting. A park, with shady walks and sparkling fountains, contains an airy pavilion, where, at six o'clock in the morning, frequenters of the cure assemble and drink milk fresh from the cow, and listen to excellent music. They get as full as possible of warm milk, then stroll around the park until ready to hold more, then go again to the pavilion, and take in loads of the lacteal fluid. In any other country this would simply be called swilling milk; here it is a "cure." Fat Germans bloated by beer, or overfed beef-eating Englishmen, go to Interlaken, live on milk a few weeks, give their overtaxed stomachs a rest, and pay high prices because it is a "cure." Living on peasants' diet of black bread and milk would work a quicker cure, besides having the advantage of greater economy.

The Grimsel Pass is one of the highest in Switzerland. The last two hours of the way lies buried in the snow; it is safe to attempt its ascent only in the day, and in favorable weather. Within half an hour of the summit is a hospice, a solid granite structure, built to withstand the fierce storms of that bleak region.

It was nearing night when we reached that point, and I was for postponing the passage until morning. The Professor, however, protested.

"The charge for a bed here," he said, consulting his guide-books, "is four francs (eighty cents). I don't mean to break my record of cheap lodgings. We can easily push over the Pass to-night."

And push we did. We traversed those vast fields of snow as the last rays of the setting sun faded beyond the distant mountains. When at last we stood on the extreme summit among lofty peaks and crags, the keen wind sweeping across the avalanches, chilling with its icy breath, it was night. A more weird and dismal scene cannot be imagined than that viewed by night from the summit of the Grimsel. All is desolation— a frozen wilderness. A few yards from where we stood in that vast solitude is a frozen sea, the grave of thousands of soldiers; for as wild and inaccessible as is this spot, it has witnessed two nights of bloody strife. First, in the Middle Ages, the Bernese and the people of the Canton Wallis fought here, and the dead were buried in the frozen waters of the lake. Again, in 1799, Napoleon wanted to drive back the Austrians. The lofty Grimsel was impregnable, until a peasant of Guttannen turned traitor and led the French by a secret path around and across the head of the Rhone Glacier to the hospice. The battle was brief but bloody. The impetuous French drove the Austrians back across the fields of snow, and down into the valley. Many dead were left behind, and these found their last resting-place in the icy Todtensee—"Deadmen's Sea," so called since the bloody fray of 1799.

The traitorous peasant received a large tract of land for his treachery, and Napoleon got Switzerland, and shortly afterwards Italy; for he pursued the Austrians into the lowlands, whipped them at Marengo, and reduced all northern Italy to French control.

Two hours' rapid walking down the steep and rugged path that leads into the Rhone valley brought us to the Rhone Glacier Hotel. Here quite an adventure occurred. The Rhone Glacier Hotel was evidently for first-class tourists; "no tramps need apply" seemed written all over its fashionable exterior.

What was to be done? The nearest village was distant three miles, and it was already midnight.

Across the way was a small châlet, the stopping-place of the guides and teamsters.

"We must rouse them up there," said the Professor, and going to the door he began pounding away, until a woman with a candle appeared rubbing her eyes.

"Was wollen sie?" (what do you wish), she said, in an injured tone.

"Lodging, if you please," replied the Professor, suavely.

"This is not the hotel. It is across the way."

"But we do not wish to go to the hotel. We are poor journeymen."

The woman looked at us hard and suspiciously.

"I have no place," she said.

"But you must have *some* place," persisted the Professor. "In the barn, on the floor — anywhere, only that it is somewhere."

This persistence increased the good woman's suspicions. She called to her husband, and between the two we suffered severe cross-examination. The Professor stuck to his story of being poor *Handwerksburschen* (journeymen), pleaded economy as the reason for not going to the hotel, and at length they consented to admit us. We lost no time in shedding our clothes and seeking our mattresses, which, though of straw, were as welcome as eider-down.

So far the economical plan was working admirably. The hospice or hotel would have charged about a dollar; our beds in the châlet only cost ten cents, and the whole bill next morning, breakfast included, was but fifteen cents apiece. The very smallness of the amount helped to get us in the predicament that followed. There was absolutely not a centime of Swiss money in our treasury!

It was our custom to carry our funds in English bank-notes, that being the most convenient form in which to carry money; we bought small change from time to time as needed. Our supply of Swiss money was exhausted, the smallest bill we had was a twenty-pound Bank of England note—about five hundred francs, a small fortune in the eyes of the frugal Swiss. It was unpleasant to have to present so large a bill, but there was no other alternative. It was impossible to slip away and get it changed.

"Madam," said the Professor, timidly, "can you change a note?"

The woman looked at us in our blouses, and seeing we were too poor to go to the hotel, doubtless thought it a poor little five or ten franc note that we had been treasuring.

"Certainly," she said, and reached out her hand.

A bomb-shell would not have astonished her more — five hundred francs! Without saying a word, she stepped out of the door, and returned in three minutes with an officer of the gendarmes. In as many minutes more we were on our way with that officer to the next village.

Appearances were certainly against us. It is not the custom in Switzerland for tramp journeymen to go about with small fortunes in their pockets. We were put to our wits' end to prove that the money was lawfully ours. This our American letters and papers, and fluent command of English, was at length able to do. We were dismissed with the warning that "an eye would be kept upon us." They did keep a pretty sharp eye on us, as I shall relate.

Three days afterwards, when we walked into Lucerne, we were as dilapidated as any American professional tramps. Our shoes were worn, our blouses stained and dirty, our whole appearance shabby in the extreme. Depositing our knapsacks at a lodging-house, we went out on the quay to look at the boats and the river, and consider the question of once more dressing like gentlemen. I proposed celluloid collars and cuffs as having the advantage of economy, not having to be washed or ironed, and also the advantage of looking neat and dressy. The Professor at once fell into one of his odd philosophical moods.

"Celluloid," said he, speaking in German—we talked in German for practice—"celluloid is a dangerous compound. It contains gun-cotton; heat, a sudden blow might produce an explosion."

In this absurd strain he continued, using the biggest words he could think of simply for the pleasure of hearing himself talk. In the midst of his harangue a man who had been lurking near approached and addressed us.

"Was sind Sie fuer Landsleute?" (what nationality are you).

We imagined him a guide or cheap-hotel runner. To avoid his importunities, we answered in an off-hand manner that we were "Handwerksburschen aus Berne" (journeymen from Berne), then resumed our celluloid conversation. The supposed hotel runner stopped us again.

"You must go with me," he said, opening his coat and displaying the badge of the secret police, and once more we were honored by the State's attention.

When before the city authorities, the man testified that he had heard a very suspicious conversation of bombs and explosions, and had reason to believe we were German Socialists, bent on disaffecting the working-classes and stirring up mischief. The brass-buttoned officials eyed us severely.

"Who are you?" was demanded.

"Americans."

"Show your passports."

The mischief was, neither of us had a passport. A passport costs five dollars. We had saved that five dollars, and at that moment regretted our unwise economy.

"No papers?" said the officer, with an ominous scowl. "How, then, can you prove that you are Americans?"

A happy thought darted into the Professor's mind. He had a draft on a bank in Lucerne; the bank had his signature. He wrote his name for the police authorities to carry to the bank and compare with the signature there. As this comparison was satisfactory, and there was really nothing against us, they were compelled to release us, as it seemed to me, very unwillingly. They could not understand why young men with money in their pockets should live like peasants. During our stay in Lucerne we were shadowed by the police. Switzerland is the refuge for Socialists, Nihilists, Anarchists, and political offenders of all sorts, making an element the Swiss consider dangerous. So many Nihilists congregate in Zurich that the Czar not many years ago issued a ukase commanding all good Russians to leave that canton on pain of banishment and punishment for treason if afterward found in the Russian empire.

Before leaving Switzerland, I went to Schaffhausen to see the Falls of the Rhine. While taking a stroll early one morning I stopped at one of the numerous small inns and ordered a glass of milk. "Cold, sweet milk," I said twice to the waiter, as otherwise they bring, as a matter of course, either hot or sour milk—two favorite ways of taking milk among the Germans. To my surprise, even after having thus given my order twice, and each time very distinctly, the waiter brought me a pitcher of boiling hot milk. I repeated my order for a glass of cold milk. The waiter said he had none. I arose to go.

"What!" he exclaimed, "you will not pay?" and, without waiting a reply, he snatched my hat from my head and gave it to the proprietor, who at that moment entered. I looked at them with a sort of admiration. Never had I seen such pure assurance, never men with so free-and-easy a method of collecting payment for goods neither ordered nor used. Gazing some moments at the good-natured host and his waiter, I took down his name and number, and repaired bareheaded to the police-station. There I related my story of a hat. The officers consulted, and finally decided the matter was not within their jurisdiction.

"Go," they said, "to the Friedensrichter" (peace-justice).

The Friedensrichter was a grave, bald-headed man, with a portly paunch that betokened acquaintance with much beer. As I was about to state my case, the learned man raised his hand and bade me stop.

"Do you not know," he said, "that my fee must first be paid?"

"But, sir, I have a charge of assault to make.   Must I pay for notifying an officer of a breach of the peace?"

"You must.   The fee is two and a half francs."

This was odd.   I wanted light on the subject, and requested the address of a lawyer.   The Friedensrichter gave me one. Half an hour later I knocked at the door of the man of law, only to learn that he was away serving his annual three weeks in the army.   The maid, however, told me of another lawyer, and he, upon payment of a fee for legal services, told me the law was on the milkman's side, but that I could go to the "Gerichtspraesident" if I desired still further information.   I went to the Gerichtspraesident.   He, too, said the law was with the hot-milk man.   Then I went to the rascally land-lord.

"I pay you," I said, handing him the money and taking my hat—"I pay you, not for the milk I did not order and did not drink, but for the information you have been the means of my acquiring."

"What information?"

"That a stranger may be assaulted here without redress."

The churl laughed scornfully.   But I got even with him. My first act, on reaching German territory, was to send the po-lite Swiss landlord a large package by express: the charges, about one dollar and forty cents, I did *not* prepay.   There was nothing in the package excepting a lot of sawdust, and a sheet of paper with this single line:

"Zum Andenken an den Mann dessen Hut Sie gestohlen haben" ("souvenir of the man whose hat you stole").

On arriving in Germany, I bought Dr. Feller's English-German conversation-book, designed for the use of Germans travel-ling in England.   Some of the doctor's specimens of "conver-sation" English are unique.   The following, for the stage-coach traveller, is given verbatim et literatim et "punctuatim:"

"*She.* Would you be kind enough to change places with me, sir?"

"*He.* With much pleasure, miss; pray make no ceremony."

" *She.* Shall we endeavor to arrange our legs? My left foot is gone to sleep.

" *He.* You are right. Place your right leg here and take your cloak to cover yourself with.

" *She.* Do you snuff, sir?

" *He.* A little, I thank you. There is the town where we are going.

" *She.* Thank God! I am tired of sitting."

Imagine some unsophisticated German with Dr. Feller's conversation-guide asking an English lady to " arrange her legs!" Here is a sample of his railroad English:

" Conductor, why are we detained?"

" To take in water and hang on more second-class carriages."

" Very well, I shall go into the restoration in the mean time."

On Shipboard. " Oh dear, there lies the gentleman and the beefsteak."

" Why are the engines stopped?"

" To take in the pilot. One cannot see the land for the thick atmosphere."

In a Hotel. " Have you a comfortable room in front?"

" Oh yes, but it is three stories high."

" That is too high, for my breath is very short."

The doctor must have meant that the room was on the third floor; the questioner, however, regarding what was said, not meant, very naturally declined the room. A room " three stories high" is altogether too high for a man with " very short breath." Polite conversation in English runs thus, according to Dr. Feller:

" Sir, what is the matter with you? How long have you been ill?"

" Since the day I had the honor of seeing you at my uncle's."

To Servants. " There are stains in my blue coat; you must take it to be scoured. Comb me carefully. You lace me too tight. Let them a little looser."

Hitherto Ollendorf, with his " where-is-the-blue-umbrella-of-my-grandfather's-red-mule" sort of question, has stood at the head of this peculiar kind of literature, but he will have to yield the palm to Dr. Feller of Gotha. As the Professor remarked, the doctor's name should be spelled with an "h" instead of two "l's" (Fehler instead of Feller). As "Fehler," in German, signifies "mistake, error," I quite agree with the Professor. Certainly it would be difficult to concoct an English conversation-book with more errors than Dr. Feller has succeeded in getting in his little work.

Strasbourg has many interesting features; there is the clock, the cathedral, the peculiar-looking houses, the fortifications. What to me was more interesting, however, was the peculiar relation of the city to the German Government. The people talk German, they look German, they belong to Germany, but their love and affection are all for France. True, it has been but a few years since they belonged to France; but when I saw the city, talked with the people, and found them so Teutonic in manner and language, I expected to find their sympathies for Germany as much as if they had never owed allegiance to France. It was hard to believe the city really French in sentiment. I became convinced only after questioning all sorts of people, and in one instance getting myself into a scrape.

The better to mix with the workmen, I wore the blue blouse of the German "Dienstmann" (service-man). Speaking German with some fluency, I was taken for a native workman, and had my questions answered freely. On one occasion I was unfortunate enough to forget the rôle I was playing. It was in a cheap coffee-house. The remarks of one of the working-men so interested me I took out my note-book and began to note them down. The sudden cessation of talk, the sudden stillness, made me look up; every eye was fixed upon me, angry suspicion in them. I had not the least idea what I had done to lose their confidence. Then I heard the word, "Spion" (spy) hissed out. It was taken up by one and then another, until the air was full of angry "Spion," "spion," "spion." I declared at once my nationality.

"Sie sind so wenig Amerikaner wie ich!" (you are as little American as I am), yelled a big, burly house-painter in overalls, daubed with paint, as he shook his fist at me.

I believe the infuriated crowd would have given me a drubbing had it not been for a policeman who was attracted to the place by the noise and hubbub. As I walked away with the officer he explained the affair. From my ready use of the pen those workmen jumped to the conclusion that I was a spy employed by the German Government to take note of the disaffection of the people towards Germany, and their love for France.

"You think it strange," said a man with whom I was conversing on the subject, in a more reasonable company, "that the people here love France more than Germany. You must remember for one hundred and eighty years we belonged to France. In that time we learned to love the country, even though we learned not the language. In another one hundred and eighty years Strasbourg will learn to love Germany; that is," he added, with a significant smile, "if France does not have her back by that time."

In Italy soldiers are very numerous. In Switzerland the supply is altogether too liberal to suit American ideas. Germany surpasses them all. In Germany the American traveller feels as if he were in a vast military camp.

I took a walk in the suburbs of Strasbourg. I saw soldiers throwing up intrenchments, building bridges, drilling; the aspect of the country looked more warlike than peaceful. On the main street of Strasbourg one afternoon, in about half an hour I counted five hundred soldiers—five hundred, not in a body, but singly—five hundred off duty, merely strolling about. Soldiers are compelled to salute all officers. As officers are almost as numerous as soldiers, the result is interesting. You look down the street, and see a crowd of men lifting their hands stiffly and awkwardly in the air, crooking the elbows, and bringing the fingers to the rim of the cap; then unbending the arm and letting it fall to the side, to be raised again, however, before it has been there two seconds.

This saluting is irksome. It is about the only work many officers have to do; and from the reluctant manner in which they respond to the private's greeting, I imagine they do not like to do even that. The salute on the part of the soldier is obligatory. Once, when looking in a shop-window, a soldier happened by, and also stopped to look in the window. Suddenly he stiffened straight as a poker, wheeled, and brought his hand to his cap. He had seen the reflection of an officer in the window.

"Must you even go out of your way to salute?" I asked the soldier, after the officer had passed.

"Not seeing the officer," he replied, "is sometimes accepted as an excuse, but not always. 'If you didn't see me, you ought to,' an officer will sometimes say, and give you ten days or two weeks in the guard-house."

This soldier told me of a case where an officer, to punish a new recruit for "stupidity," ordered him to aim and discharge his gun at the sun. The recruit did so, and was stricken blind. At first nothing whatever was said of the matter; when, finally, the surgeon reported the case to headquarters, the only punishment accorded the inhuman officer was a reprimand. One day in the park, pointing to a passing soldier, I asked a little boy,

"Willst du Soldat werden?" (do you want to become a soldier).

The little fellow eyed the brass buttons, the bright red stripes and glittering helmet, and seemed about to say yes; but he hesitated.

"No," he said; "my papa was a soldier, and my papa had his eye shot out. No, Herr, I don't want to be a soldier, and have my eye shot out."

Nevertheless, if that little boy lives to become a man, and the present government lasts until then, the strong arm of the law will seize him, and rob him of the fairest years of his life, putting him through fatiguing drills, in tiresome barracks, and in wars where he may have his eye shot out as was his father's.

On the way to Baden-Baden I found myself face to face with

an insane woman; but at first I had no suspicion of her insanity; so when she craned her neck forward and pointed upward, and asked me if I saw that big balloon, I craned my neck and stared at the cloudless sky, and wondered why I too could not see the big balloon. Then the woman laughed loudly and triumphantly.

"Fooled! fooled!" she screamed; "oh, what fools you men are! What poor fools! Ha, ha, ha!"

I stared in amazement, and she went off into screams of laughter, becoming so excited that a strong-looking woman by her side felt it necessary to interfere to soothe and restrain. Then I discovered that the poor woman who thought men such fools, though possibly right on that point, was wrong on others.

She had on a strait-jacket, and the muscular woman by her side was taking her to an asylum.

The first thing one notices in Baden-Baden is the sign announcing the rate at which visitors are taxed. One person per year pays thirty marks ($5.00); a family of two pays thirty marks; of six, forty-eight marks; per day, it is half a mark—twelve cents. Payment of this tax gives access to the public gardens, parks, springs, etc. Life in Baden-Baden is monotonous. In the morning you drink water, eat breakfast, take a stroll, bathe in the mineral waters at eleven, sleep, lunch, and at 3 P.M. go to the "Conversationshaus" and listen to music and watch the children play. A big German in knee-breeches and swallow-tail coat is employed to amuse the children: he is a success, for he amuses the grown folks as well as the young ones. I spent a very pleasant hour watching his burly form rolling on the grass and performing all manner of jolly tricks. At the conclusion of his performance he sent up a variety of queer-shaped balloons—some made to resemble horses, others elephants, fishes, men, etc. These odd figures hung a few hundred feet over our heads like a flying menagerie.

CHAPTER XV.

AFOOT IN GERMANY.—POVERTY OF THE STUDENTS.—ADVENTURES OF A DUTCHMAN.—THE BOOZY LOVER.—MARRIAGE AND FUNERAL CUSTOMS.

THE stranger entering Heidelberg is apt to think there has been a bloody riot, and that the Heidelbergians got the worst of it. The town is full of students, and almost every student is slashed and gashed with sword-wounds. Some have their ears and nose slotted, others have their cheeks cut from jaw to skull. These are wounds received in duels which are fought twice a week in a little white house across the river. On the morning of the duelling-days streams of carriages may be seen crossing the bridge on the way to the little house. Each carriage contains only one student and a dog, so that it requires a number of vehicles to get all the dogs and all the students over. Mark Twain, in his "Tramp Abroad," airily says:

"In the interest of science, I told my agent to procure admission, and on the appointed day was prompt on hand to witness the proceedings."

It is provoking that Mark did not explain how his "agent" procured admission. While the duels are in progress sentinel students are posted about to give warning of the approach of strangers. Only corps students and their intimate friends are admitted to the sacred precincts.

The old Heidelberg Castle is still a romantic place. Portions of its wall have been blown to pieces by the French, and parts have suffered sadly from the ravages of time; still, much of the old-time grandeur remains. Often I strolled by night through its gloomy underground passages, its deserted moats and dikes, imagination going back to the time when the castle

was full of stirring life, when stern soldiers stood in the now
empty sentry-boxes, and brave knights, all clad in steel, galloped
across the drawbridge, and war was the general work of life.
Though war yet seems to make a big part of German life, still
there is an improvement : modern times are a little more peaceful than past times.

One evening I sat by the spring in the court-yard—the same
spring whose cool, clear waters the knights and ladies of old
had drunk from.   The shadows grew deeper and deeper as the
moon sank behind the ruined walls.   The sound of an old German folks-song came floating to me on the still night air.   The
voice sounded sweet and young.   The situation, the hour, har-
monizing with my thoughts, all conspired to rouse within me
the feelings of romance, of poetry, which doubtless is latent in
every breast only twenty - two years old.   My heart gave a
bound ; I listened breathlessly and eagerly ; gazed, not only
hoping, but actually expecting, to see a fair lady shine out from
the gloom.   So I was not the least startled when a white figure appeared in one of the upper windows of the castle.   Just
as I was about to address her in Romeo style—"Fair spirit,"
etc. —another voice interrupted the singer—a good, substantial, every-day voice of a good, substantial, every-day German
Frau.

"Louisa," said the voice—"Louisa, have you brought in the
wash ?"

And the sweet singing stopped, and the sweet voice screamed, "I'm agoing to, now !"

That ended my Heidelberg Castle romance.   I learned next
day that the rooms looking out on the south end of the castle
are occupied by the custodian's family.   His daughter, the
sweet singer, is a solid, red - cheeked German lassie weighing
fully one hundred and fifty pounds.   The wife of the custodian speaks four languages ; and when she shows the castle,
rattles off her descriptions in French, English, German, and
Italian.

In Germany as in Italy it was my custom to stop at work-

ing-men's cheap hotels and lodging-houses. They afforded a
better and closer view of the classes the study of which formed
the object of my trip. Moreover, they are economical. The
highest price demanded in such places for a room is forty pfennige (nine cents). The usual rate is only fifteen or twenty
pfennige (three or four cents). One afternoon in Frankfort-
on-the-Main, while lying down in the room of a workman's
hotel, resting after a long tramp, there was a timid knock at
the door, and a moment later a head poked itself in, followed
by the very shabbily dressed body of a very shabby-looking
man. He looked at me hesitatingly, then said, in an humble,
apologetic tone,

"Pardon, mein Herr. I am hungry. I have had nothing to
eat."

"Nothing to eat!" I exclaimed, rising from my couch.

"Yes," he said, "nothing for two days. I am very hungry."

"But would they give you nothing at the farm-houses? Will
they give you nothing here in the hotel?"

"Ah, Herr, I have not dared to ask. It is forbidden to beg,
forbidden to ask for work."

The man seemed honest, yet it looked hardly credible that a
man should be forbidden to ask for work. I took him to the
nearest eating-house and ordered a substantial but cheap meal.
The poor fellow was ravenous. He had eaten nothing for two
days, and on an empty stomach had dragged himself forty miles.
When he had done eating he told me his story. He was the
son of a South German bricklayer. His father had given him
a common-school education; but being ambitious above the
ordinary, he had worked hard, saved a pittance of money, and
gone to the university at Leipsic. He was now on his way home
to earn a livelihood, as he hoped, by teaching. His statement
regarding begging and asking for work I found to be literally
true. An observer entering a German town may see the an-
nouncement that beggars of alms and persons *asking employment* will be sent to the workhouse. I gave my young student
a mark (twenty-four cents), enough to pay his way for the next

two days' journey, whereupon he took his departure with many blessings and expressions of gratitude.*

Frankfort's main recommendation to the tourist is its historical houses—houses in which great men either lived or were born. On Jew Street is still standing the shanty where the first Rothschild was born. In 1872 seventeen houses in the neighborhood fell down and killed thirty-four people. New buildings have taken their places; the Rothschild shanty, which somehow did not fall, is the only one of the old houses left. The head office of the Rothschilds, just around the corner from the birthplace of the founder of the firm, is in a very common-looking house; from outside appearances one would never imagine that behind those windows and gratings was the money centre of Germany, if not, indeed, of all Europe. Jew Street was formerly a kind of Jew prison. There were gates at each end; a bell rang at sunset, and any Jew caught off Jew Street after that hour was severely punished.

Visitors are shown the house wherein Goethe was born—a simple, plain building, with a tablet over the door, merely stating,

"IN THIS HOUSE JOHN WOLFGANG GOETHE WAS BORN,
AUGUST 28, 1749."

The window from which Luther made his celebrated speech is shown.

---

* Professor Billroth comments upon the great increase of pauper students, and as examples of the straits to which these hapless hungerers after knowledge are reduced, quotes from a Berlin paper the application made by a university student who asked to be employed as a night-sweeper; a post which, however modest, would not interfere with the prosecution of his studies. In the Gallician and Hungarian universities poor students sell matches on the streets, or, if they have a musical gift, eke out an existence by playing or singing in *cafes*. Many of them, for want of books and leisure to study, never manage to pass the examinations, and settle down after thirty to the very humblest occupations, while not a few take to evil courses and swell the army of criminals. This fact I obtained from an article in the *Pall Mall Gazette* bearing upon the subject in question.

"If the way is covered with devils, yet will I go to Worms," spoke the intrepid reformer; and the imaginative mind, in gazing at the window from which he spoke those words, can picture the scene, can see the mob staring and wondering at such determination—a determination that braved the Holy Catholic Church, the mightiest power of that age. On the Steinweg, glancing up I saw a stone tablet just under a window of the second story. Translated, the inscription on the tablet runs thus:

"IN THIS HOUSE WAS THE PEACE BETWEEN FRANCE AND
GERMANY SIGNED,
1871."

There, in that room, the five milliards of francs were promised; Napoleon was already in exile—a disappointed, broken-down man. The strange career that began in the fortress at Ham was virtually closed in that second-story room on the Steinweg in Frankfort. The Kaiser Hall contains portraits of the German emperors from Conrad the First (912 A.D.) down to modern times. These portraits represent men in gowns with villanous-looking faces. In those days, to become emperor it was necessary to lay aside scruples and play the villain's part. Henry V. (1106 A.D.) has, in particular, a disagreeable face—cunning and cruel. I would not like to meet such a face on a lonely road. Most of those old fellows went crusading to Jerusalem. Crusading was by no means a pleasure-jaunt, and no doubt the hardships endured, the bloody scrimmages, the robberies and general wickedness perpetrated by those pious Crusaders, had a great deal to do in giving that ill-tempered expression to the faces pictured on the canvas.

A Frankfort window-sign reads thus: "Jeweller to their Majesties: His Majesty the King of Denmark, his Majesty the King of Greece," etc., through the list of all the kings of Europe and the Emperor of Brazil; then a list of queens: "Her Majesty the Queen of Portugal," etc.; then a list of "Excellencies, dukes," etc. The window was fairly covered with the high and mighty names, though it is doubtful whether their Highnesses and Majesties ever heard of the little Frankfort jeweller. Another Frankfort sign of interest is that of L. Levy, U. S. Consul. It is not the sign as consul that is interesting, but the sign announcing that " L. Levy, United States Consul, has a choice lot of the best dry-goods, ladies' gloves, gents' ties, etc." Mr. Levy seems to be of a mercantile turn, and displays along-side the stars and stripes a pretty big advertisement of his dry-goods business.

In Wiesbaden I went to the Conversationshaus, where, seventeen years ago, men won and lost fortunes, where noblemen threw away their inheritances in a single night. Talking, laughing, noise of any kind, however slight, was not permitted. The players sat with pale faces; the servants of rich men stood behind their masters with rouleaux of gold, handing it over silently from time to time as the piles on the table vanished from sight. Too often, after a night of hard luck, the despairing gambler would rise from the table, go out on the street—a moment later a pistol-shot, and a dead body! While walking in the spacious hall musing over the melancholy scenes, the suicides, the lost fortunes, the broken hearts which that magnificent chandelier in the grand salon had gleamed down upon, music from the strings of a harp fell on my ear. In my mind's eye I always picture a harp and a beautiful woman together. The harp is the most gracefully formed of all instruments. With the ready romance of youth I jumped to the idea that those unseen strings were swept by the fairest fingers, and that the loveliest form sat by. Softly stealing towards the door whence issued the sounds, I peeped, and saw—an exclamation burst from my lips as I saw a round, fat, bald-headed, middle-aged fellow, the sweat streaming from his red face, twanging those divine strings!

The Professor, dear old fellow, left me at Zurich. I was alone until I reached Wiesbaden, when I made the acquaintance of a musician from Amsterdam. My description of the delights of pedestrianism so pleased him that he decided to join me in

my tramp. We took the cars back to Heidelberg, and there set
out on foot through Wurtemberg and Bavaria. About ten
miles out from Heidelberg I inquired of a man standing in a
door-way if we could obtain something to eat there.

"Na," he grunted, "kann aber hiebe kriegen" (but ye can
get a licking).

My Dutch musician thought the man was joking. After a
quarter of a mile walk, however, the fact got through his head
that the man was simply surly and boorish; then the Dutchman was so mad that he wanted to go back and whip him.
The churl, I learned, was an employé of Prince Lowenstein.

We overtook, one morning, a stout peasant-woman, with a
scythe under one arm and a baby and a jug of beer under the
other. She looked at our blouses, and soon fell to gossiping.

"Ah," she said, "it is fine to be a *Handwerksbursch*" (travelling journeyman) "when one is young. It is the way to see
the world; and it pays well too, does it not?"

"Not very," I answered, carelessly, "only three or four
marks" (seventy-two or ninety-six cents) "a day."

"Three or four marks!" she exclaimed, "that is splendid.
Is it really true? Three or four marks? The factory hands
at Goeppingen make not so much. Ah, you must be a pretty
workman," and she looked at me in undisguised admiration.

When we reached the fields, this good woman deposited her
baby, her jug of beer, and bread under a tree, and began a hard
day's work with her scythe to earn twenty or twenty-five cents.
There are no farm-houses; all live in *bauerdorfs*—peasant villages. The fields are often two or three miles away, and to
reach them betimes the agricultural laborer has to get up very
early in the morning. Loss of time is not the only disadvan-
tage arising from this custom; there is also a loss of comfort
and health. A bauerdorf consists of a few miserable two-story
houses huddled together on crooked streets. Each side of each
street is invariably lined with stacks of ill-smelling manure.
One can smell a bauerdorf almost a quarter of a mile away.

The names of the inns in these villages are often odd. Once

I stopped in an inn, "To the Golden Air." Another time in one, "To the Bunch of Grapes," "Inn to the Red Rooster," "Inn to the Yellow Angel," etc. In Obrigheim, a fine bauerdorf with more than the usual number of manure-heaps, the host was a young German with a blond beard and a wonderful air of complaisance and self-satisfaction. He played the accordion, and the two old beer-drinkers who constituted his company the night we were there declared the accordion-playing divine. The old bloats looked on in ecstasy while the blond host tipped back in his chair and squeezed doleful squeaks and wheezes from his instrument. At the conclusion of the strain —I must not say melody—the beer-drinkers turned to me and, with one voice, demanded if I had ever heard such music before?

"Never!" I fervently and truthfully replied.

"Ah, I tell you," said one, a shoemaker by trade, "our host comes of a musical family. You can walk two days without finding such a player."

My Amsterdam companion was a professional of the Wagnerian school. Of course his cultivated ears were tortured; his sympathizing face showed it so plainly that I endeavored to divert attention from his disgusted looks by extravagant laudation, which so pleased the beery audience that one of them offered me snuff from his dirty box; this was worse than the music. I politely refused, whereupon he kindly volunteered advice as to my future life.

"A young fellow like you ought to know something of the world," he said. "I have been about a good deal in my day. When I was a handwerksbursch I was as far as Switzerland, and almost to Italy. I dare say you have hardly heard of those countries, eh?"

"They are a long way off," I answered, modestly, and then listened to the wonderful story of his trip to Switzerland. Thirty years had passed since he made that great trip; but a two-hundred-mile journey is looked upon as so huge a thing by a bauerdorf shoemaker that it lives in his memory while life lasts.

An old man whom we overtook carrying a bundle of twig brooms was bent with age and drudgery. I carried his bundle for him a short distance while he took breath and told me the simple story of his life. He had made brooms since his youth. Every morning he goes into the forest, cuts his twigs, and makes his brooms. In one day he makes twelve brooms, which take half of another day to sell, he peddling them from hamlet to hamlet. The brooms sell for nine pfennige each (about two and a quarter cents); so that for two days' work the poor old man makes barely thirty cents. When I gave him back his bundle he looked at me thankfully.

"You are good to help an old man," he said. "You are young now, and make, maybe, your two marks a day; but days will go by, and after a while you will want some one to help carry your brooms. Ah, it is a hard world for the old; always work, work, nothing but work;" and the wrinkled old man went on his way. From the replies he made to my questions as to how much he earned, spent, etc., I prepared the following table.

German Twig-broom Maker.

Earns per year... $68 64

Cost of Living.

	Per Day.		Per Year.
Lodging.....................	3½ cents	....	$12 77
Potatoes and sauerkraut.........	3 "	....	10 95
Bread.......................	3 "	....	10 95
All other food.................	3 "	....	10 95
Coffee and sugar..............	2 "	....	7 30
Beer.........................	2 "	....	7 30
Clothing.....................		....	7 20
Incidentals...................		....	1 22
Daily cost of food, etc......	16½ cents.	Total......	$68 64

In a country inn where I stopped for dinner, a "Verlobungs Karte" (engagement card) was hung on the wall.

"When is the marriage to be?" I asked the host.

He winked, shook his finger mysteriously, and whispered,

"Sh! *she* is over there. It may not be for years. Her man is poor."

The future bride was sitting by the window, and, despite her father's caution, overheard our remarks. She blushed a rosy red, and her fingers flew faster with the knitting. It seems the custom is to publish engagements as soon as made; from that hour the couple are looked upon as almost married. The girl sees no company, goes out but little, and is supposed to think only of the happy hour that is to make her and her beloved one — not always an easy thing to do, for that hour is too often very far off, sometimes never arrives; for it not infrequently happens that the engagements, in spite of their publicity, become broken. The girl in such cases stands small chances of ever being married. No man wants a woman who has been jilted, or who has been almost the wife of another.

Marriage and funeral ceremonies may go on at the same time in the same church. One morning about six o'clock, in the ancient town of Gmuend, on my way over the Hohenstaufen, I passed a church in the style of the Milan Cathedral, built by the same architect. The sound of music from within attracted me. I went in. A man and woman were being made one, and at the same moment prayers were being said over a corpse. Not ten feet away from the bride in her white dress was the coffin with its gloomy trappings!

One night after supper, the Dutchman, having found a piano in the beer-room of the inn, began playing heavy Wagner music. This so enchanted a boozy man who sat at a table drinking beer that he came up, embraced the musician, and called for an encore. He was almost too full of beer for utterance, but managed to tell us he was going to be married.

"And I want you to play some music in honor of the event," he stuttered.

At the end of each selection he hurrahed and cheered, and ordered more beer brought to the musician. The latter knew well how to dispose of beer; still, he was not up to the would-be Benedick's standard, and soon a row of filled and half-filled mugs began to form in front of him on the piano. The big, boozy lover was so persistent for more and more music, that the good-natured Dutchman did not make his escape and get to bed until the lover had fallen asleep, and was unaware when the music ceased.

CHAPTER XVI.

AMONG THE FACTORIES. — LIFE OF GERMAN MILL OPERATIVES. —
HOW TO FORM A BEER "KNEIPER."—THE DEAD-HOUSE OF MU-
NICH. — ANECDOTES OF BAVARIAN PEASANTRY. — THEIR SUPER-
STITION.

TWELVE miles from Goeppingen, on the high-road in the direction of Ulm, nestling at the base of high hills or mountains, is
a place called "Kuchen Fabrik," the literal signification of which
is "Cake-factory." It is, however, by no means a cake-factory.
On the contrary, cake is scarcely known there, the inhabitants
being glad if they only have a sufficiency of rye or black
bread. Kuchen Fabrik is a manufactory of cotton goods; and
the town, if so it may be called, is composed entirely of the
factory hands and employes, some seven hundred persons in
all. Around a small park forming a hollow square are built a
number of plain two-story houses, which form the habitations
of the seven hundred hands. Each house has two floors, with
four rooms to the floor. Families of five, six, or seven persons
may sometimes be found occupying an entire floor; none,
though, enjoy the luxury of an entire cottage, and the majority content themselves with two rooms, making four families to
the cottage.

In front of each cottage is a small plot of ground planted
with vegetables, which is shared in common by the inmates of
the cottage. The park or hollow square is planted with shade-
trees and provided with long tables, at which in summer the
operatives eat their dinners between the hours of twelve and
one o'clock. Work is begun at six in the morning, and continued, with intermissions during the day amounting in all to
one hour and forty minutes, up to seven o'clock. For this
day's work of eleven and a half hours and upward a good

man-spinner receives two and a half marks (about sixty cents). Women-spinners earn less. They average only thirty-seven and a half cents a day of twelve hours' actual work, and thirteen hours at the mills. Boys and girls twelve years of age work not more than six hours per day. Their wages amount to the pitiful sum of nine to eighteen cents per week. Tabulated, the statement of wages paid at Kuchen Fabrik appears thus:

Wage-table.

Spinners, men, per week of 66 to 68 hours $3.60
Spinners, women, per week of 66 to 68 hours........   2.25
Boys and girls, per week of 33 to 34 hours ....   .09 to .18
Firemen, per week of 66 to 68 hours..............   3.60
Engineers, per week of 66 to 68 hours............   3.84

A workman's ordinary suit costs $7.30; a Sunday suit costs thirty to thirty-six marks ($7.30 to $8.64). Such a suit the workman wears for years. The rent of two rooms per week ranges from thirty-eight to forty-eight cents, or $18.24 to $24.96 per year. A floor of three or four rooms costs $37.44 to $49.92 per year. Those of the employés who so desire are boarded by the mill company for sixty-five pfennige a day, or about fifteen cents. Breakfast and supper consist of two pieces of bread, and coffee. For dinner is served a soup, together with the meat of the soup, bread, and one kind of vegetable, generally either potatoes or cabbage. These prices are low, and compensate in some degree for the poor wages. But do they compensate entirely? The following account will show in detail the income and cost of living of German mill operatives of the skilled and better class. The reader may judge for himself therefrom whether the low prices in Germany make proper compensation for the low wages.

Family of German Mill Operatives.

Family numbers five: parents, two children, and the mother of the father.

Condition.—Occupy two rooms on second floor of cottage; parents work in mills; the grandmother looks after house and children; family dress very plainly; have few or no comforts.

Earnings of father per year................................... $177 00
Earnings of mother per year.............................. 122 40

      Total earnings per year........................ $299 40

Diet.—Breakfast: black bread and coffee. Dinner: rye-bread, soup, bacon or soup-meat, potatoes, beer. Supper: black bread and coffee.

Cost of Living:

	Per Day.	Per Year.
Bread..............................	15 cents.	$51 75
Soups, meats, sausages, etc.............	5 "	18 25
Coffee and chiccory...................	$3\frac{5}{7}$ "	13 55
Milk..............................	$3\frac{2}{7}$ "	11 99
Potatoes and cabbage.................	4 "	14 60
Eggs.............................	$1\frac{1}{2}$ "	5 47
Cheese and groceries of all kinds........	$27\frac{1}{2}$ "	100 67
Food costs five people.......	60 cents.	$216 28
Rent...		18 12
Clothing..		29 00
Fuel and light.....................................		12 77
Beer...		37 60
Total yearly cost of living for five persons........		$313 77
Total income.....................		299 40
Showing a deficit of................		$14 37

The German workman spends a great deal on beer. It costs ten pfennige ($2\frac{1}{4}$ cents) a glass; the host of the one saloon permitted in the settlement said each man averaged three half-quart glasses per day. I took dinner under the trees with the men. It was a sight to see them, seven hundred in all, every one with a foaming glass of beer. Several thousand glasses are consumed every day at this one factory. The word " Gemuethlich," which Germans so fondly declare has no rival or equivalent in any other language, is simply a polite expression for " bumming." No other one thing is so destructive of domestic happiness as this German custom called " Gemuethlichkeit." Almost every beer saloon has one or more private rooms cosily furnished with easy-chairs and tables. These rooms are rented to beer " Kneipers " (clubs). A beer club is easily formed. Ten or twelve neighbors agree to go once a week to the nearest saloon and drink as much beer as they can hold; that is a beer "Kneiper." Every week, on the appointed evening, they go to the private room, sit around the table, smoke and drink beer until midnight, or even later; this is called "Gemuethlich" (sociable). There is no discussion of politics, of literature, of philosophy, no flow of wit—only a flow, one continuous flow, of beer. One man orders a round; the glasses hold half a quart, but the last drop is drained and another of the party returns the first man's treat. A second round comes and goes. Another man feels called upon to respond to number two's treat, and so it continues until the whole party are heavy and boozy.

This evil, far from abating, is increasing, and so rapidly that even the Germans themselves are becoming alarmed. In 1870 there were in Prussia alone 120,000 licensed saloons and 40,000 public-houses where liquors were sold. In 1880 the census showed an increase of 38 per cent.—in other words, the number of saloons had risen to upward of 200,000, and the average consumption of beer per day was four glasses for every man, woman, and child in the kingdom! Twenty-seven per cent. of the male lunacy in Prussian asylums is attributed to drink. These are some of the direct effects of beer, admitted by all; its indirect effects may not be so readily seen or admitted, they are, nevertheless, as sure and injurious. Look at the distended paunch, the bloated face, the unnatural redness of the veins, the dull eye of the practised beer-drinker; consider his diseased liver, his fat, overlaid stomach, overworked kidneys, and it will occasion little surprise to learn that the average life of beer-drinkers is less than that of the non-beer drinkers—is less than thirty-three years.

One night at Kuchen the country singing-master arrived from a neighboring village. The members of the class went through their exercises in the hall of the public-house, accompanied by the teacher on a squeaky fiddle. At the close of the lesson my Dutchman sauntered up to the singing-master, and asked if he might look at his violin. The country musician eyed the Dutchman's blouse, took him for some village clodhopper, and naturally hesitated to trust him with his beloved fiddle. But the Dutchman insisted, and gained his point. The astonishment that followed upon the apparent Handwerksbursch's first sweep of the strings is indescribable. As the flood of melody and harmony poured forth, the simple country master and factory-hand pupils sat breathless, drinking in the sounds in ecstasy. They realized that they were in the presence of a master. That Dutchman who had so often tormented me when on other matters intent with his eternal whistling and humming, was one of the foremost violinists of Holland. Never had that old fiddle spoken so eloquently. The singing-master and his scholars called for an encore; more beer was brought, and until far in the night the Dutchman stood there in his blouse, now melting with soft, melancholy strains, now firing his hearers with some wild gallop or Hungarian theme. The following night, at the singing-master's earnest entreaty, a regular concert was arranged; when we left the Kuchen Fabrik it was in a blaze of glory.

In Baden I bought some stamps and postal-cards. In Stuttgart they were worthless. Stamps bought in Wurtemberg are not good in Bavaria. Wurtemberg, Baden, and Bavaria have their own money and their own postal services. They have, in addition to the emperor, local kings and dukes, which of course is a heavy burden on the people. For instance, Bavarians have not only to pay the old Kaiser Wilhelm, but their own mad king also—mad king, for such the present king is. His predecessor, who so recently drowned himself, was the man who had an opera company all to himself, who built romantic castles with subterranean passages, and battlements and moats and drawbridges in the style of the Middle Ages. Ludwig II.'s salary was 4,231,044 marks—about $1,100,000; but on that beggarly pittance he was utterly unable to meet his expenses; only a short time before his suicide he found himself obliged to borrow $2,000,000 to pay some of his more pressing creditors. Notwithstanding his enormous debts, the king continued building castles to the last. That of Herrenchiemsee, which was begun twelve years ago, has already cost upward of thirty million marks, yet it is hardly one-third of the way towards completion. Just before his death another castle, which was to be called "Falkenfels," was ordered. "Lindenhof" is still another unfinished castle of Ludwig II.

"For what purpose are these castles?" asked a German paper bolder than the rest (*The Frankfurter Zeitung*, July 16, 1885). "Where will it stop? Who can tell whether there are not more projects for squandering money? What is the object of so many castles? They are built in so peculiar, so romantic a way that they will suit no other owner. They are constructed regardless of expense, as if money were grabbed out of the air. The tradesmen creditors of the king have not been paid for ten years. Some of them are on the point of bankruptcy. The eight million loan served as a sop for a while, but what next? Will the State intervene? No minister will dare to introduce such a measure, and no chamber would support it. It is useless to hope for a change for the better; the catastrophe is unavoidable, and such a catastrophe as Bavaria has never experienced before!"

The catastrophe was avoided by the suicide of the mad king in June, 1886. The father of the present king was extravagant, but his extravagance was at least productive of a little good, was not all thrown away on useless castles. The art galleries and museums that ornament Munich are almost entirely due to the taste of King Lewis I., who died in 1868. In the Pinakothek is a collection of some of the finest modern works of art. A large painting in that collection by Piloty * is entitled "Thusnelda in the triumph of Germanicus." Tiberius is on the throne, a man of dark, treacherous, sinister look. Thusnelda, proud, haughty, unbroken, passes the throne head erect, her very attitude betokening defiance. Her boy, a little fellow of five or six, is by her side with dazed look, as if not knowing what to make of the strange men around him. In the background a

* Died July, 1886.

Roman soldier is pulling the long beard of a German prisoner. Lying on the ground is a pile of captured arms and shields. The whole painting is admirable in design and execution. It is virtually a Roman triumph upon which you gaze—Varrus and his legions are avenged.

In the same room and by the same artist is another striking painting—"Seni before the Corpse of Wallenstein." The grim old hero of the Thirty Years' War is lying on the floor of his study, the table-cover half pulled off, the books scattered, the globes overturned, indicating the violence and suddenness of the death. Seni the philosopher stands melancholy, as if lost in reverie, gazing at the dead body of his friend. The canvas is very large, the coloring and perspective so accurate, you feel you are really in the room and presence of the stern Wallenstein.

The Maximilaneum contains thirty of the largest paintings in Germany. One represents the Battle of Arminius, where the Germans are overwhelming the Romans. On a knoll in the rear the women and old men are inciting the warriors to greater efforts. "The Building of the Pyramids" shows the swarthy Egyptians raising great blocks of stone by means of inclined planes and mechanical apparatuses. This painting is considered one of the finest in the collection.

But Munich is celebrated not alone for its art. As a beer centre it has not its equal. The Court Brewery is nightly thronged by thirsty beer - drinkers. There are no waiters. You walk into the court-yard of the brewery, hang around a man who you think will soon be through with his glass, grab the glass when he has finished, take it to the pump, and wash it yourself; then you are ready to get beer, if you can—if you can, because unless patient and strong you will not get any. The rush is like that in some American cities after Patti opera tickets. There is a cue; you have to take your place, and only get your beer when your turn arrives. Once the possessor of a quart of the foaming liquid (quart jugs are the smallest used), you can go out to the court-yard, stand around, and look at the crowd.   I remained there one night until one o'clock watching a crowd of young men getting drunk.   At first they were mere-ly hilarious—sang, rollicked, and playfully kicked off one an-other's hats; then they became boozy, then sleepy, then dead drunk, and had finally to be put in cabs and carried away.   The Court Brewery is only one of many such places in Munich.

In the Munich Cemetery I saw a house full of corpses.   One whole side of the house was of glass, through which the ghast-ly inmates were plainly visible.   The dead in one section were surrounded with flowers and wreaths; in the other section there were no wreaths, no flowers, only plain biers devoid of all trimmings or trappings.   The one was the section of the rich, the other was for the poor.   The corpses in both sections are connected with electric bells; the slightest movement rings an alarm and arouses attendants.   The dread of being buried alive prevails, and every corpse must lie in this house twenty-four hours before burial.   A crowd of curious, morbid people constantly surround the windows and flatten their noses against the glass walls, gazing at the ghastly scene within.   I asked a Munich physician if any one had ever been saved by these pre-cautions.

"Yes, though not often," was the reply.   "Once the body of a man lay there nineteen hours without a motion, then sud-denly his hands twitched, the bells instantly rang, and he was saved.   He lived several years after that.   As a rule, those who come to life again live only a short time.   In their en-feebled state they cannot withstand the shock of waking up and finding themselves surrounded by the dead."

This same doctor mentioned an incident occurring in his practice which illustrates the superstition of the lower classes. A peasant had broken his arm, and the doctor put it in a splint-board.   The arm having healed, the doctor called one day for his splints.   They were gone.   The peasant stammered, hemmed and hawed, that was all.   He either could not or would not pro-duce the boards.   Some six months afterwards, happening to be in the village church, what was the doctor's surprise to see on the altar his old splint-boards, painted and decorated with this inscription:

"OFFERING OF HERMANN SCHWEBEL, WHO WAS SAVED BY THE HELP OF DR. F—— AND THE VIRGIN MARY."

It is the custom among the Bavarian peasantry for a father, on becoming old, to turn over his hut and few acres of ground to his married sons; the sons in their turn are obligated to give their father a lodging-place, and food and drink. This, said Dr. F., the Bavarian sons often do most grudgingly. In one case the old father fell a victim to small-pox. The sons deserted him, and the priest they sent to minister to his spiritual wants was afraid of the disease and dared not enter the door. Standing without the window, he shouted, "You are forgiven of all your sins!" and returned to the village. For such louts the discipline of the German army seems a good thing. In the three years they serve, a little of the boorishness is drubbed and beaten out of them. The soldiers are often detailed to act as servants to officers. In America that is forbidden by law; the law, however, does not amount to much. When a guest of Colonel H—— at Fort S——, Indian Territory, I learned that the officers' cooks and waiters were soldiers.

"The inspector stopped with me once," said Colonel H——, "and when he saw I had a soldier for a cook he made a big to do—called me at once to order. I said nothing, simply sent my waiters and cooks to the barracks. The next morning when the inspector came down to breakfast there was no coffee, no beefsteak—no anything excepting cheese and soda-crackers. The inspector had much consideration for the inner man. His heart fell at sight of the meagre breakfast.

"Colonel," he said, while munching a dry cracker—"colonel, I think you had better send for your cooks."

"I did, and I never heard any further objection about hiring soldiers for domestic duties."

A church in Munich has a glass case in which is the skeleton of a saint decked with diamonds, rubies, and pearls.   In the palace of the king is a bed of the fifteenth century which cost $400,000, and required forty persons ten years to make. In the museum is the faded purple coat, the saddle, pistols, and walking-cane of Frederick the Great.

These are a few of the curiosities of the Bavarian capital.

CHAPTER XVII.

IN A SALT - MINE. — TWO THOUSAND FEET UNDER THE EARTH.—
TROUBLES OF A PEDESTRIAN IN AUSTRIA. — I PERFORM IN THE
OPERA BEFORE AUSTRIA'S EMPEROR.—A GRATIFYING SUCCESS.

THE finest church music I ever heard was in Salzburg, Austria. Strolling through the town early one Sunday morning, I passed the cathedral, heard music, and entered. It was grand. The choir contained fiddles, flutes, and harps; the volume of sound increased and swelled until the vast edifice was filled with melody from floor to vaulted roof and lofty dome. It was while listening to that grand music that I remembered that I was in the birth-town of Mozart. A statue of the great composer is in the square opposite the cathedral; elsewhere in the town the tourist is shown two houses in which he was born.

A charge is made for showing these houses. Mozart, while he was about it, should have been born in a dozen houses, and thus still further added to the revenues of his native Salzburg.

The Hallein salt-mines near Salzburg are among the most noted in Europe. The Romans once worked these mines, and from first to last it is probable they have yielded upward of a million tons of salt. The whole mountain is honeycombed with tunnels and passages, which every year are extended deeper and deeper. The visitor to the bottom of the mine must now go some two thousand feet below the level of the top of the mountain.

I walked there one day from Salzburg, and paid three florins to go through the mines. A curious costume was provided for the trip. First I was put into a baggy suit of sail-cloth; then a heavy fez was clapped on my head. A thick piece of sole leather was next tied around my middle, and finally a pair of heavy leather gloves were fastened on my hands. The reason for this singular outfit was at first not apparent; it soon became so. After going about a mile through a horizontal passage five feet high by three wide, my conductor suddenly made a turn, and I found myself at the head of a steep, sloping shaft, the only means of descent down which was by a sliding skid. A rope lay along-side the skid. Grasping this rope serves as a brake, thus checking the rapidity of the descent. Like a pair of school-boys sliding down ballusters, we took our places, the guide going first. Soon we were whirling down that black and fearful shaft at a rate that almost made my hair stand on end. I griped the rope for dear life; the friction was too much even for the thick leather glove I wore: it burned my hand and I was compelled to relax my grasp. When finally I shot on to the landing one thousand five hundred feet below, I thought I was going at a velocity of sixty miles an hour! Fortunately, no bones were broken; I was able to pick myself up and view the enchanting scene that surrounded me. It seemed like dreamland! A subterranean lake illuminated by a thousand lights! We were ferried across this lake; then came a short slide of only a few hundred feet, and we were at the very bottom of the mine, under the lake and under the mountain.

Notwithstanding the nature and astonishing rapidity of the descent, two thousand feet into the very bowels of the earth, I had time to wonder how the ascent was to be made. The greased pole of the country picnic would be easy compared with those slick, almost perpendicular slides. How were we to get out?

The question was very pleasantly answered. After walking around the bottom of the mine, looking at the way the men got out the salt, my guide conducted me to where two men were in waiting with a singular conveyance. It was a narrow board about ten feet long, raised a couple of feet above the ground and fixed to four small wheels. The guide straddled this board, I did likewise.   A lamp to serve as head-light was strapped on the guide's breast; then the two men, one in the rear, one in front, shoved and pushed the board-wagon along at a dangerous pace, considering the darkness and narrowness of the passage.

Through miles of crooked galleries they ran.   Fearful of losing my balance, I clasped my arms around the guide in front of me, almost afraid to breathe lest I might topple over and dash my brains out against the salty walls.   At last a speck of light became faintly visible in the dim distance.   It grew larger, still larger, until finally the speck of light became an opening, and we emerged once again into the world and the light and day.

We had entered at the summit, we were now at the base of the mountain.   The men slide down to their work in the morning, and when through, slide clear down to the bottom of the mine and leave by way of the horizontal shaft.

The mines are, of course, damp and dark.   Indeed, the mere going and returning from work involves a considerable amount of labor.   The wages for such work should be good.   I made inquiries, and found that an able-bodied miner averages only forty-five kreutzers (about twenty-one cents) a "turn" of six hours.   The following extract from my note-book will show the condition of the average miner at Hallein:

Austrian Miner.

Family numbers three: parents and small child.

Condition.—Occupy one room in a tenement-house; the father works in six-hour shifts in salt-mines—six hours on and six off; the mother does a little work on hand-loom, most of time attends to house and baby.

	Per Day.	Per Year.
Earnings of the father.................	40 cents.	$134 80
Earnings of the mother.................	20 "	60 40
Total earnings.............	60 cents.	$195 40

Diet.—Breakfast: black bread and coffee.   Dinner: black bread, beer, and potatoes; in winter, sauerkraut, and occasionally a bit of salt pork or bacon.   Supper: black bread and coffee.

Cost of Living:

	Per Day.		Per Year.
Bread................................	9 cents.	....	$32 85
Coffee...............................	2½ "	....	9 12
Milk.................................	2½ "	....	9 12
Beer.................................	8 "	....	29 20
Potatoes.............................	15 "	....	18 25
Groceries of all other kinds...........	14 "	....	51 10
Food costs three people.....	41 cents.	....	$149 64
Rent at three florins per month...........................			14 40
Clothing (92 florins).......................................			26 80
Incidentals of all kinds, including fuel, light, religion, etc.......			12 50
Total yearly cost of living......................			$203 34

I will give another itemized statement of the income and expenses of a working-man's family, this time for a family of nail-workers living in one of the Danube villages west of Vienna.

Austrian Nail-makers.

Family numbers eight: parents, boy aged fifteen, boy aged fourteen, four children from four to twelve years of age.

Condition.—Occupy one room in a miserable, ill-smelling house; room is close, no ventilation. Straw mattresses are spread on floor at night; in day-time are removed, and room converted into workshop. All the older members of family work at nail-making, averaging thirteen hours per day. General condition is one of abject poverty.

	Per Week.		Per Year.
Earnings of father.....................	$2 44	....	$126 88
Earnings of boy of fifteen..............	1 00	....	50 84
Earnings of all other members of family...	1 14	....	59 28
Total earnings..............	$4 58	....	$233 20

Cost of Living:

	Per Day.		Per Year.
Bread...........................	23½ cents.	....	$85 78
Potatoes and cabbage................	8½ "	....	31 02
Coffee.............................	4 "	....	14 56
Milk...............................	3 "	....	10 95
Bacon and sausage...................	3⅗ "	....	12 48
Groceries of all kinds, as soap, starch, sugar, etc., and beer..............	2⅘ "	....	45 36
Food cost eight people.....	55 cents.	....	$200 15

Cost of Living, continued:

	Per Year.
Brought forward	$200 15
Rent (at $1.24 a month)	14 88
Clothing	19 25
Various incidentals	9 00
Total yearly cost of living for eight persons	$243 28
Total income	236 20
Showing a deficit of	$7 08

The reader will doubtless conclude from these instances, as I did from personal observation, that the German mechanic and laborer receive miserably insufficient wages; that they live huddled in close, crowded quarters; that they work too many hours and have too little to eat—that, in short, their life is one of hopeless, unceasing drudgery.

My Protectionist friends had said that high tariffs made high wages.

What a pity, I thought, that they do not communicate to the German Government this simple secret of prosperity.

I called on a prominent official to inquire in the matter. The official said:

"Germany a free - trade country? Not a bit of it! Our tariffs are very high. The duty on pig-iron is $2.50 per ton, about twenty per cent.; on bar-iron it is three times as high, or sixty per cent. On manufactured iron goods a duty is levied of from $7.50 to $37.50 per ton. On cotton goods two-eighths of a cent per pound is levied; on woollen goods it goes as high as sixty-five cents a pound. Ready-made wearing apparel is taxed over a dollar a pound; so are ornamental feathers and thread-lace. Asses are taxed $2.38 a head."

Somehow the high tariffs do not succeed in making wages high in Germany or Austria.

On emerging from the salt-mines, I walked over to Berchtesgaden and to the Koenigsee, one of the wildest and grandest regions in Europe. The lake is hemmed in on every side by lofty mountains, rising for the most part precipitously from the water's edge. When the boatman fired a huge blunderbuss of a pistol, the noise and reverberation was as that of thunder.

> "Far along
> From peak to peak the rattling crags among,
> Leaps the live thunder."

The sound dies away; you think it is over; when lo! some still more distant crag takes it up; it comes back again and again, every time fainter, less distinct—like the dying rumble of retreating thunder.

The villages between Salzburg and Linz, on the Danube, are not of an inviting character. Passports are very frequently demanded in Austria, and more than once did my lack of the proper papers occasion trouble. One little town that I entered about nine o'clock at night, after a thirty-mile tramp, possessed just three inns. At each I sought a lodging-place, and at each was refused because I had "keine Schriften" (no passport). The hour was late, I was worn and weary. To walk to the next village, possibly only to meet a similar reception, was out of the question. I determined to fall back on my friends, the peasantry. I saw a light through an open window. A man and some women and children were sitting at a rough table drinking beer. I boldly approached them.

"Meine Herrschaften, ich bin Amerikaner. Ich habe keine Schriften.—I am American. I have no papers, but I have a little money. They will not take me at the inn. Can you give me a place to sleep? I will give you thirty kreutzers."

They all stared at me.

"Ei, Platz genug auf dem Boden" (plenty room in the loft), said the mother, and so it was arranged.

The loft in the high gable-roof was reached by a rickety ladder. My fat old hostess went ahead with a tallow candle to light the way. A pile of straw was heaped in one corner.

"Koennen dort schlafen" (can sleep there), said the old woman, and with a grunt turned and descended the ladder.

It was pitch dark. Fortunately, in my knapsack there were a few matches and a candle; I soon had a light. Hardly two minutes elapsed when up bobbed the head of my hostess again, panting and blowing like a porpoise. She was in a state of extreme excitement.

"Was dann," she cried, "you want people to know we take you in? Mein Gott, it cost us zehn Gulden!" and with a big puff she extinguished my light and left me to find my straw couch in the darkness.

In another village I paid two cents extra for a promise that the other bed in my room should not be rented. It was sweltering hot. In the vain hope of keeping cool, I removed every article of clothing before going to bed. About nine o'clock a stout peasant-woman entered, eyed me coolly as I lay in my airy garb, then proceeded to put herself in a similar state of nature. In a few minutes she was peacefully sleeping, while I lay thinking what strange bedfellows pedestrianism throws together.

I arrived in Vienna at 6 P.M. on the emperor's birthday. At the Imperial Opera-house Verdi's "Aïda" was to be given. The emperor himself was to be there. The occasion was one it would not do to miss. I hastened to the Opera-house only to learn that, with the exception of a few five and ten gulden places, there were no seats left. What was to be done? A brilliant idea occurred to me.

"The emperor has never seen me act," I thought. "Why not let him have that pleasure to-night?"

In the opera of "Aïda" an Egyptian army is represented on the stage. Several hundred "supes" are required. It was now 6.45 P.M. There was no time to lose. Repairing from the ticket-office to the rear of the building, I joined the line of "supes" that had formed at the stage door. Pedestrianism makes one bronzed and sun-burnt—the very thing for an Egyptian soldier. I was at once taken by the manager at a salary of forty kreutzers the night.

Modesty forbids my speaking of the glorious success of my first appearance on the imperial boards of the Austrian capital. I will merely say that as I passed in review bearing aloft the

banner of the good King Rameses, my heart swelled with pride
at the warm approbation of Austria's emperor.   Of course, as
it was my first attempt at opera, I could not help being aware
that his applause was mostly given to me.   It was gratifying.

Vienna is truly an imperial city.   The Ring Strasse, which
encircles the old original city—the city the Turks used to be-
siege—is built up with a collection of public and private buildings which, for solid, imposing magnificence, are not excelled
even in Paris.   The Prater-Stern quite rivals anything of the
kind in the French capital.   Here, where twenty years ago
were fields and woods, are now thousands of houses, beer-gar-
dens, concert-halls, theatres, etc.   Every afternoon and evening
the avenue is thronged by all classes and grades of humanity,
from the emperor down to the scullion and chamber-maid off
on a half-holiday.

There are Punch-and-Judy shows, " Flying Dutchmen," ten-
kreutzer museums, shooting-galleries, and a hundred other catch-
penny places of amusement.   It is here that the "lady" orchestra is seen in its native lair.   Vienna was the originator of
that institution.   The players are selected not so much for
their musical ability as for their beauty.   Result—it is much
pleasanter to *look* at a Vienna "damen capelle" (lady orchestra) than to listen to one.   The leader of one band that I used
to go to see—I mean, to hear—was a dark brunette with wavy
hair, and a pair of the prettiest dancing black eyes I ever saw.
The bass fiddler was also a comely lass.   Unluckily, the fiddle
was as large as she was, and almost hid her from view.

In the basement of the Capuchin Church are the sarcophagi
of Maria Theresa, Joseph II., and others of the imperial house
of Austria.   Externally the church is gloomy-looking; internally it is positively funereal.   The great lead or bronze coffins
(of the material I am not certain) are stowed away in a dark
basement.   The monk who accompanies visitors gives in a solemn monotone the names of the dead, when they died, and who
they were.   Among the rest I noted the coffin of Maria Louisa
and the young Duke of Reichstadt.   What stories lie buried in

those two leaden boxes! When Napoleon was storming Vienna with shot and shell Maria Louisa lay sick in her palace. That sick girl afterwards became the mother of his only son. Mother and son were banished from Paris, and now lie side by side in the gloomy Capuchin Church of Vienna. The father lies a thousand miles away in his gorgeous mausoleum in Paris. I stood over the coffin, read the inscription, thumped the hollow case, and wondered if I really was within a few inches of the skeletons of Napoleon's wife and son. Shortly afterwards I saw the cradle of the Duke of Reichstadt. It is a short distance from cradle to coffin. The cradle is in the Treasury Museum, only two blocks from the funereal church of the Capuchins.

The cradle is ornamented with pearls; the canopy is of the richest satin, the trimmings are gold. Oft has Napoleon bent over that cradle, building grand air-castles for his son and heir. Little did the poor, second-rate Corsican lawyer, Charles Bonaparte, dream that his son would be emperor of the French, the mightiest man of his age; and in turn, little did the mightiest man of his age dream that his son would die unwept, unmourned, in a foreign land, not even known to the French whose emperor he expected him to be!

CHAPTER XVIII.

A FEW miles from Vienna the traveller down the Danube
passes the island of Lobau. Here, in 1809, Napoleon and his
army of 150,000 men were locked for five days. It was a bad
box, the swift Danube on both sides and the Austrians waiting
to get at him; but the great captain was equal to the emergen-
cy. He threw bridges across the river, beat the enemy at
Wagram, and came out victor where defeat had seemed inevitable. From my place in the prow of the boat I saw traces of
the French fortifications.

The boat landed at Buda-Pesth at nine o'clock. I at once set
out in search of a cheap hotel. It was hard to find one. The
Exposition was in progress, every place was full. I was finally
forced to content myself with a bed in the attic of a second-
rate inn, having to pay therefor the extortionate price of one
gulden—forty cents—the highest price I had yet paid in Europe.

The inhabitants of Buda-Pesth do not seem to bear the
Austrians much love. They have their own coin, their own
parliament, their own post-office department, and in general appear to have little in common with Austria. All the streets
are marked with Hungarian names, the German equivalents
having been removed a year or two ago by order of the government—a patriotic action, perhaps, but hard on strangers.
For instance, such names stare one in the face as,

"Szakirodalom," "Tejgazdasagj," "Varoshazter," "Wlasz-
lovitsj."

The great market of the Hungarian capital is held on the bank of the Danube in front of the city. The situation is highly picturesque. Frowning guns look down from the fortress on the hill opposite, seven hundred feet high; near by is the palace of Maria Theresa; at either end of the city are the graceful arches of two great bridges. In the early morning the peasants begin to arrive from the country, usually bringing their wares on their backs, and spreading them out on the rough stones of the levee to await purchasers. The men wear an odd kind of dress: the skirt, of some coarse cotton material, falling just below the knee, and a slouch hat and jacket of coarse white stuff. Some have their legs swathed in cloth up to the knee, a thick piece of leather being strapped under the foot a la sandal; the majority, however, go barefoot and barelegged. This is the every-day costume; their dress for feast-days is more gaudy. The greasy hat that has been in use perhaps ten years is replaced by a more fashionable affair only two or three years old, and decked with a gaudy rooster feather; the short jacket is of some bright-colored material, red, blue, or green; the knee-skirt is gayly trimmed. Altogether, the Hungarian peasant presents a novel spectacle when attired in his holiday dress.

The Hungarian women also wear short dresses. When they wear any kind of foot-gear it is generally high boots. A red turban-like covering is worn on the head. Every morning by ten o'clock a thousand or more of these queer-looking people are collected on the river-bank. The men, with their dresses and feathers and greasy hats, stroll about chatting and flirting with the barelegged, red-cheeked women — apparently never in a hurry, never seeming to have much business on hand. They look as though they had a thousand years before them as well as behind them. I bought some pears of a woman. She handed me back change. This act was not astonishing, but the manner in which she did it was astonishing. Her pocket was on the inner side of her dress; to get at it she lifted her dress considerably above her waist. Afterwards in other markets the same thing occurred. I came to the conclusion that the women of the lower classes in Hungary are not sticklers for the rules of propriety.

In the celebrated mineral baths, maintained at expense of the Hungarian government, I saw men and women bathing together, no clothing of any kind and not the slightest sign of embarrassment among either sex. There were seventy or a hundred bathers in the pool at the time of my visit; about half of that number were women. While I was looking on, a young peasant-girl came in. She gave one glance at me, then proceeded to undress as unconcernedly as if I had been blind or a thousand miles away. She hung her clothes on a hook and waded out into the pool; there she splashed about in the water with the men, women, and children. I visited the mud baths. The water was almost as thick as mush. The bathers sit in that dirty slime hours at a time. It reminded me of the backwoods in America, where one sees hogs wallowing in mud.

The Exposition which was in progress at Buda-Pesth afforded an insight into the nature of the resources and products of Hungary. In articles made by hand they seem abreast with the age; where machinery is concerned they appear to be backward. There were no steam-ploughs, no steam brick-machines, weaving apparatuses, printing-presses, etc. Steam-ploughs and threshers seem almost unknown in Europe. I saw none in Spain, Italy, Switzerland, Germany, or Austria. In Russia I saw an American reaper. This was the nearest approach to the advanced American style of agricultural machinery that I saw in all Europe. Another thing in which Europe is behind America is in her newspapers. Vienna, for instance, a city as large as New York, has not a single paper as large, or with half the news, editorials, or general literature, as will be found in the papers of small American towns. One reason of this, perhaps, is the unwieldiness of their language. The words are so big it is a hopeless task to attempt to give much news in one sheet. As a sample of the intricate and involved style that the Germans love, I translate a sentence from a story which I read in

Buda-Pesth. I translate literally, word for word, in the order in which they come :

" And as the horse-dealer to him without him to answer the letter handed so clapped this worthy man to whom the shameful injustice which one at Tronkenburg upon him practised had on which consequences Herse even perhaps for the lifetime sick there lay, known was, upon the shoulder, and said to him," etc.*

The author starts out to say that a worthy man clapped a horse-dealer on the shoulder. He got his verb in at the right place, but the poor shoulder had to wait a long time to be clapped.

The fare from Buda-Pesth to Constantinople (second-class) is one hundred and ninety-one Austrian florins — seventy-six dollars and forty cents. I had less than sixty dollars in my pocket, yet I determined to make the trip. Steerage on the Danube to Rustschuck costs six dollars. Thence I could walk through Bulgaria to Varna on the Black Sea. Steerage from Varna to Constantinople costs two dollars and eighty cents. In this way transportation was to cost, all told, only eight dollars and eighty cents, leaving ample funds for living and seeing the country on the way. I bought ten pounds of bread, some cheese and sausage, and set out on the trip.

The departure from Buda-Pesth was at night. The long line of lights on both sides of the river twinkled and reflected on the water. The grim fortress loomed up from its lofty height black and forbidding. We bade the city good-by in silence, for the hour was late, and few people were astir as the boat glided from its moorings. When at midnight the lights of the Hungarian capital had completely faded away in the distance,

---

* The above sentence is from an historical romance called " Michael Kohlhaas." The sentence in the original runs thus :

" Und da der Roszhaendler ihm, ohne ihm zu antworten, den Brief ueberreichte, so klopfte dieser wuerdige Mann, dem die abscheuliche Ungerechtigkeit, die man auf der Tronkenburg an ihm veruebt hatte, an deren Folge Herse eben, vielleicht auf die Lebenszeit, krank danieder lag, bekannt war, auf die Schulter und sagte ihm," etc.

I bethought myself of a place wherein to pass the night.   The company was not select, the choice was not of two evils, but of a hundred.   Bulgarian shepherds, Spanish Jews, Turks, Russians, Hungarians, and a dozen other nationalities, crowded the boat and disturbed the still night air with the Babel of many tongues.   The best corners were already occupied, and I was forced to content myself with a space on the upper deck.   The boards of the deck did not prove a soft bed, yet I could have slept there peacefully enough had not the Fates disturbed me.   The moon became obscured by clouds, the wind increased, and about two o'clock in the morning the big drops of rain came dancing on my face.   The balance of the night I spent downstairs under the cook's table, surrounded by my fellow-passengers.   Of the lot, the Bulgarian shepherds looked the strangest and wildest.   They dress, if not in skins, in something very like skins.   A coarse white sail-cloth serves as a cloak; sail-cloth breeches come to their knees; to their feet are attached by leather thongs the rudest sort of sandals.   They eat black bread and raw bacon, a diet at which the American plantation darkey, even in the days of slavery, would have rebelled.   This coarse food seems to agree very well with these shaggy Bulgarian fellows.   The bag which they carry slung over their shoulder invariably contains a huge hunk of raw bacon.   The great pones of black bread are bought every two or three days as needed.

The Danube presents various sorts of scenery.   From Linz to Vienna there are high hills, ruins, castles, curious towns.   From Vienna to Buda-Pesth the same on a smaller scale.   From Buda-Pesth on, the river winds its way through the vast Hungarian plains, where all is flat and dreary.   Both the banks and the water are very muddy.   One is at a loss to imagine Strauss's reason for calling his waltz the "Blue Danube."   If he had styled it the "muddy" or the "yellow" Danube it would have been more in keeping with the truth.   There is no sign of "blueness" in the Danube from its source in Germany to its mouth at the distant Black Sea.

At intervals along this part of the journey the river is dotted with floating "mill-villages"—small houses built on boats anchored a hundred yards or so from the shore. The current turns the wheels in a languid way; this suits the miller, for people in those parts are languid, and do things in a languid way. Whenever we passed settlements of these out-of-the-way places, the millers ran to their doors and stared at us while we stared at them. They were worth staring at. Half-naked, covered with flour, and with strange, Slavonic faces, they never ceased to attract my interest and attention.

The cook's table was protected by only a leaky tarpaulin, and the steady rain which set in on the second night proved too much for it. The water leaked through, trickled on my face, down my neck, and I got up and retired to the hold, which, though too crowded to afford even a seat, was at least dry, and presented an interesting array of queer characters. A band of gypsies had been taken on at some way-landing. They spent their time sitting cross-legged like the Turks, puffing villanous-smelling cigarettes. The women passed their time in the same way. With their deep-set eyes, haggard faces, and sallow complexions, they were rather uncanny objects to look upon. They wore fezes of coarse cloth, ornamented by long horse-hair tassels. During almost the entire three days that they remained on board, these queer people kept in this squatting posture, puffing their cigarettes and toying with their horse-hair tassels. Before curling up at night, and on uncurling in the morning, the members of the band saluted one another with kisses. Their tobacco-stained mouths seemed fit for almost anything rather than kissing.

After Buda-Pesth, the first city worthy the name is Belgrade, the capital of Servia. Here one begins to note clearly the receding tide of Turkish power. There are Turkish mosques and minarets, but they are dilapidated, and decaying from neglect. There are Turkish inhabitants, but they look meek and dispirited. It is no temporary decline; it is a decline forever. It has taken a long time to effect this result. In 1521 the city fell into the hands of the Turks. In 1688, one hundred and six-

ty-seven years after, Maximilian of Bavaria besieged the city
with half a hundred thousand men, and restored it to Christian
rule.   Two years later, however, it again fell into the hands of
the Turks.   They kept it about twenty years, then had to yield
it to Austria.   In 1739 they took it again, keeping it this time
upward of fifty years, when they lost it for the short term of
three years, after which they remained in undisturbed possession until 1807.   In that year there was an uprising of the people, and Turkey was successfully withstood for five years.   In
1812 Turkey again bobbed up serenely, and this time kept the
upperhand until 1867, when, at the intervention of Austria, the
Turks were compelled to give up Belgrade, which they had held
off and on since the time of Solyman II., in 1521.

This city, which has so long been the bone of contention between Christian and Turk, is now the capital of Servia.   It
stands on a high bluff overlooking the Danube.   From its long
Turkish occupancy it still presents an Oriental appearance.   The
promenade along the river-front is daily thronged with a crowd
of loungers, for the most part attired in Turkish and Oriental
costumes.

The lower classes in Servia seem to live somewhat after the
communistic plan.   A number of persons ranging from ten to
seventy band together, forming what is called a " Zadrouga."
A head or chief is chosen by vote of the Zadrouga, each adult
male having one vote, and this chief allots the land and specifies
to each one the work he shall do.   A father generally lives with
his married sons, cultivating the land or performing other work
as the chief may direct.   Women are treated with contempt,
being regarded as slaves, and rarely spoken to by the masculine
members of a family.   Five acres of land are exempt from seizure for debt.   There is a primary school for every three thousand inhabitants.   In time of peace the standing army is limited
to seventeen thousand men.   Citizens are permitted by law to
carry arms.   These are a few of the privileges enjoyed by this
Eastern people.

At Nicopolis I saw the remains of the fortifications thrown

up by the Russians in 1877. A heavy storm of shot and shell was hurled at the city, and the garrison of six thousand men very soon capitulated. Plevna is directly south of Nicopolis, distant only twenty or twenty-five miles. The heavy battles which took place in this vicinity during the Russian-Turkish war of 1877–78 are still remembered by the public.

A day out from Buda-Pesth Mohacs is passed—the scene of Hungarian disaster and Turkish triumph. It was here, near this town in a swamp, that King Lewis II. perished in 1526. The Hungarians were routed, and their country for more than a century remained under the Turkish yoke. In 1687, in the same place, near Mohacs, the Hungarians again met the Turks in battle-array, and this time it was the Turk who was beaten. He was compelled to retreat, and Hungary ruled herself once again. Thus historically Mohacs is interesting; intrinsically it is dull and tiresome. It is a miserable-looking place, in a swampy region reminding one of the swampy Mississippi bottoms during an overflow. It is not until the Kazan Pass is reached that the scenery becomes really grand. The shores grow more rocky, the river more narrow and confined, until at length the Danube enters the defile, only one hundred and eighty yards wide. The precipitous mountains shoot abruptly from the water's edge to the dizzy height of two thousand feet. There are constant turns in the river; one moment it seems as if the vessel is locked in on every side by stupendous walls; then, just as you catch your breath, expecting the prow of the boat to dash into the granite bluff, there is a sharp turn, and you glide into another section of the river which appears like another lake. After the days of dull, monotonous mud-banks, this wild scenery strikes the traveller as peculiarly grand and beautiful.

Eighteen hundred years ago the Roman emperor Trajan built a road along the Danube. Where the rocks rise so precipitously from the water, holes were drilled in the granite walls, beams were fastened in the holes, and the road wound its way through the wild defile supported by these jutting beams. The holes for the beams are still there. The boat passes so near the bluff that the observing traveller can see the inscription which Trajan ordered to be made in the rock to commemorate his war with the Dacians.

At Turn-Severin the boat tied up all night, and advantage was taken of the opportunity to get glimpses of a typical Roumanian city. The town was a mile or so from the river. The night was very dark, but there was not the slightest difficulty in finding the way. A dozen bugles were blowing the signals for bed; the sound floated to me from the barracks, and guided my steps to the town.

Turn-Severin is a primitive-looking place. The houses are all white, are only one story high, resembling somewhat the houses in Mexico. The people also have a Mexicanish look— swarthy, yellow complexions, black hair, dark eyes. I stopped in a grocery to replenish my stock of provisions; the proprietor spoke only Greek, and I left. At other groceries Roumanian, Bulgarian, Turkish, and similar third-rate languages were fired at me, but no English. With the exception of a little German, the Turn-Severinites know as little of the world-languages as do the Turks. I was finally obliged to abbreviate my wants, and negotiate for those few by shrugs and signs. I bought several loaves of bread, paid for them in leu and bani, the money of the country, and went on my way rejoicing.

A detachment of Bulgarian soldiers boarded the steamer at Widdin, and from that time on the voyage was extremely uncomfortable. Every foot of space was taken up by either the soldiers or the other steerage passengers of whom I have spoken. There was no place to lie down. I passed the time talking with one of the soldiers who had been to Vienna and knew a little German. He told me the Bulgarian field-hands get forty to sixty cents a day; bricklayers, carpenters, etc., from eighty cents to a dollar. These wages are higher than in Germany or Italy. The difference, however, is only in appearance, for the cost of living is dearer. One dollar will go no further in Bulgaria than sixty or seventy cents will go in Italy.

The Bulgarian soldiers remained the greater part of the night on the upper deck, singing with voices more powerful than musical. I noted down one of their rude airs; it ran thus:

This refrain they repeated again and again with never-failing vim and energy. The pay of the Bulgarian soldier is \$1.20 a month. He is provided with a uniform, and rations of soggy bread, uncooked meat, and black coffee; apparently not a very nourishing diet, yet in the revolution which occurred shortly after my visit to the country they endured severe hardships and did some pretty hard fighting.

We reached Rustschuck at five in the morning; there the long steamboat trip ended. It was a treat to tread solid land once more. A still greater treat was the bath which I took in the Danube. I sported in the swift current half an hour, then shouldered my knapsack and set out on the tramp. Rustschuck was pretty badly battered in the war of 1877–78. I should say that it has not yet recovered. It could hardly present a more dilapidated or woe-begone aspect than it does to-day. I walked through its principal street, stared at the swarthy inhabitants, and was stared at. That is about all I have to say of Rustschuck. I got out of the miserable place as soon as possible.

At Radujewatz, in Wallachia, an Austrian *Handwerksbursch,**

---

* The Handwerksburschen (strolling journeymen), though not so numerous as formerly, still exist. They are constantly met on the highways strolling from town to town, not so much with the expectation of making a living as of seeing the world and rubbing off the " sharp corners " before settling down. At the age of nineteen or twenty the men are put into the army, and their abilities for a period of three years turned in non-proa sign-painter, got aboard as a steerage passenger. His original intention was to walk from Schiurschewo to Bukureschti in search of work; but we became acquainted on the steamer, and on learning my intention to walk through Bulgaria, he decided to walk with me. I was very glad to have his company. The uncouth people among whom we tramped spoke only Bulgarian and Turkish. It was a relief, after so long a silence, to have even a Handwerksbursch to converse with.

After pedestrian trips through flowery Italy, through picturesque Switzerland, and through Germany between the two lines of fruit-trees which in that country adorn the highways—after all this, it was a sad change to the sandy, shadeless roads of Bulgaria. The dilapidated villages in Mexico which excited my wonder when in that country a few years ago are palatial in comparison to the villages of Bulgaria. The houses are made of sun-dried mud; the roofs are thatched, not in a workmanlike manner, but covered loosely with straw or hay. They are not above six feet high. I think a hard rain would dissolve and wash away a Bulgarian peasant village. The people in these villages seemed to have nothing in particular to do. They sit on the shady side of their huts gazing idly at the parched fields around them. Occasionally we saw women threshing wool with twig brooms. The men did no threshing, but they appeared quite pleased with looking at the women thresh.

The heat was so intense we tried walking in the night and sleeping in the day. Walking at night was all right, but not so with the sleeping in the day. It was impossible to sleep under that burning sun, so we were compelled to give up the plan. My companion Ludwig ran short of money. My own supply was dwindling down to so fine a point I was unable to

---

ductive directions. Another three or four years are lost as Handwerksburschen, so that the German and Austrian mechanic is twenty-five or twenty-seven years old before he settles down and begins the real business of life. This tardiness in becoming producers, together with their inordinate fondness for beer, are, in the opinion of many, two very important causes of the unsatisfactory condition of German labor.

help him. We agreed to stop at the little town Sindschere-Kujudschuk for Ludwig to get work, if possible, to replenish his funds. It was a forlorn hope. That wretched, baked little town looked as if it had never even seen a sign. The sign-painter's occupation was not gone—it had never existed. From noon (the hour of our arrival) until bedtime we strolled through the rambling streets, Ludwig stopping at every shop, explaining as best he could his trade and asking for work. At every place the same reception was met—a stare and shake of the head. One man, a dealer in cowhides, chickens, and eggs, spoke a little German.

" Where are you from ?" he asked Ludwig.

Ludwig told him.

" And where is your friend from ?" pointing at me.

" From America."

" America?" repeated the cowhide dealer. " Where is America ?"

Where is America? When a small boy I could answer glibly enough, but I failed in my attempt to make that worthy Bulgarian understand the whereabouts and immense importance of my native land.

The next day we set out on the sandy road, glad to be rid of that little town with the big name and unspeakable shopkeepers, who did not have the good taste to adorn their stores with one of Ludwig's artistic signs. In the first bauerdorf (peasant-village) another halt was made, this time not with the hope of getting work at his trade, but with the idea of turning " Landsmann," as Ludwig expressed it; that is, working in the fields. In our blouses and knapsacks we doubtless looked as strange to them as they in their heavy boots and short white skirts appeared to us. On neither side was there too much confidence. We managed, however, to come across a man who had not gathered all his grapes. The heat was injuring them, and he agreed to give Ludwig four piasters a day. The ordinary pay of a field-hand in Bulgaria is ten or twelve piasters a day—fifty take a mean advantage, that I advised Ludwig to let his grapes alone, and see the man in a hotter place than we then were in, rather than do his work for twenty cents a day. I had made a careful calculation, and thought that with economy I could help Ludwig, and still make my funds hold out until I received my next remittance at Kijew, Russia. Accordingly, the plan of getting work in the interior of Bulgaria was abandoned. Indeed, at any other time the idea of working for even ten piasters a day would have seemed preposterous; but we were now living on ten or twelve cents a day, and in relation to the cost of living, ten piasters—forty-eight cents—was by no means a ridiculous figure.

We had little to do with the inhabitants along the way. We could not speak their language, and they seemed little inclined to show us kindness or hospitality. When our provisions gave out, we bought bread and grapes. The latter were very cheap, and were refreshing. They were similar in taste and shape to the Malaga grape, only much sweeter. We paid twenty-five para the ocho—about one and one-third cents the pound. This was simple diet—bread and grapes. Lovers of roast-meat and juicy beefsteaks think hard work or active exercise cannot long continue on a bread-and-fruit diet. I think my pedestrian tour proves the contrary. I walked twenty-five miles a day for days at a time, living the while entirely on black bread and grapes, figs or other fruit. On those hot marches through Bulgaria, I have no doubt but that it was the simple and wholesome diet of bread and grapes which enabled us to stand the fatigue, and even to improve in health and vigor.

We passed a lot of rude stones marking the place where lie the remains of many of the French soldiers who died during the Crimean war, of cholera and other diseases, and then tramped, dusty and tired, into Varna, on the Black Sea. The same afternoon we boarded the Austrian steamer for Constantinople.

CHAPTER XIX.

THE STEERAGE TO CONSTANTINOPLE.—A TURKISH FLIRTATION.—
SEARCH FOR CHEAP QUARTERS.—THE GREEK RESTAURANT.—A
BILL OF FARE IN FOUR LANGUAGES.—HOW I SAW THE SULTAN
AHMED MOSQUE FOR ONE HUNDRED PARA.

At the time of which I am writing there was cholera in
Spain. I do not know that there was cholera anywhere else;
nevertheless, the Sultan, who is morbidly afraid of cholera, had
ordered a quarantine against vessels from Varna, and for two
days we lay at anchor in the Bosporus, so near and yet so
far.

There was a Bulgarian ex-Jew in the steerage who aided not
a little to pass the time. He was a thorough German scholar,
well read in history and philosophy. We had grand dis-
cussions on the Darwinian theory. The ex-Jew was a Christian missionary in the Turkish capital. I did not understand
then, and certainly do not know now, how he made the two
beliefs compatible, but he declared his implicit faith in the
Mosaic account of the creation and in Mr. Darwin's theory as
to the evolution of the species. When not discussing philosophical questions with the Bulgarian missionary, I watched
the strange characters around me. There was one fellow, a
Tartar, with extraordinarily strong lungs. He sat, or rather
squatted, cross-legged on the deck for hours together, singing
all the while a hideous and monotonous chant. His complexion
was a muddy yellow, his hair was coarse and straight like that
of a horse's tail. There were half a dozen other Tartars in his
party, but fortunately they refrained from singing. Had they
all made the same horrible noise at once, I would have been
deafened for life.

A treacherous-looking Turk with an unusually long, dirty

beard and dirty turban had his wife with him. She was swaddled from the crown of her head to the tips of her toes in a kind of loose gown. The end of her nose, which stuck out just enough to get a whiff of fresh air, was all of her that was visible. The old Turk watched her jealously from morning till night; he rarely spoke to her, merely treated her as a piece of valuable baggage, seeming to think it sufficient if he kept her unpolluted by the impious gaze of Christians. Once I took my knapsack to the corner of the deck where the poor thing had been sitting all day, without daring so much as to move, and squatting down near the railing, I took out my pen and ink and note-book, and under pretence of writing watched her narrowly. I discovered that she was young and pretty. There were some figs in a paper in her lap. Thinking me too busy with my writing to see her, she lifted her veil to eat the fruit. She had an exquisitely shaped mouth, and the whitest, prettiest teeth I ever saw. Her complexion was soft and creamy, her eyes black and dancing. I did not take her to be above seventeen years old. The hoary old Turk, old enough to be her grandfather, had doubtless just bought this young and beautiful girl to displace an old and withered wife. So absorbed did I become in these observations and speculations that I did not stop to think what the husband might have to say of my sitting so near his valuable freight. I was called to myself in a way more startling than pleasant. While gazing at her as she bit off the stems of the figs with her dazzling teeth and admiring her bright eyes, and wondering at her curiously dyed finger-nails and eyebrows, there was a whiz, a flash, and the same instant a big watermelon burst on the railing eighteen inches from my head. I looked and saw the Turk glaring like an infuriated beast. That portion of the vessel no longer had charms for me. I left. After that the poor slave was guarded more strictly than ever. Until quarantine was raised, she hardly moved from her pallet in the corner by the ship's railing. At certain hours her villanous old husband turned his face to the East, and prayed and prostrated himself, and thumped his head on the deck. Except when engaged in these pious duties, he sat by his wife, keeping close vigil. At meal-times he turned her face towards the sea, so that no eye might behold her, then fed her as he would a child or a dog.

At last, thanks to Father Time, the days of probation expired. We steamed into the Golden Horn, the anchor was dropped, and we were in Constantinople! Before the ship had come to a stop, a swarm of Turks were on board, making the air hideous with their cries and yells. They surrounded the vessel in their small boats, and clambered up the sides like monkeys. I was leaning over the railing looking at the city, when suddenly a turbaned head stuck itself in my face. The ship was still in motion. I had not seen the man as he stuck his grapple in a ring in the side of the vessel and clambered up. Fortunately, my knapsack was strapped tight on my back. Had it not been, the impudent fellow would have seized it despite my most vigorous resistance. The Turkish boatmen who ferry passengers to the wharf are veritable pirates. They are shameless in their demands; if you do not accede to them, they hold or confiscate your baggage. It is not often that a traveller arrives with so little baggage as I had. My ferryman, when I refused to pay more than twenty cents, became furious. I had no baggage on which he could levy; my knapsack was fast to my back. I laughed in his face as he fell to raving and cursing in his heathenish tongue.

As I was passing through a gate at the landing, an official extended his hand for my passport. I handed it to him. He looked at it, turned it upside down, pretended to read it, then handed it back. I walked on through the gate. The Austrian Handwerksbursch who came behind me fared not so well. The Turk scowled at his passport, and instead of returning it ordered the inoffensive Austrian to retire to an inner room. What dread ordeal he there underwent I know not. He came to the door in a few minutes, and said he was a prisoner, that he was not allowed to leave the room. It afterwards transpired that his passport was not *viséd* by the Turkish consul.

Neither was mine, yet the custom - house official made that difference between us. I was allowed to go, while the Austrian was detained until his consul came down and vouched for his nationality.

The cheapest hotels mentioned in any of the guide-books for Constantinople charge from three to four dollars a day. Accordingly, when I landed on the shores of the unspeakable Turk, I set out to find a hotel *not* mentioned in the guide-books. I found a very nice room on the Rue Vöivöda, within two doors of the German and French post-offices. The price was one hundred and sixty para a day—about seventeen cents. My meals I got at a Greek restaurant for forty to fifty para—three and a half to four and a half cents—the meal consisting of a piece of bread and a plate of rice, macaroni, or potatoes. It was a curious little place, this Greek restaurant. The oven was in the broad sill of the front window, looking on the street. There, over a fire of hot coals, were the different pans from which the guest selected his meal. The one contained potato-and-meat hash, another macaroni, another rice, etc. A guest on entering goes to this window, surveys the different viands, makes his selection, and it is served on a tin plate on a table in the back of the room. Some of the dishes eaten at this restaurant were peculiar.

Rice is cooked with pepper, honey, fruit-sauce, and maize. Boiled fish, filled with cucumbers, pumpkins, or rice, is much liked. Another favorite is a kind of hash made of fish mixed with cabbage, salad, etc. Kaimaik is a dish of roasted noodles dipped in honey. Jaurt, a sort of sour milk, is eaten in soup or with raw cucumbers. Geese, ducks, and similar fowls are not eaten, being considered unclean. A hog once broke into a mosque; since then no good Mussulman will eat hog-meat.

The majority of these dishes I found impossible to learn to like; the potatoes and rice, however, were always palatable and filling. I avoided the high-priced European hotels, and stuck to the Greek restaurant. One day a Greek soldier came in. He wore a tiny bit of a cap, a bobtail jacket, and a white skirt eighteen inches long, that stuck out like the starched skirt of the ballet-dancer. White hose reached to where the absurdly short skirt left off, and covered his legs down to the feet. This curious and ridiculous-looking fellow so absorbed my attention, hungry as I was, I forgot to eat my dinner.

The steerage is not the cleanest part of a ship. The first thing I did after finding a room was to take a Turkish bath. There are so-called Turkish baths in America. They are only so-called. The genuine article is not to be found out of Turkey. On entering, the visitor finds himself in a large domed salon, in the centre of which is a refreshing fountain. A grave, courteous Turk meets you; you take off your shoes and climb upon the platform that stands out from the wall circling the salon. An attendant takes off your clothes, puts a sheet around you, gives you a pair of wooden clogs, and conducts you through a door into the first room of the bath—a large room with marble floors and not the slightest sign of water. A mat was spread in the middle of the floor. On this mat I was laid to reflect and sweat. While thus gradually melting and dripping away, a door was softly opened, and before I knew what was up, a naked and swarthy Turk had jumped upon my body, and was stamping me with might and main. The onslaught was so sudden, and I was so unprepared, that resistance was impossible. I was sore and aching in every joint before the villain released me. The kneading and pinching which followed seemed, in comparison to the first treatment, or rather *mis*treatment, mild and pleasant. When my body had been beaten and pinched black and blue, the Turk took me to another part of the room, and laying me flat on the floor, began with a kind of curry-comb to rub and scratch the skin off. There were numerous other processes. I was doused in hot water, a tub of soapsuds was poured over me, while another attendant kicked and beat me. This and the various other indignities to which I was subjected lasted an hour and a half; then, wearied and dejected, I went back to the gallery where I had undressed, and lay on a couch covered with sheets, to rest and recuperate. On leaving, the dignified Turk who had first greeted me presented a small hand-mirror, on which I laid a piece of money. The Turk is supposed to be above counting or even looking at the money; if you put any faith in this supposition, test the matter sometime by putting on the glass less than two hundred para—twenty-five cents—the usual amount charged for a bath. The howl which that Turk will set up will very speedily convince you of your error.

I counted one day in front of the German post-office sixty-seven dogs and eighteen puppies. Lazy Turks were squatting on the sidewalk smoking long pipes and eying the dogs as they scratched off the fleas. It was difficult to get about without stepping on one of the canines: some one is constantly treading on a tail or a leg, and the air in consequence is filled with a frightful howling and barking. It would not be so bad if they cleaned up after the dogs; this is not done, on account of the scarcity of water. Water is sold by peddlers on the streets at so much a glass. There are a few baby fountains where by turning a faucet a tiny stream is produced. These are constantly surrounded by a crowd of thirsty people. The generous Italian fountains running volumes of water are unknown.

A native Turk speaking but one language would almost be regarded as a curiosity. Hotel bills of fare, shopkeepers' signs, etc., are printed in Greek, Arabic, Armenian, and French. On the Stamboul bridge one may hear a dozen different languages at once—Greek, Arabic, Kurdish, Turkish, Armenian, Bulgarian, Servian, Albanian, Wallachian, Jew-Spanish, Italian, and French. Many of these people are beggars. They line both sides of the approach to the bridge, and expose their horrible sores in the hope of exciting pity and receiving alms. In my tenderness of heart, the first time I saw these poor devils I made a trifling donation. The whole tribe came hobbling after me; to escape them I was literally compelled to take to my heels and run. The streets of Constantinople are so hilly and crooked that the street-car companies find it necessary to have a man run ahead of each car to warn pedestrians. This *avant courier* is provided with a horn, which he blows, not with his mouth but with his nose! The sound is hoarse and snorting. The first time I saw one of these barefoot fellows tearing along, blowing a brass trumpet with his nose, I thought it merely an individual eccentricity; it seemed, however, to be quite usual.

Most of the great powers have their own postal service in Turkey. An Englishman in Constantinople, when he wishes to mail a letter, takes an English stamp, puts it on his letter, and drops it in the English post, where English clerks take care of it and forward it to its destination. Germany, Italy, France, etc., have posts in the same way. The Turkish post is a very shabby affair. It is in a little wooden shanty in Stamboul, at the end of the bridge over the Golden Horn. In one corner of this rickety building is a glass case, where are displayed the letters which the department were unable to deliver. The letters were addressed in Arabic, Hebrew, Greek, and other " chicken-scratching " characters. Around this case of dead letters squat a number of men who make a livelihood as scribes. They are generally surrounded by a crowd, who watch the hieroglyphics and stare at the veiled women dictating their letters. The prettiest sort of a girl came up while I was there. If I may judge from the sparkle of her roguish black eyes, I should say the letter she dictated was a love missive. She wore the thinnest of veils, through which the contour of her face was quite visible. The handsome Turkish women are not a little prone to thin, gauzy veils. Only those of unusual homeliness insist on wearing veils entirely opaque— at least I so imagined.

Nominally the government of Turkey is constitutional—only nominally. In reality the Sultan possesses absolute power over the millions of beings who inhabit his provinces in the three continents of Europe, Asia, and Africa. Yet, paradoxical as it may seem, the Sultan is not even his own master. He is a prisoner in his own palace. The Sultan Abd ul Hamid II. is morbid on the subject of assassination. His palace is surround-

ed by high walls. Soldiers guard every entrance. He never
goes out unless accompanied by a large body-guard. I saw
him one Friday on the way to prayers. Former sultans attended the Ahmed Mosque in Stamboul. Abd ul Hamid
dreads going so far. He prays exclusively in the Mosque of
Tschiraghan, only a few hundred yards from his palace gates.
By paying forty para to the proprietor of a coffee-stand in
the neighborhood I obtained a place in the window, whence
I had an excellent view of the procession as it passed. Lines
of soldiers stretched up and down the street, beyond the palace
walls on the one end and beyond the mosque on the other. No
civilian was permitted on the street. At length there was a
loud huzza; the thousands of Turks who were craning their
necks to get a glimpse of the Sublime Porte shouted and threw
up their fezes. A carriage drawn by four horses approached.
The carriage contained two very brilliantly uniformed men,
and a black-bearded man of medium stature and sallow look.
The two men in uniform were pachas; the black-bearded man
was the Sultan. The soldiers presented arms, the drums beat,
the fifes and horns tooted, and his Highness, the Sun and Moon
and Light of the World, disappeared behind the walls of the
mosque, there to pray or not, as he chose. No one is allowed
to enter, and the soldiers look to it that no prying eye peeps
to see what is passing within.

It goes without saying that none but true believers are employed in the Government departments. The Government takes
care its employes do not let their faith grow rusty. Adjoining
the bureaus are provided apartments where clerks can step out
at short intervals and pray. Passing through the corridors of
the High Porte in Stamboul, where are the offices of the grand-
vizier and other high dignitaries, I glanced into a room next to
where a number of clerks were writing. A dozen or so men
were in the room, barefoot, praying, and knocking their heads
against the floor. When through, they hurried to work again.

When I called on the American consul, he told me, among
other things, that Americans had been granted a place in the

British cemetery. This was gratifying news. I immediately visited the cemetery. It was a bleak, barren, cheerless-looking spot. The grass was burnt and parched by the fierce sun, a few willows afforded a scanty shade. It is very well to bury Americans here who die in Constantinople ; but why bring those dying in Brusa and other distant Asiatic cities ? It is hard to believe that the cemeteries of those places can be more forsaken-looking than the cemetery at Constantinople. Some of those buried in that cemetery died in Brusa and at Jerusalem !

The lower classes of Turkey are veritable beasts of burden. The streets of Constantinople are steep, crooked, and unpaved ; vehicles cannot go over them. The heaviest loads are carried on the backs of men. A kind of saddle—a big hump of leather—is worn on the back. When the porter carries a burden he leans forward almost at a right angle, and carries loads often of two hundred or three hundred pounds. I have seen them, thus bent double, carrying bales of goods or huge boxes, the sweat trickling from their faces in streams. For this severe labor the Turkish porter receives the munificent sum of twenty or twenty-five cents a day. Similar to the porters are the fruit-peddlers. They carry on their backs great baskets of grapes, figs, pomegranates, etc., which they sell at ridiculously low prices. For fifteen para (not quite two cents) you can buy as many grapes or figs as you can eat—and such grapes and figs ! I have never seen them equalled, even in Spain or California.

Everybody on arriving at Constantinople buys a fez. Why they do this I cannot say. It is a silly little concern—no brim, giving not the slightest protection against sun or rain—still, it is the fashion. My first wrestle with a Turk was in an attempt not to pay eight times as much as the ordinary price of a fez. They are sold by street peddlers. The peddler has a big bag, in which he carries several hundred fezes. When your selection is made you step into a " pressing " shop (one is at every turn) and have the fez ironed and a tassel sewed on ; then you are ready to join the rest of the ninnies and walk about in the sun with a brimless thing that lets your nose burn red as fire.

My fez, pressing and all, cost two hundred para—about eighteen and a half cents; the foot-baths that I afterwards took to
bleach my nose cost twice that sum.

Turkish women go to one extreme, Turkish men to another.
The women hide even their faces, the men seem careless about
exposing their entire persons. I saw, one night, on a business
street in Stamboul, shopkeepers sleeping out on the street in
front of their shops almost in a state of nudity. Most of them
were small provision dealers, and had chickens in coops for sale.
Quilts were spread upon the coops, and there the nearly naked
Turks lay snoring as peacefully as if in the privacy of their
harems, instead of in a public street, with dogs and cats and
donkeys and prowling sight-seers around them. The night I
took this stroll happened to be the anniversary of the Sultan's
accession to the throne. The city was illuminated by feeble
candle-lights and dim lanterns. As a pyrotechnical display it
was despicable. It was only interesting as a sample of the
kind of Fourth of July the Orientals can get up. The half-
naked Turks asleep on their chicken-coops looked peculiarly
strange and weird in the different-colored lights of the illumi-
nation.

The thing in Constantinople most suggestive of Roman origin is the Hippodrome in Stamboul. Here, where in ancient
times the Romans held their races; where, as Gibbon tells us,
the factions of the Blues and the Greens heaped the ground in
a few hours with forty thousand corpses — here one sees the
outline of a Roman forum. This Hippodrome, once brilliant
with the decorations of prodigal emperors, once alive with the
gayeties and pomp of a luxurious court, is now bleak and barren. Of all the works of art that once adorned its ample
space only three relics now remain — the Egyptian obelisk,
erected by the Emperor Theodosius, the Byzantine obelisk,
and a spiral column of brass. The first column, originally
erected in Heliopolis in Egypt, b.c. 1600, was brought to Constantinople by Theodosius. The Byzantine obelisk was formerly ornamented by bass-reliefs; they have long since disap-

peared, and the shaft stands now a mere skeleton of its former self. The spiral column is one of the most ancient and interesting relics of antiquity. It was erected by the Greeks in the Temple of Apollo after the battle of Platæa and Salamis, to commemorate their victory over the Persians. So venerable is this column it occupies a page in the history of Herodotus. Since it was transported from Delphos by Constantine to its present site the level of the Hippodrome has risen fourteen feet. The earth immediately around the column has been excavated, but the visitor is not permitted to descend into the excavation, and is therefore unable to read the inscriptions, still remaining, which the Greeks graved in the column centuries before Christ.

To the east of the ancient Hippodrome is the Mosque of the Sultan Ahmed. It was a hot day. To get into the shade as well as to see the mosque, I took off my shoes and entered the sacred edifice. Scarce had I done so when a coolly attired Turk, that is, attired in a short white petticoat, naked legs, and half-naked body, came running up and demanded "backsheesh." I took out a one-hundred para piece—about eleven cents—and handed it to him. He took it, gazed at it scornfully, and said,

"Bere garush" (two piasters).

I refused, upon which he motioned me to leave. I was willing to leave, but not without my one hundred para. I extended my hand to take back the money; the Turk extended both his hands, the one for more money, the other to expel me from the mosque. There was no sign of my one hundred para. I looked the Turk square in the face, and told him in good English to "go to the d—l." He will doubtless obey the injunction later on, but at the time he showed no inclination to do so. On the contrary, he put both hands upon me, and endeavored to put me out of the door. I dislike being swindled even in small matters. The sickly little Turk was smaller than I. In my turn I put my hands upon the Turk, and in so ungentle a manner that he receded, I might say fell back, several yards. Then I extended my hand and intimated as well as I could that I meant either to see that mosque or have my money.

Of course he could not think of returning the money, and thus it happened that I saw the Mosque of the Sultan Ahmed to the east of the ancient Hippodrome at a cost of one hundred para—more than enough.

The great central dome of this mosque, the culmination of a number of small domes and half domes, is mosaicked with small blue stones, set here and there with a dazzling star—the whole a wonderful representation of the vaulted heavens. Inscriptions in Turkish on shields thirty feet in diameter afford inspiration to devout worshippers. The prodigious central dome is supported by four fluted marble columns, fifty or sixty feet in circumference. From what I saw, I do not think Mohammedans regard their mosques as very sacred. True, Christian dogs are made to take off their shoes on entering, but they allow themselves much liberty. While looking around the interior of the mosque, I heard sounds of the most hilarious laughter. Squatting on the floor near one of the huge marble columns was the festive Turk who had tried to rob and then eject me; there he was holding his sides, and laughing till the dome echoed the sound again. His brother pirates seemed equally amused and boisterous. One day when visiting another mosque I saw a man of venerable aspect, long gray beard, and wrinkled face, sitting cross-legged on the floor, surrounded by a dozen or so younger men, who were busily engaged in writing. The old man had a pillow or cushion in front of him, on which rested a book. He was a professor; the young men were his pupils. Sometimes half a dozen professors may be seen holding their classes in a mosque at the same hour. Mosques are selected on account of their roominess and coolness. The thought of sacrilege in using a religious edifice for secular purposes does not seem to occur to them.

The Mosque of St. Sophia is intrinsically not so interesting as the Sultan Ahmed. It is larger, but not so imposing. Historically, of course, St. Sophia is the most interesting edifice in Constantinople. It was beneath St. Sophia's dome that the great Roman Empire breathed its last. Here, on that same marble floor, surveyed and trodden by nineteenth-century tourists, that great fabric which had been feeble and tottering for a thousand years received its death-blow from the furious Turk. For centuries the Roman Empire of the East had existed but in name; still it *had* existed. The Palæologi, those feeble Greek emperors, could still walk the walls of Constantinople, could still read of the ancient glory of the empire, and indulge in dreams of a happier future; but that fearful day which saw the streets of Constantinople running with blood, which ended with a horrible massacre beneath St. Sophia's dome—that day put an end to such hopes forever!

The Emperor Palæologus lay buried under a heap of dead, and with him lay the withered corpse of the Roman Empire!

CHAPTER XX.

WALKING through a narrow alley in Stamboul one day, I was
overtaken by a Turk who addressed me in tolerable English.

"You want guide?" he asked.

I told him no, but he continued walking by my side.

"Maybe you not know me?"

"Certainly not. How should I?"

"Why," he said, "you ought know me. Me in Mark
Twain's book. You remember Mark Twain's book? Me Far-
away-Moses."

Did I know him? I should think I did. What American
does not know, and has not laughed over, Far-away-Moses?
Here was I in the very presence of that celebrated man. I
gazed a moment in silent admiration, then squeezed his hand,
and treated to a Turkish pastry at the first booth we came to.

A day or two after this event, I was again walking in Stamboul, and again was I approached by an English-speaking guide.

"No, I don't need a guide," I told him. "I can paddle my
own canoe."

"But me very good guide," insisted the man. "You don't
know me, gentleman; I tell you who I am. You know Mark
Twain's book? Me Far-away-Moses!"

Had the great Far-away-Moses changed so in three days?
It was impossible. The only solution to this remarkable incident was that there were *two* Far-away-Moseses. A day or two
later still another Far-away-Moses turned up. Before I left
Constantinople I began to think the woods full of them. That

the guides should think the mere name Far-away-Moses a passport to your good graces is a great compliment to Mark Twain. There was a sequel to this little adventure in Antwerp several months afterwards. I was visiting the Turkish bazaar at the Exposition then being held in that city. I spoke to the man in charge of my recent return from the East.

"Ah, you were in Stamboul?" he said. "Perhaps you saw Far-away-Moses?"

I had seen several of them, but I did not tell him so. I merely said "Yes." His face lighted with a smile.

"Tell me," he said, "how did he look? Far-away-Moses is my father!"

It is very possible the sons were as numerous as the father, but I saw only this one.

The cistern of the thousand and one columns is a gloomy place. It was originally three stories deep. The two lower stories have been filled with dirt and débris, and at the present day only the third or upper floor is accessible. A number of silk-spinners carry on their work in this cistern forty feet under the earth. They smoke while they work. One hand is busied with the whirling spinning-wheel, the other hand manipulates the long tube of their pipe. Although there are not literally a thousand and one columns, there are several hundred; they present the appearance of a forest of marble shafts. It is supposed Philoxenos built this cistern. Several others are in the same vicinity. That of the "Forty Martyrs" was built by the tyrant Phocas. The exact purpose of these immense underground reservoirs has never been precisely ascertained. A plausible supposition is that they were destined to collect the storm-water to use in case of fire.

In Scutari, Asia Minor, a steep and rugged street leads to the cloister of the howling dervishes: an ordinary-looking house in a garden surrounded by a high wall. I had no guide, and could not have found the way but for persistent repetition of the word "Tekke," Turkish for cloister. I repeated that open-sesame word to every one I met, and at last reached the

right place. In the anteroom or hall leading to the main apartment was a coal-black negro, who upon my entering promptly
ordered me out. At any rate, I presume that is what he said,
for he followed his remark with a gentle but firm seizure of my
arm, leading me to the door. From his pantomimic action I
discovered that I had neglected to remove my shoes! Having
rectified my error, I humbly sought admittance again, and this
time with success. The turbaned black gave me a stool, and
made me understand as well as he could by signs and gestures
that the ceremonies had not yet begun. I amused myself in
the interim by observing my surroundings. Lying on the floor
were a dozen or two men, some of them dervishes, smoking
pipes and sipping coffee, which the negro served in very small
cups. In the garden were graves of devout dervishes, over
which waved the boughs of fig and pomegranate trees, and the
leaves of grape-vines. At intervals of ten or fifteen minutes
the turbaned black who had put me out, and who seemed to be
head - manager of the coffee department, went out into the
garden and carried on a little pious performance all by himself. First he would bow and strike the ground with his head ;
then arising, he would give vent to doleful howls, as if afflicted with a horrible case of stomach-ache! After howling and
butting the ground for several minutes, thus relieving himself
of superfluous religious ecstasy, the turbaned fellow returns to
his post and resumes the duty of ladling out coffee.

I have witnessed the war and medicine dances of the Indians
in the North-west; I have visited a number of lunatic asylums ;
but neither among the Indians nor among the lunatics did I
ever see so grotesque or fearful an orgy as that of the howling
dervishes of Scutari.

The ages of the dervishes varied from tender youth to extreme
old age. They wore loose, white gowns. In the beginning all
were squatting on lamb-skins in the centre of the floor. There
they howled and rocked backward and forward a quarter of
an hour ; then of a sudden all leaped to their feet, and backing
against the wall, began a more hideous howling than ever. They

howled in unison; as they did so they swayed backward and forward, up and down, distorted their faces, jerked their heads about, and writhed as if in convulsions. As the moments flew, the distortions became more violent, the movements more rapid, the hoarse grunts and screams more and more furious. I observed that the antics of the coal-blacks were wilder and fiercer than those of lighter-complexioned dervishes. A tall black in the uniform of an officer of the army was so violent in his contortions that I momentarily expected to see him tumble over in a swoon. He sprang up and down, screamed, roared, twisted his neck; his eyeballs glared, the long tassel of his fez flew hither and thither—he was a horrible sight. This man had the strength of a Hercules. He was the last to give in; to the last his writhings and hoarse shouts retained their full vigor and perfection. He sunk suddenly, from nervous exhaustion. Some of those who took part in the ceremonies were Turkish officers and medical students. The women were penned in a closely latticed gallery. Through the bars I saw that they were swaying back and forth, marking time to the mad music going on below.

When, after an hour of this mad tumult, all the dervishes collapsed to the floor, the Scheich, or head-priest, enacted a still more revolting performance. A number of children ranging from six months to ten years of age were laid on the bare floor face downward; then the hoary sinner called "Scheich," a man weighing fully one hundred and sixty pounds, deliberately walked over those children. The little fellows screamed with pain. As each child was trod upon it was picked up by an attendant and presented to the Scheich, who blew in its face and made magic passes in the air over its head. If the infant survives this treatment it is holy; if it dies (as it often does) it is not holy, and ought to die. Such is the barbaric belief and practice of the howling dervishes.

The dancing dervishes of Pera, though happily less barbaric than the howling dervishes, are as curious and interesting. Their "Tekke" is an octagonal building. The floor of the large central apartment is waxed very smooth. Along the eight sides of the octagon are rows of straw mats. The dervishes sit on these mats, and begin their ceremonies by long, monotonous chants. The orchestra consists of a flute with a cadaverous tone, a kind of violoncello with one string ("A"), and a kettle-drum of bad quality. At the ceremonious introduction, after an unearthly yell by all the dervishes in concert, the following melancholy strain,* with its original instrumentation, begins:

Hereupon several of the dervishes arise and chant the following melody, during which the dancers gradually enter:

* These melodies of the dervishes were noted down on the spot by Mr. Arnold Strothotte, of St. Louis, Missouri.

FINAL CHANT WITH ACCOMP.

Dance continues.

This music continues until the Christian visitor begins to think the show a fraud; he gazes at the Arabic inscriptions, looks out of the window at the ships gliding along on the Bosporus, and at the hills of Asia beyond. From this occupation his attention is suddenly diverted. While the chanting is in full blast, as if never to end, a drum sounds an alarm, a wheezy flute begins a melancholy strain, the dervishes spring from their squatting postures, at the same time throwing aside their cloaks, revealing their long white gowns. The Scheich stands at the centre of one of the octagonal sides; the dervishes file before him, each one stopping as he passes to kiss the hat of the Scheich, who bends over for that purpose. Immediately on kissing the hat each dervish spins off towards the centre of the room, where he continues revolving like a teetotum. When the last man has kissed the hat the room is full of the whirlers. They hold their hands out at right angles, their heads droop, their eyes have a glassy, trance-like look. The perspiration pours from their necks and faces; still the wild rotary motion continues so rapid as almost to make the on-looker dizzy; it seems to have little effect on the dancers.

When the dance has continued for an almost incredible time, considering its nature, the wheezy flute gives the signal to stop; the living tops spin slower and slower, and finally stand still. At this moment they look like men awakened from a dream. Standing still a few minutes, as if to collect themselves, they once more file around the room, pass the Scheich, kiss his hat;

then a side door is opened, they file out, and the ceremony is over. The founder of this sect was Mevlana Dschelaaleddin Rumi, of Konia. The howling dervishes were founded in 1182, or thereabouts, by Asketan Seïd Ahmed Rufâi. Each sect go through their ceremonies once a week. Europeans are permitted to look on upon payment of two hundred para—eighteen cents—a modest enough sum. Four hundred para is charged to look at a mosque, neither as strange nor as interesting as the ceremonies of the dervishes.

Stamboul, the ancient Byzantium and the real Constantinople, is situated on a small triangular peninsula. The Golden Horn and the Bosporus form the defence of the city on two of its sides; a wall was once the city's defence on the land side. This wall is now in ruins. In places it has been torn down altogether. Hoary trees grow on its summit, vines and weeds cling to its sides. Before this wall once ran a ditch one hundred feet deep. Four hundred years ago this ditch was filled with thousands of bloody corpses; it is now half filled with earth. Figs, pomegranates, and orchids grow where besieged and besiegers once met in a death-struggle. In this ditch successive centuries saw vast hordes gather one after another, until the final catastrophe in 1453. A thousand years ago the followers of Mohammed stood here, heaped curses and darts upon the heathen Christians, and after a thirteen months' siege ignominiously retired. Eight hundred years later they again marshalled their forces in front of the ditch and the wall. This time Mohammed had cannon instead of curses and darts; the ditch was filled, the wall was battered down—the Roman Empire ceased to exist even in name.

Napoleon at one time had Prussia trampled under his feet. The Allies, after Waterloo, had France absolutely at their mercy. But the consequences were insignificant in comparison to the consequences of Mohammed's conquest of Constantinople. That was more the annihilation of a nation than a conquest. People, religion, manner, language—everything changed as a result of that day's work before the walls of Stamboul. To this day, after a lapse of centuries, the results are still present and still felt.

The view from the wall is fine. Stamboul with its forest of minarets is on one side, the luxurious gardens and cypress forests on the other; afar off are visible the blue waters of the Bosporus, the Sea of Marmora, and the outlines of the Balkan Mountains.

When returning one night through the labyrinth of steep streets from a trip to the ancient walls, my reflections were suddenly disturbed by loud cries and blowing of horns. People hurried hither and thither, and presently a squad of half-naked men rushed by, waving lanterns and giving forth the most unearthly yells.

There was a great fire in the city. Those men were the firemen. A mob was running in the direction of the fire. I joined them. It was a curious sight. A large harem was burning. The miserable Turkish women for the once left off their veils and saved themselves as best they could. The close lattice shutters which keep them from the fresh air as well as from the gaze of men were thrown wide open. At some of the windows stood human figures, shouting and wildly gesticulating. On the surrounding hills were thousands of fezzed and turbaned spectators. The firemen did little more than scream and shout. Their toy engines, worked by hand, throw at best a small, feeble stream; two-thirds of the time it threw no stream at all, for lack of water. There are no cisterns, no water-mains; the sole supply is the water brought from the sea in leather bags on the backs of men. I watched these water-carriers as they rushed about in wild confusion. Their bags hold two gallons. It is often a mile or more from the scene of the fire to the sea; as the bags are leaky, only a small portion of the two gallons remains when they arrive upon the scene of action (or *in*action). Such efforts are, of course, vain. I watched the harem until it burned to the ground.

Among the passengers on the Black Sea steamer was a Damascus silk-merchant. The Bulgarian missionary acted as interpreter, and before the landing at Constantinople the Damascus silk-merchant became quite friendly.   He wrote his name and address in my note-book in Arabic, and invited me to call upon him at his Stamboul residence.

During my frequent journeyings across the Golden Horn I fell in with a street gamin, a bright little fellow ten or twelve years old, who had learned Italian from Italian sailors.   For two hundred para this ragamuffin agreed to find the address of the silk-merchant, and to act as interpreter during my call.   The Arab seemed glad to see me.   He was just going to the bath, and insisted on my accompanying him.   Unfortunately I consented.   The indignities described in speaking of my other bath were heaped upon me, together with other still deeper atrocities. After a villanous Arab had stamped upon me and nearly dislocated all my bones, another fellow of a sudden threw himself on me, and before I could remonstrate had begun to shave my body with a keen-bladed razor.   Afraid to move lest he might cut me, I was forced to submit to his treatment.   The silk-merchant, lying on a marble slab near by, regarded me calmly ; my scamp of an interpreter, who stood a few yards off, clad in a towel, stuck out his tongue and grinned when I commanded him to tell the attendant to release me.   Thus was I obliged to endure it to the bitter end.   I felt glad that the villain spared the hair on my head ; it was about all he did spare.

The next day, accompanied by my Italian-speaking interpreter, I went to the Arab's, by special invitation, to dine.   Turkish dwelling-houses are divided into two parts, which are entirely separated one from the other.   Into the " Haremlik " no man is ever allowed, excepting the husband and his eunuchs. Visitors are admitted to the half called " Selamlik."   There is not much furniture, even in houses of the rich.   Around the walls are divans ; a few vases, lamps, smoking apparatuses, and coffee sets complete the furnishing of a room.   The floor is covered in summer by fine straw matting, in winter by rugs. The centre of the room remains empty.   The reception-room of my Arab friend was hung with bright Damascus silks ; over the door was an inscription in Arabic.   At exactly twelve o'clock the meal began. The drapery over the door leading to an inner court was deftly thrown aside, and a servant appeared bearing a large, round bowl of soup. He set it upon the low table, we took our places on cushions about ten inches high, and without further ceremony dipped our spoons in the big bowl and began eating, each one taking from the side of the bowl nearest him.

The second course consisted of some kind of curiously cooked meat. It was brought in on a large platter already cut in pieces. There was no knife nor fork, so I proceeded to help myself with my wooden spoon, which I had taken the precaution to keep. My host looked in astonishment at my attempt to dish up meat with a spoon. Laying one hand gently on my arm, with his right hand he selected and handed me a choice piece. I took it from his fingers and ate it with the best grace I could. The third course was rice cooked in the Turkish fashion. It was covered with oil and tomato-sauce. I was glad I was not called on to eat that with my fingers. The wooden spoons were brought back once more. We dipped our spoons in together, eating from the common dish. There were several other courses, including some delicious peaches from Damascus. At the conclusion we retired to the divans, where we reclined, sipped coffee, and conversed. During the progress of the dinner there was little conversation; the Turks do not like to distract their thoughts at meals. They speak in monosyllables or not at all. A napkin and a piece of bread is at each place. They help themselves with the fingers of the *right* hand. It is annoying to them to see guests help themselves with the left hand. Europeans, of course, often commit this breach of Turkish etiquette through ignorance. It is in part on that account Turks dislike dining with Europeans. After each course a servant brings water with which to wash your fingers.

I had considerable difficulty in persuading my friend Mohadin to accept my invitation to dine with me at the Hotel d'Angleterre in Pera, the principal European hotel of the Turkish capital. After much coaxing my interpreter told me he consented, and I made preparations that night to receive him.

When, the next day, we walked into the grand dining-room of the Hotel d'Angleterre, the guests there stared as if they had never seen an Arab before. Mohadin was as much at a loss with knives and forks as I had been the day before without them. He made one or two awkward attempts to cut his meat, and succeeded so badly that I called the waiter and made him cut it for him.

During my stay in Constantinople I saw much of this friendly Arab. He introduced me into some places generally closed to Europeans. The morning I called to bid him good-by he seemed quite moved. Grasping my hand he gave me his blessing in Arabic; at this moment his servant handed him a neatly tied package. Mohadin gave me the package, and speaking through my interpreter, said,

"My young friend, you are going home again. You will look back on this strange land as on a dream. Take this as a souvenir of your friend Mohadin. I had a son not long ago. He was your age; his complexion was yours. You resemble him; but he is dead now. He died in Jerusalem."

I pressed the old man's hand and departed. It had been remarked that the liking which Mohadin had for me, a stranger of another land and race, was something unusual. This fancied resemblance to a lost son explained the mystery. When I opened the package I found a handsome Turkish costume—a fitting souvenir of my trip in the East and of my Oriental friend.

At the time of my visit Mr. Jacob Spori was a Mormon missionary at Constantinople. Mr. Spori's predecessor was a man of the Ananias type. Once a week he wrote to the Salt Lake Saints, giving wonderful accounts of his success, of his many conversions, and of the marvellous spread of the true faith. That the Turks, already familiar with polygamy, should accept the Mormon teachings seemed reasonable. The Saints received the missionary's reports for nine months without suspicion.

"Then," said Mr. Spori, "he made another requisition for funds to transport his converts. The last time money had been sent him for that purpose no converts ever appeared.

Suspicions were awakened. I was sent over to investigate. The missionary did not even await my arrival. He set out for some remote province in Asia. I shall not bother with him further, but shall devote myself to undoing the mischief he did here."

Mr. Spori said he was born in Switzerland, that he early became converted to the true faith, and has since labored as missionary. When I called upon him he was studying a Turkish grammar preparatory to translating Mormon tracts into that language.

"I prefer monogamy," said Mr. Spori, "but polygamy is a tenet of my religion."

How can reason be used with such people? When in Salt Lake City I asked Amelia, Brigham Young's widow number seventeen, whether a woman could feel herself really beloved when there were so many to share her lord's affection. She smiled a frigid smile.

"Why not? Does a child feel unbeloved because there are sisters and brothers to share the parents' affections? We all loved and respected the President, and he loved us. There were nineteen of us. We never had fewer than seventy-five at the family breakfast-table. It was lively and sociable."

The stores in Stamboul are small, box-like affairs. A shop ten feet square by seven feet high is considered large. The proprietor squats in the middle of the floor, his goods piled around him. There he smokes his long pipe, or dozes, or plays a hand-organ. The hand-organs are used to attract customers. Many of the shops hire boys to grind on these hand-organs all day.

Dogs are made special pets in Stamboul. They are publicly fed every Friday between twelve and one o'clock. An English physician, desiring to remove a few hundred of the surplus dogs that congregated round his door, imprudently attempted to poison them. He narrowly escaped being mobbed.

Fountains are few and far between. When you find one a curious scene repays your trouble. Around the fountains of the city may be seen at almost all hours a crowd of donkeys, rude carts, and water-carriers. One day I came across a caravan of camels. There were about one hundred and fifty of the beasts; they had evidently made a long journey, and their drivers were busy drawing them water. The camels were divided into gangs of eight or ten, each gang fastened together by a light chain. The poor beasts were loaded with mountains of baggage, cooking-utensils, skillets, pots, pans, etc. They lie on their stomachs, their legs curled under them in what seems a most uncomfortable position. After watering them the drivers went around with oil-cans and oiled their beasts under the legs and belly.

Nominally, slavery in European Turkey has been abolished. It is an open secret, however, that girls of Georgia and Tscherkessina are sold in Tophane. It is here that the harems are supplied. It is said the slaves are treated well. Their children are treated the same as the children of the master. Male white slaves are no longer made eunuchs, as was formerly the custom; only blacks are now so treated. The Sultan selects for his harem a number of pretty slaves; the one bearing the first male child becomes his official wife, and is regarded with great jealousy by the less fortunate concubines.

Girls begin at ten years of age to wear veils. A long mantle covers the body from head to foot. Underneath is worn a shirt and a peculiar sort of trousers. Corsets are unknown. The bosom is covered by the end of the veil. Fashionable women color their finger and toe nails, the palms of the hands and the soles of the feet, a bright red. Women are forbidden to visit the European bazaars; the order is, however, frequently disobeyed. Under Sultan Mahmud, Turkish women took to visiting European bazaars to such an extent that an edict was issued commanding the shopkeepers to employ only old men in their bazaars.

Although the Koran permits wives to the number of four, monogamy is the rule, on account of the expense entailed by a plurality of wives. The average Turk marries early. At eighteen or twenty he buys a slave who, after the birth of the first child, the law makes his legal wife. Divorce is easy. All that is necessary is mutual consent. A man can separate three times from his wife; if he marries her a third time, the law compels him to stick it out to the end.

The life of a well-to-do Turk must be a trifle monotonous. They lounge about on divans, napping, or smoking cigarettes, sipping coffee, eating sweetmeats, or, accompanied by a maid, they ride in "caïques" on the Golden Horn, shop at the bazaars, and visit the baths. They are treated as children or playthings. The Turk regards his wife merely as a means of gratifying his desires.

The Turk is not provident for the future.

"We Turks," they say, "are better Christians than you. We obey the injunction, 'Let to-morrow take care of itself.' Christians forget that; in their scramble after gain they lose faith and reverence for God."

Of the many different peoples subject to the Sublime Porte the Albanians are the handsomest. They have tall, slender figures, and are extremely graceful. They make splendid soldiers. A great part of the Turkish army consists of men of this race. Twenty years is the time of service; three years in infantry of the line, three in infantry of the reserve, four years in the land reserve, class 1; four years in class 2, and six years in the militia. Christian subjects can purchase exemption from military service upon payment of a certain sum of money. The Turkish year is shorter than the solar year by eleven days. It consists of twelve lunar months of twenty-nine to thirty days each. The reckoning is begun from sundown. The sun sets at a different hour every day, so Turkish clocks require to be altered every day or two. It takes a skilled mathematician to keep the run of Turkish time.

Estimating my expenses after a trip to Asia Minor, I found I had spent upward of eight thousand para. The figures sound appalling. I reduced it to American money, and it was not so bad. Eight thousand para are not more than six or seven dollars. It requires forty para to make a piaster; a piaster is nearly equal to eighteen pfennige; five pfennige make a shade more than one cent. With this data the mathematician may calculate the exact amount spent in spending eight thousand Turkish para. When I bought a stamp at the German post-office, I handed the clerk a two-hundred-para piece, worth about eighteen cents.

"Do you expect me to change that?" asked the clerk.

"Certainly. Why not?"

The clerk saw I was fresh from foreign shores. He condescended to explain.

"Do you not know, to change that would cost me twenty para? Small money is scarce. You must get it changed at a broker's."

Such is the fact. The toll over the Golden Horn bridge is ten para; if you hand the guard a forty-para piece he will return only twenty para. He charges ten para for toll, and ten for changing your money. It need hardly be remarked that this system works a great hardship on the poor, who are paid their wages in a lump, but buy their supplies from time to time in small quantities. They lose from twenty to twenty-five per cent. at the money-changers'.

CHAPTER XXI.

WHEN preparing to leave Constantinople for Russia, I was told that permission from the Russian consul would be necessary. I hurried to that official and presented my card and passport. He scanned both closely as he demanded,

" Who are you ?"

I pointed to my card and passport.

"How do I know that is your name or passport? Go to your consul. You must show me that you are yourself."

The American consul knew no more of me than did the Russian ; but for the sum of 1500 para (about $1.40) he very obligingly certified that I was whoever I claimed to be, and, armed with the document he gave me, I returned again to the charge. The mighty man looked at the pass carefully, scanned it from every point of view, then demanded why I was going to Russia ?

" To see the country."

" For nothing else ?"

" Nothing."

" What is your business?"

" Travelling."

" Are you married ?" and so forth and so on through a long and severe examination.

When finally his numerous questions had been satisfactorily answered, a huge book was brought forth, and the long columns searched to see if my name was among the list of exiles or "suspects." Apparently it was not, for after a while he

shut his big book again, and with rather a sour look, as if
disappointed at not finding me on the list banished to Siberia,
told me my application would be granted, and to return the
next day for my pass and the *vise*.   I went back the next day,
paid the Russian consul four hundred para, and received the
necessary papers.   Then came another struggle, this time with
the Turk; for without the permission of the "Sun and Light
of the World," of the Sublime Porte, no one can leave the
realms of Turkey.   Happily the American and Russian *vises*
were not without an effect, and after only a slight delay the
heathen pocketed his fee, scratched something on my pass in
Arabic, and intimated that I was free to go.   At the harbor
there was one last struggle.   The customs-officers went through
my knapsack to see that nothing was being carried away that
should not be carried away; and then I hired a skiff—"caïques"
they are called in Turkey—and started for the steamer, which
lay at anchor in the Golden Horn a hundred yards from the
shore.

One would suppose that after providing all these official
documents, and undergoing such an array of formalities, there
would be no further trouble in leaving their blessed land.   The
heathen Turk, however, for "tricks that are dark and ways that
are vain," can "see" the heathen Chinee and go him a hundred
better.   Hardly was the caique afloat than I was signalled by
a small boat in the middle of the stream, which in a few moments pulled up along-side, while a villanous-looking fellow,
black as a coal-miner, climbed over into my boat and signed me
to unstrap my baggage.   He was another customs-officer, and
possessed of a wonderful amount of impudence and boorishness.   Before touching my sack he said,

"Backsheesh?" (drink-money).

I refused to give anything, whereupon he began a search as
if expecting to find stolen diamonds.   Everything was dumped
out on the bottom of the caïque.   He took out my letters, un-
folded them, shook the envelopes.   Every few seconds he
would say, "Backsheesh!" and on my continued refusal he

would renew the examination with still greater vigor. Of course it was a mere attempt to extort money. He even went into my pockets, and required me to show my watch and pocket-book. When at length he had exhausted even his resources for annoying, he climbed back into his boat fairly shaking with rage, while I looked him in the face and laughed. He had worked over the baggage half an hour, and still had extorted no "backsheesh." The thought made him furious.

"Englishman," he muttered, "no give backsheesh. Englishman damn fool!"

On board of the Russian steamer my passport was again examined. Not until the vessel was fully under way did I feel at all certain that I would be allowed to get out of the country.

Leaving Constantinople, it is three hours before the steamer passes out of the Bosporus into the Black Sea. During that time the eye is feasted on both the European and Asiatic shores, with a view of long lines of forts and bristling guns. The spot where Mohammed's big cannon was planted, and the old castle that he erected to the terror and dismay of the feeble Emperor Palæologus, are passed; the towers and minarets of the Eastern capital become dimmer and dimmer in the distance, and at last the steamer emerges in the open sea. Two days and nights pass; then on the morning of the third day the traveller awakes, and knows he is in Russia by the strange faces and uniforms around him. They are there to see that none leave the vessel without authority. And no one is given authority to leave until he has submitted to the doctor's inspection and produced his passport.

It was a motley crew the doctor had to examine that morning. Europeans, Turks, Tartars, Arabs, and specimens of a dozen other people passed before him in single file while he looked at their tongues or punched them in the ribs to ascertain their physical condition. Fortunately, all were in good health, and we were permitted to land as soon as the officers had finished examining the passports.

In entering Russia it is necessary to be circumspect with regard to the literature you take with you. Books are examined at seaport and frontier stations, and those advocating freedom or denouncing tyranny are confiscated. As for newspapers, those that do not fill all the requirements of the Russian censorship are run through an inking machine and then ironically returned to the owner. A disagreeable thing about this business is, that often the official does not understand the book or paper he is examining, and, to be on the sure side, condemns it to the daubing-press. In this way it not infrequently happens that the most innocent poems or fairy-tales are returned to their owner only after being daubed with ink and rendered wholly illegible. Byron's works are not permitted in Turkey. His poems are considered too democratic, and calculated to arouse the Greek and reawaken his dreams of liberty.

Odessa presents a very handsome appearance from the sea. The buildings are modern and imposing. There is a magnificent flight of marble stairs a hundred feet wide, leading from the sea to the summit of the bluff on which the city stands, while the streets seem, to one just from the labyrinth of winding, filthy alleys in Stamboul, a collection of the finest and handsomest avenues in Europe. They are broad and well paved, and on each side, flanking the sidewalks, is a double row of shade-trees. This is not the case on one or two streets only, but the great majority are so shaded, adding no little to the general elegance and beauty of the city.

One of the first things that strikes a stranger's attention in Russia is the peculiar appearance of the cabmen, or of the " Iswoschtschik," as they are called in Russian. They wear a long, clumsy dress that touches the ground. In the middle, for a foot above and below the waist, it is plaited and thickly padded with cotton or wool: a very good sort of cushion, but when cabby (iswoschtschik) stands up his great gown protrudes in the middle in a way most suggestive and ridiculous. His bushy head is generally surmounted by the tiniest sort of queer-style Derby hat. The cab he drives is almost as absurd. The dash-board, and indeed the whole front part, is made of sheet-iron; the seat is very small and uncomfortable; and as there is no cover or back it is often a difficult matter to stay seated when driving over rough stones or turning a sharp corner. Over the horse's neck is an arch or hoop sticking up two feet or more, and hung with bells.

The overcoat of a fashionable Circassian contains on the breast a row of cartridge-pockets, and at his side he carries a sword or hanger. These gentlemen wear their trousers stuffed in very high-topped boots, and present quite a fierce and forbidding air as they saunter through the streets, occasionally toying with the gun or sword at their side. I saw several of them in Odessa. As I gazed upon them from a respectful distance, they brought up thoughts of the festive cowboy in the Far West. The Far West and the Far East agree in this respect if in no other — both can show some wild and weird specimens of humanity. I will not assert that Russian ladies partake in this peculiarity, but certainly, if some things which occur in Odessa may be taken as a criterion, they too have a little of the Western *chic* about them. It is not at all unusual to see the nicest-dressed ladies spring on and off a street car while it is in motion. The sight of a lady smoking excites in Russia no more remark than does a man's drinking a glass of beer in Germany.

Russia is like a vast prison. The prisoner in a dungeon can walk within certain limits as freely as the freest. It is only when he would go farther that he encounters the walls, and is stopped. So, in Russia, as long as you remain within a narrow limit, you may possibly forget that you are in a prison. It is not easy to forget it when you would stir. Walls—that is, officers—meet you at every turn.

On arriving at a hotel the first thing demanded is your passport, which you must carry to the police and have registered and stamped, you, by-the-way, having to pay for the registration and stamp. When you leave a city the police must again be notified; and from beginning to end it seems as if every new-comer is suspected of being a Nihilist or Dynamiter. It is dangerous to converse on social or political topics; each one suspects the other of spying. It is so easy to be denounced, so easy to be waltzed off to Siberia, that the truth of the proverb, "Silence is golden," is appreciated in no other part of the earth as it is in Russia.

Some thirty years ago, when the first big railroad was projected in Russia, two cities disputed as to which should have the road. The matter was referred to the Czar.

"H'm," said his Majesty, "not at all a difficult matter to decide." And laying a ruler between the two termini, "Build your road *here*," he said.

As a result of this simple method of adjusting matters, railroads in Russia run pretty much in straight lines. The stations are anywhere from two to ten miles from the towns. As if to make up for the inconvenience he thus occasioned, the Czar sent to America for Ross Winans, an American engineer, and engaged him to introduce the American system of railroading.

Russia, alone of all the European States (excepting a portion of little Switzerland), has long, open coaches instead of the miserable little boxes called compartments. On the trains they have not only one conductor, they have half a dozen. The head-conductor on the train out of Odessa was the most gorgeous and imposing individual I ever saw. His boots, glistening with polish, came above his knees; his belt was very broad, and was as shiny as his boots; his coal-black beard came down to his waist. A fur cap surmounted his head; his uniform gleamed with decorations and medals. Whenever this mighty Mogul deigned to take up tickets, two sub-conductors preceded him, announced his approach, and shook by the shoulders such of the passengers as were asleep, to prepare them for the great man's arrival.

At stations there is a great deal of ceremony connected with starting the train. The first conductor nearest the engine blows a whistle; the second conductor, a little farther down the line, blows his whistle; and so it continues to the Grand Mogul, who, looking majestically around, blows *his* whistle, whereupon the blowing starts back on the line to number one again. Number one gives another blast, the engine answers, and at length the train moves out.

Russian peasants are inordinately fond of tea. The train never stopped but that a score or more wild, shaggy-looking fellows rushed out with their tin pots for hot water, which they brought back into the car and converted into tea. Before beginning a meal the Russian peasant takes off his hat and crosses himself; he does the same whenever a church is passed. I was often surprised to see every man in the car take off his hat and begin a series of salaams and prostrations. On survey ing the surrounding country the reason became apparent; the gilded dome of some church was visible.

It is not in every country that one can see one's fellow-passengers get down on their knees and bump the floor with their heads.

An incident which occurred the morning of my arrival in Odessa was encouraging. A man whom I stopped on the street said,

"Italian-sky?" meaning if I were Italian.

"No," said I, "American-sky."

The man seemed to understand perfectly, and elated with success, I tried him further. I said,

"What-sky is the name-sky of this-sky?"

Alas! The plan failed to work to that extent. American-sky and Italian-sky were about the only words of Russian that I mastered. In the Black Sea ports Italian is of some slight help, and in Western frontier towns German is occasionally understood. Generally speaking, however, the only language of any use in Russia is Russian.

The Russian peasant and workman is a marvel of superstition—such greediness, such filth, such degradation and cringingness! I have seen more than one churl, clad in a suit of cowhide, enter an eating-house, deposit scythe, bags, and other baggage on the floor, and then fall to eating with ravenous haste. They fill their mouths to overflowing with great chunks of greasy meat and black bread, and before disposing of one mouthful they take in another.

As wretched a sight as is the Russian laborer himself, his home is more wretched still. I was approaching one day in South Russia, on the Black Sea, what seemed a lot of hay-stacks, but which proved to be a " Bauerdorf "—peasant village. Each hut was covered quite deep with hay. Into this hay the cattle eat, so that by spring or summer the hut is uncovered. The village seemed as if it had been set down in that spot temporarily, and then forgotten. All around was a vast, tree-less plain, across which the wind swept, biting and cutting like a knife. The miserable straw-covered huts, each about eight by twelve feet by six feet high, are arranged in one long, straggling street, and that street made of the sticky, black soil which characterizes that whole part of the country.

The creatures who inhabit these villages dress in skins; their hair and beard grow long, and are seldom or never cut. They look wild and shaggy. Very rarely is one able to read. Their lives are spent in the hardest toil, with no other thought than to fill their stomachs with gross food, to keep off the freezing cold of winter, and to obey the priests in this world that they may be sure of a free passport into the next.

Ask a Russian bricklayer or carpenter what wages he re-ceives, and he will reply, a ruble and a half, or, if skilled, two rubles, a day—that is, from seventy cents to a dollar. So far this appears quite as good as wages in other European countries, but there is another side to the story. The Russian bricklayer may earn two rubles a day, but his terrible climate only allows him an average of about one hundred working-days a year. Two hundred days it is too cold to work (snow lies on the streets of St. Petersburg one hundred and seventy-one days out of the year), and fifty or sixty days are consumed in cele-brating religious holidays. The small sum received for the remnant of time left in which it is possible to work must suffice to support him the whole year. Generally, employers make contracts by the year. One hundred and forty to one hundred and sixty rubles will represent the yearly wages of the average bricklayer or carpenter. In Italy, where one can pluck grapes from the vines and live in the open air, it is possible to conceive a man supporting a family on eighty dollars a year; how, though, is it possible in a land where the winter's snow endures eight months out of every twelve? where the great struggle of life is to keep warm? I put this question to a Russian in Moscow. Said he,

"The Russian workman is like the bear in one respect—he is a hibernating animal. Most workmen own or rent a small piece of land on the plains, within a few days' journey of the city wherein they work. The workman only comes to the city in summer; with cold weather's approach he returns to his mud or straw-covered hut, and remains buried there until summer comes again. He wears a suit of skins; this suit he lives in, sleeps in, eats in, in short, he very rarely removes it in the course of a whole winter, or from August to May, or even June. His food in winter does not cost ten kopecks—five cents —a day. His clothing is a small item, as one suit lasts ten or twelve years. Almost the only fuel he has is the peat dug from the swampy plains surrounding his hovel."

In Russia there is not that division of labor which the practice of other nations has found desirable. For instance, there is no hod-carrier. A bricklayer brings his own brick and mortar.

A "dessatim" of land—about six acres—in the vicinity of Moscow is worth fifty rubles (twenty-five dollars). Better land costs in the neighborhood of two hundred rubles per dessatim. The land around Moscow is poor. It is too sandy, and the plains surrounding the ancient capital are almost totally uninhabited.

CHAPTER XXII.

IN an eating-house in Southern Russia I fell in with a long-haired student who spoke broken German. It had been weeks since I had spoken a word. I passed a day in the student's society with considerable pleasure. He related a curious story, which he called "Das Elixir der Schnelligkeit" (The Elixir of Rapidity).

"Near the mouth of the Ural River, on the Siberian frontier of Russia," said the long-haired student, "was at one time a small hut which, in an isolated section of the country, was encircled with so thick and impenetrable a growth of fir and Polish wierzba trees as to escape the detection of the few travellers whom necessity or adverse fortune cast in that desolate region. The low hut, without window or chimney—probably in years gone by the retreat of some fugitive Jew—had until recently been deserted. There were cobwebs in the dark corners; the yard lying around the hut, shut in by a palisade of thickly-set firs, was overgrown with rank grasses, with the ruta, the roza, and other herbs peculiar to Western Siberia. The faint plash of the Ural as it rippled on its way to the Caspian Sea was the only sound that disturbed the solemn stillness. The sun had set behind the snow-capped peaks of the Ural Mountains, a dull light flickered out into the darkness through the chinks and cracks of the dilapidated hovel.

"Lying on a pallet in one corner of this low room was a man of Eastern dress and appearance. His furrowed and bronzed face was framed in long locks of white hair, his beard was flowing and gray. Near, on a stool, his face resting in his hands, was a man of exactly opposite type—youthful as his companion was aged, dress after the North Russian style, and his hair and mustache as black as that of the sage was gray. But with all his youth and health, his mien seemed that of extreme dejection.

" 'Tell me, O son of the West!' said the old man, raising himself and observing his companion's dejection—'tell me, art thou lonely in this dreary hovel? Do thy studies interest thee no more?'

" 'Oh, father!' exclaimed the youth, impetuously, turning and meeting the eye of the patriarch as it gazed searchingly into his, 'of what use are my wanderings, my studies? My thoughts are ever away, away in Nishni-Novgorod with one who my heart tells me is lost to me forever.'

" For some moments the graybeard made no reply to this outburst, but, wrapped in silence, gazed thoughtfully into the smouldering fire. At length he spoke:

" 'Allah is great, Allah is powerful! What is it weighs on thy heart? Thou hast saved Allah's servant from the Russian dog of a Christian—Allah will help thee; what is it weighs on thee?'

" 'Oh, if your conjurer's art and magic *could* help me!' exclaimed the youth. 'They wanted to burn you for a sorcerer; if it be true, if you are master of magic, you can, you will help me.'

" The old man gravely nodded his head; the young man went on with his story:

" 'A year ago the handsomest girl in all Nishni-Novgorod promised me her heart and hand. I was happiness itself. But her cruel father declared none but a millionaire should ever marry his daughter. I was moderately rich, but where was I to get a million? It was then near the time of the great races. In an evil hour I determined to risk my fortune on the racecourse and win my ladylove or lose all. Day after day I was the first at the betting-stand, and day after day my purse grew thinner and thinner ; and then came the last day when, of the inheritance left me by my father, there remained but a single thousand rubles.'

" ' " What if it is lost ?" I thought. " As well without a kopeck as with a beggarly thousand rubles ;" and so going to the betting-stand, I placed my last ruble.

" ' The bell was tapped, the jockeys drew their horses in line, the signal to start was given, and forth they shot like arrows. Around they flew almost as the wind ; now at the half-mile post, now obscured by a cloud of dust, now again in sight, the jockeys plying their whips, the fleet-footed animals straining to the utmost. My heart fairly rose to my mouth as I looked at those horses and thought of the wife and fortune that were at stake for me. So far it seemed even, then of a sudden the blue jockey bounded half a length ahead.

" ' " The Blue ! the Blue !" shouted a thousand voices, as the horses came tearing down the home-stretch. The Blue is ahead —it will, it must win ! I was almost overcome with excitement. There was a loud cry, a cloud of dust hid the riders from view. When it floated away, there lay the blue jockey pinioned to the ground by his fallen horse. The race was lost—I was ruined !

" ' I left Nishni-Novgorod and the woman I loved, to wander whither I knew nor cared not. Chance led me to the Asiatic frontier. One day, at Saratow, an Oriental was displaying the mysteries of his Eastern magic. The superstitious rabble attacked the sage. I came to the rescue. You know the rest —how we left Sarotow by night, how we crossed the Volga, and, after a weary march across the mountains, at last found refuge in this deserted hovel. Such, oh father, is my story. Of what use then are the mysteries you teach me, since they do not, cannot restore to me my Nikolajewna, my darling, my lost love ?'

" During the recital of this story, and for some moments after its conclusion, the patriarch remained silent, as if lost in deep meditation. At length, drawing his shrunken figure to a sitting posture, he turned to his companion, and in low, measured tones thus addressed him :

" ' Allah is great, Allah is powerful ! Though he loves not to aid the unbeliever, thou hast preserved his servant, and through his servant will he help thee. Thou wouldst regain thy love— 'tis well. The servant of Allah will help thee.'

" 'But how, oh father, how ?'

" 'Is not Allah great and powerful ?' asked the sage, with rebukeful tone. 'Bring me my chest; the servant of Allah will help thee.'

"Obedient to this request, the youth brought forth from a hidden recess a small chest which, the sage opened, disclosing cases of phials, powders, acids, scales, a crucible, and a quantity of strange plants. The Oriental's eye glistened as he gazed on these instruments of his mystic art. Quickly arranging the cases before him, he selected from the many varieties of plants in the chest one of large leaf and long, juicy stem. These he placed in the crucible and subjected to a high temperature. As the plants sizzled and parched, a strong incense filled the low apartment, and a pungently odorous liquid was distilled in the bottom of the vessel. These precious drops the sage watched with careful anxiety ; when the leaves were parched dry, the drops were poured in a blue phial, and the baked and crumbling leaves were minutely pulverized. Long into the night was this strange work continued, while the youth sat looking on in distrusting wonder. Noxious gases floated out through the cracks in the rickety walls ; the gurgle of liquids poured from one phial into another, telling of strange mixtures and compounds, sounded faintly on the still night air; the desolate hovel was, as by enchantment, transformed into a magician's or chemist's laboratory.

" At length the Oriental paused. Slowly sifting a white, silver powder on the glowing embers, he began an incantation in his strange Eastern tongue. As he spoke, a drowsy incense filled the room ; the youth's head fell on his breast, his eyes closed in sleep. It was in the gray of the morning before he awoke. The sage lay reclining on his pallet.

" 'Allah's will is done,' said the sage. 'Thou wilt be happy. Go bring from the river a turtle, that I may make clear to thee.'

"On the youth's return, the sage, stretching the turtle on its back, withdrew the legs from under the shell, and proceeded to make a slight incision in the muscles of each leg. Then producing the phial of distilled drops and a hypodermic syringe, he injected in each of the incisions a small quantity of the liquid.

" ' Now set him without the door.'

"The command was obeyed. The sluggish animal started around the circle within the palisade of firs. As he went, his legs moved faster, he fell into a trot; in a few seconds the turtle's speed had increased with such astounding rapidity that the black shell on his back was scarcely visible—he was literally flying around the ring! The youth stared in amazement at this miracle of turtles, the sage stood calm and smiling.

" ' Allah is great; his will is done,' he said. ' My son, thou art an unbeliever. It is not permitted to reveal the secret of this compound to the unbeliever, but this phial may be intrusted to thee. A single drop of this oxygenated liquid hypodermically injected in an animal's leg-muscles will result as thou seest in that turtle. It is the Elixir of Rapidity!'

"Now, now the youth understands: with this elixir he may regain his fortune and his love! Falling on his knees before his benefactor, he attempted to pour out his thanks. The patriarch smiled benignly.

" ' Arise, my son. Thou owest me no thanks. I but repay the debt I owed thee. The spirit of Allah is in this elixir; Allah will restore thee thy love. But the servant of Allah must go; he has dwelt long enough in the land of the Christian. Let us part here on the banks of the Ural.'

" The Oriental extended his arms with a parting salaam, while the eyes of the youth filled with tears. His heart had learned to love this lonely wanderer, whose life he had saved from the superstition of a Russian rabble. The sage, who had injected a few drops of the fluid through the skin of his own thighs, began to slowly move away. As the powerful liquid assumed its sway, he waved his companion a last farewell; his weird figure and long gray hair streaming in the wind, faded rapidly out of sight as, his speed increasing, he ran with incredible rapidity towards the mountains in the East. The Elixir of Rapidity had borne him away almost like the wind, leaving the youth desolate and alone in that dreary hovel.

"It was race-week at Nishni-Novgorod. Baron Nikolaus's celebrated racer had been entered, to the terror of all competitors. The baron himself, accompanied by his beautiful daughter Nikolajewna, occupied a seat in his carriage near the grand stand. So great was the fame of the baron's horse, it was doubtful whether there would be found any bold enough to enter against him. The president of the club was on the point of requesting the baron to withdraw, when a stranger, stepping forward, quietly remarked that he was ready to match his horse against the baron's racer.

"'You!' ejaculated the president. 'Are you aware whom it is you encounter?'

"'Perfectly,' replied the stranger, coldly.

"'And where is the steed you have the temerity to enter against the fleetest racer in all Europe?'

"'Already on the track.'

"Following the stranger's glance, the president beheld, a few yards from his stand, a scraggy-looking animal, halting in gait and blind in one eye.

"'What mean you, sir?' he exclaimed, indignantly. 'What mean you by running such a—a—a scrub, sir? This is no place for foolery.'

"'Nor do I mean foolery,' said the stranger, with a cynical smile. 'Do you see this? It is an unlimited letter of credit on the Rothschilds at Frankfort. Say to the baron I will wager a million rubles on the success of the animal you call a scrub.'

"The message was conveyed to the baron, and quickly spread through the crowd. 'Some wealthy lunatic anxious to be rid of his money,' was the universal verdict.

"'A madman!' the baron exclaimed, indignant at the idea of

the scrub running against his fleet racer. It was observed, however, that the baron was not averse to winning the stranger's money, even though he were a madman.

"'We must teach him a lesson,' he said; and the enormous wager of the stranger's million against the baron's fortune was soon arranged. Baron Nikolaus was reputed worth, at the least, five million rubles, but the odds, five to one, seemed nothing when one looked at the two horses. The idea that the stranger's hobbledy, lame-footed scrub had the slightest chance of winning appeared too monstrous to entertain for a moment. As the judges were on the point of giving the starting signal, the stranger requested permission to examine his animal.

"'I make it a rule to see that all is right before starting,' he said, with a queer smile.

"'Certainly,' the judges replied; 'and if you can right the hobbledy gait and blind eye of your scrub you may win after all.'

"The stranger, making no reply, approached his horse and began to examine his limbs. None of the thousands of eyes that were fastened upon him knew what was going on when, with a small syringe, he hypodermically injected in the fore and hind legs a few drops of a liquid taken from a phial carried in his pocket. So quietly and skilfully was this operation performed that it was unobserved; nor, had it been seen, would the public have understood its connection with the subsequent amazing event.

"The signal to start was given. The baron's racer shot forth like an arrow; the stranger's miserable scrub ambled slowly off at a hobbling gait, amid the jeers and hoots of the populace. But their shouts and laughter gradually lessened, and finally gave way to amazed silence as the scrub, seemingly aided by magic, increased his speed with marvellous rapidity, gaining every moment, and in ten seconds shooting by the baron's racer like a gust of wind. Before his competitor had made the first mile, the scrub had made the complete circuit, dashed by the judges' stand, and was flying around on the second mile. Judges, people, all too amazed to speak, sat dumfounded, while the stranger's horse continued flying round the course with such astounding rapidity as to be scarcely visible.

"Towards the fifth mile, long after the baron's racer had left the course, the strange steed's speed began to slacken, and finally he drew up before the eyes of the dazed crowd, quivering in every nerve, the perspiration dripping from every pore. His jockey, who, after the first mile, had given up all attempt at curbing his speed, and simply held on, clutching him around the neck with might and main, now tumbled to the ground almost paralyzed with fear. It is impossible to describe the uproar and confusion that ensued. The senses of the people were paralyzed; one thing was clearly apparent: by some un- heard - of, some inconceivable means, the stranger's scrub had won, and the baron was a ruined man. That night Baron Niko- laus received a letter:

"'Two years ago,' began the letter, 'I had the honor of be- ing a suitor for your daughter's hand. You said the winner of your daughter's hand must be the owner of a million. I have now a second time the honor of suing for her hand. My present suit will, I trust, be successful. I have the pleasure of signing myself the possessor of five times the necessary million.

"'PAUL PETROWITSCH.'

"Of course the baron gave his consent; but it was not until after the marriage that he learned that his son-in-law and the winner of his fortune were one and the same."

CHAPTER XXIII.

IN THE HEART OF RUSSIA.—HOW TAXES ARE COLLECTED.—THE PIL-
GRIM CHURCH AND THE WONDERFUL PICTURE OF THE MOTHER OF
GOD.—ARRESTED FOR WRITING IN MY NOTE-BOOK.—THE CZAR'S
PALACE.—MOSCOW AND ST. PETERSBURG.

I ARRIVED in Kiev one Sunday night in a freezing rain. It
was bitter cold. Wearied with long nights and days of journeyings, I never before felt so dispirited. I had managed to
get a little troubled sleep by spreading my rubber coat on the
floor under the benches of the railroad car; but it seemed to
me my eyes had hardly closed before the black-bearded conductor pulled me out and I found we were at Kiev. I stepped
on the station platform feeling utterly lost. I was in the heart
of Russia, ignorant of a single word of the language, and, worst
of all, with a pocket-book depleted to an alarming thinness.
The next morning I hurried to the post-office. The draft I
was expecting had not come. I walked to the heights overlooking the Dnieper and the adjacent swampy plains. As I
gazed on those vast swamps extending hundreds of versts towards Moscow, the possibility of having to make the journey
on foot was anything but cheerful. I was greatly relieved next
day on receiving the draft.

In Kiev I saw what seemed the side-show of an American
circus. There was a squeaking hand-organ, a ticket-vender
with his (presumably, for it was in Russian) "Step this way,
gentlemen, right this way, for the greatest show on earth."
On broad sheets of canvas, to afford an idea of the unparalleled
wonders within, were hideous lying pictures. I paid twenty-
five kopecks (twelve and a half cents) to see this aggregation
of marvels. What did I see? An Edison phonograph!—that
was the entire show. It reminded me of a show I saw in Rome,

where, when returning from the Vatican, a flaming poster on a little side street caught my eye. It announced that in the "Stabilimento grandioso" adjoining was to be seen the most marvellous collection in Rome, all for the modest sum of forty centessimi—eight cents. I paid eight cents, and saw—a lot of photographs! They were lying on a table in a heap. I, who had just seen the originals in the Vatican free of charge, paid eight cents to see poor photographs in the "Stabilimento grandioso!"

The Pilgrim Church of Kiev is surrounded by a high wall. Half a dozen or more gilded domes surmount the roof; its appearance is Oriental. When you enter the gate of the big wall you pass between two lines of beggars, and find yourself in the church amid a labyrinth of narrow and crooked passages, the walls of which are decorated with most doleful and lugubrious-looking frescos of saints and apostles. Pictures of Christ and the Virgin are numerous, and are set in frames of gold and jewels. Some of these frames contain jewels worth half a million dollars. The celebrated painting of the Virgin at Moscow is valued at even greater figures, on account of the brilliant stones in its frame. The Moscow Virgin is used to heal the sick and bring back to life the dying. The picture with its dazzling frame is placed on a car with great ceremony, and drawn by six horses to the house where the miracle is to be performed. To Americans accustomed only to read of miracles, not to see them, this ceremony is interesting. A grand cavalcade of priests and people starts from the little church opposite the Kremlin to accompany the Virgin's picture on its holy mission.

The Pilgrim Church at Kiev has nothing to rival the miracle Virgin painting of Moscow; it has, however, other features as interesting. Three hundred thousand people visit the church every year. Pilgrims are met on the road-side long before the church is reached — some in skins, some in rags, some without shoes, their feet blistered and almost bleeding from cold and fatigue. They walk hundreds of miles, and a few, it is said, come from the distant provinces of Siberia. Surrounding the church was a large encampment. The shaggy, strange-looking people were camped out with their pots and kettles and skins. One old woman was bent double under a load of pans and kitchen effects. The pilgrims come many miles, pray in the church, camp on the plains for a few days' rest, then trudge back to their distant hovels and resume their daily rounds of drudgery.

Within the Pilgrim Church I saw several hundred long-haired, wild-looking people kneeling, crossing themselves, and every moment or two striking the floor with their heads. One gray-haired old man, with a bag of potatoes and black bread slung over his shoulder, kissed nearly everything in the church. He kissed the floor, the walls, the corners, the pictures — in short, everything that was kissable he kissed. I almost feared to turn lest he might kiss me too.

The market of Kiev is in a rough, cobble-paved square. The venders squat on the pavement under the open sky, their goods and wares around them. Old moth-eaten furs, high boots that reach to the waist, cucumber pickles, horseshoe nails, railroad spikes, scrap-iron—these are a few of the articles that may sometimes be obtained of one and the same vender. They sit there in that open square, rain or shine, hot or cold. When it rains they hoist their old umbrellas; when cold they draw their skin coats and dilapidated furs closer around them; when it turns hot—well, when it turns hot they simply remove superfluous clothing. The Russian peasant studies convenience rather than appearance. The men seemed to me to have very long bodies and very short legs. The throat is short, the neck thick and muscular. Their hands and feet are often small and well formed. They allow their beard to grow; the hair is also worn long. Russian women possess the same general characteristics as the men. They have not as good teeth, the reason of which is their inordinate fondness for sweets.

The rate of taxation in Russia is so high that the lower classes and many of the smaller merchants not only cannot pay their taxes, but have no hope or idea of ever being able to pay them. Two methods are taken by the Government to remedy this. First, when a town or village fails to come up with its quota of tax, the leading or most well-to-do men of that town or village are called to the metropole's office and told that the tax *must* be paid; that *they* will be held responsible. By this simple device, when a community is unable to pay its taxes, one or two rich men pay for the community.

The other method for rebuking delinquent tax-payers is to flog them. One does not hear much of this in the papers, for they dare not mention it. The traveller into the small interior towns of Russia, however, may not infrequently see citizens tied to posts and thoroughly flogged for not being able to pay their tax. If the merchant is a "leading" man, his wealth is confiscated; if he is a poor man he is flogged. Verily the lot of the Russian tax-payer is not a happy one.

So much for internal taxation. Tariff taxes at the frontier are as burdensome. The list of dutiable articles is as long as the words of their language. Even pies are subject to an import duty. Four dollars and eighty cents is charged on every thirty-six and a half pounds of pie imported into Russian territory! Is this a blow aimed at the New England pumpkin-pie industry? If so it calls for retaliation. In a note at the end of this volume will be found a partial tariff-table for Russia as well as for the other countries I visited. In the same note will be given a comparative wage-table. The reader may determine from those tables whether or not high tariffs make high wages.

My greatest difficulty in Russia, especially in the south, was in purchasing railroad-tickets; and indeed it was often only by accident that I even found the railroad-station. In one small place the station remained obstinately hidden full half a day. There was not a soul in the village with whom I could speak. I stopped a man on the street and imitated as best I could the sound of a locomotive. "Toot, toot, toot; 'psh, 'psh, 'psh; ding-dong, ding-dong," I cried, and ran up and down the street working my arms like the arms of a driving-wheel. The result of this brilliant idea was, a crowd collected; they began to hoot and jeer; a gendarme came up, and I was walked off into durance vile. My passport saved me serious trouble, but it was twenty-four hours before I succeeded in getting away. The railway-station was three miles and a half from the village.

It was next to impossible to make the agents understand where I wished to go. In Kiev I worried the ticket - agent half a day before I succeeded in making him understand that I wanted to go to Moscow. I pronounced the name in forty different styles, got out my map, pointed out Kiev, then Moscow, and pantomimed that I wanted to go there. This seemingly excellent scheme had its drawbacks; my map was printed in German. The official did not know one word of German, and I knew nothing of Russian letters. I never even attempted to learn the Russian alphabet, with its "Rs" turned backward, its "Bs" standing on their heads. In the scramble for letters the Italians got nearly all the vowels and the Russians all the consonants. This makes it hard for strangers. When finally, after a day's work, I got the railroad-agent at Kiev to give me a ticket, I was not at all certain he had given me a ticket to Moscow. At every junction and change of cars I wondered if I were not on the wrong train—on the way to the North-pole or Siberia. Not until the tiresome forty-two-hour ride ended, and I reached Moscow, did I feel entirely relieved.

The Wossnossensky Cloister is in the rear of the palace in the Kremlin. In the chapel of the cloister is a wonderful picture of the mother of God, and a number of red-covered coffins containing many royal remains, including those of the scheming sister of Peter the Great. In the Wossnossensky Cloister priests and nuns officiate together. I saw a pale-faced nun in deep black reading the service as if propelled by steam; so fast did she rattle it off it seemed impossible that even a Russian could understand her. A priest stood near by. When the nun's rapid performance ceased, the priest began rattling away almost as fast as the nun, as if determined to get in as much as possible in the short time allowed him.

Actions most harmless in other lands may prove very unsafe in Russia. Near one of the Kremlin gates I observed that all passers-by crossed themselves and bared their heads. The fact seemed odd; I took out my note-book to make a note of it. While scribbling away, a bushy-bearded gendarme with a savage look and a long sabre stepped up and addressed me in his forty-syllabled tongue. I did not understand, whereupon, without further ceremony, the man of savage look and bushy beard seized my arm and took me to the nearest station. There I produced my note-book and passport for the inspection of the captain of the police. He examined both closely, held a consultation with another uniformed official, then said to me in German,

"You may go this time, but I warn you, young man, not to stop again on the streets to write your notes."

Such leniency and moderation were overwhelming. I left the great man's presence with many inward thanks at his forbearance in not sending me to Siberia.

Not much is heard now of the Government's sending people to Siberia; it does not follow that the Government has ceased doing such acts of despotism. The Government, adopting the tactics of the Nihilists, works in secret and in the dark. A man is seen in his house, in his accustomed haunts to-day; to-morrow he is not seen. The next day and the next, and the next he is still missing. People ask each other:

"What has become of X——?"

They ask, but are never answered. A case of this kind occurred in Moscow about the time of my arrival in that city. X—— was the book-keeper and trusted agent of one of the most prominent houses in the city—a young man of excellent education, of family and means. One day an officer appeared in the counting-room of the firm and told the young man he was desired at the office of the metropole (governor of the city). Young X—— shut up his books, locked the safe, stuck

the key in his pocket, and started out with the officer. An
hour, two hours, three, four passed; he did not return. The
head of the firm wondered what could detain his agent. Finally he supposed X—— had been kept late at the metropole's,
and had gone thence direct home. Thinking, therefore, no
more of the matter, the merchant closed his offices for the night.

But the next day the young man still failed to appear. His
family came to the merchant to make inquiries, and for the
first time it was known he had been neither at the counting-
room nor at home. The merchant was acquainted with the
metropole.

"I will go to him," he said to his young clerk's friends—"I
will go to him, and all will soon be clear."

He went, but alas, all was *not* made clear; nor will it ever be.
The metropole received his acquaintance coldly.

"I know your mission," he said; "I must ask you to seek
no explanation. Of course you may insist, but"—significantly
—"but I tell you it will be better if you do not. Your young
friend is gone. You will never see him again."

And the world not only does not see him again, but never
even hears of him—knows not whether he has suffered a midnight execution, or is still living, toiling in the depths of some
Siberian mine! He has disappeared—has been literally blotted
from the face of the earth. Such incidents are not noticed in
the newspapers; the editor daring to mention it would himself be spirited away. The affair of young X—— was related
to me by a Russian in Moscow, who had lived several years in
England, and who regarded with sadness the darkened condition of his native land.

The morning I went to the commandant's office in the
Kremlin to obtain a permit to visit the Czar's palace a pour-
ing rain was falling; the streets were converted into small
rivers. I wore a rubber coat and a very broad-brimmed hat in
lieu of an umbrella. When ushered into the mighty official's
presence, dripping, I was about to say, from every pore, I felt
my heart quake within me. I realized for the first time how

sorry a specimen I was to appear before a servant of his imperial majesty the Czar and Autocrat of all the Russias! The commandant eyed me with looks of mingled indignation and scorn, then slowly said,

"Did you come in a cab?"

I surveyed my dripping coat and soaked shoes. There was no chance to conceal the truth. I had not come in a cab. I so told the commandant.

He gave me another indignant look, and eyed me from head to foot.

"Did you come also without goloshes?"

I had come without goloshes. What then? Was I to be sent to Siberia? No; but the punishment was severe. The mighty man pierced me with his eyes again.

"You come without a cab, and without goloshes, and expect a permit to visit his Majesty's palace?"

He said no more; more was not necessary. I bowed silently and withdrew. Afterwards I came with the cab and the "goloshes," and this time received the permit. It was a bitter pill to go back to that haughty man, but the Czar's palace was so rare a sight that I put my pride in my pocket and swallowed the pill with the best grace I could. The palace was well worth the sacrifice of pride I had to make. The Czar's Winter Palace in Moscow contains grand audience-chambers, gilded saloons, brilliant halls and galleries that make an American, accustomed to Republican simplicity, stare. Nor is the palace lacking in historical associations. The visitor is shown the "Red Staircase" where the barbaric Czar Iwan the Terrible used to receive his messengers. Those who brought good news were flattered and caressed; the unfortunate bearers of ill tidings were assassinated on the spot by the Czar. The same Czar, after the completion of the Cathedral of Saint Basilius, had the architect's eyes put out so that he never could plan another such masterpiece! Napoleon occupied this palace in 1812. A number of relics of his stay are shown; among others, the iron bedstead which he used during the Russian campaign. The chair in which the mad Charles XII. was carried after the battle of Pultowa, in 1709, has a place near Napoleon's bed. Both are interesting relics of the past. The horse that Peter the Great rode at the battle of Pultowa, and which was stuffed and for a time kept at Moscow, is now in the museum at St. Petersburg.

The tower of Iwan Weliky, near the palace of the Kremlin, is three hundred feet high; from its summit a fine view of the city is obtained. Madame de Stael, when she stood on this tower, broke out with an exclamation of delight,

"Voila Rome tatare!" (There is the Tartar's Rome.)

Joseph II., in 1780, and Napoleon and his marshals, in 1812, surveyed the Russian capital from the Iwan Weliky tower. Marshal von Moltke wrote:

"It would never occur to one viewing Moscow from this point on a warm sunny day, that he was in the same latitude in which, in Siberia, reindeer graze, and in Kamtchatka dogs draw sleds on the ice. Moscow makes decidedly the impression of a southern city. One can almost imagine one's self transported to Bagdad, Ispahan, or some other similar place, where the romances of Scheherazade are recalled — places we might have dreamed about, but never expected to see."

At the base of the Iwan Weliky tower is the celebrated bell, the largest bell ever cast. It fell many years ago from its position in the tower, and now rests on the ground where it fell, as large as a small house. The piece which was broken out in the fall measured four or five feet in length. The opening thus made serves as a door-way to this odd house.

The most magnificent church in Russia is that of the "Saviour." It cost upward of ten million dollars. It is constructed of polished marble; all the quarries of Europe were drawn upon to furnish their finest and most beautiful specimens. The church was erected to commemorate the deliverance of Russia from the French in 1812. Another church I went to see bore the laconic name of

"BLAGOWJASCHTSCHENSKYKATHEDRALE!"

Russian words are so long that those of more than seven sylla-
bles are counted as two by the telegraph companies. There is
one thing in which the Russian thinks he is more terse than the
rest of mankind. He uses no " Mr.," " Mrs.," or " Miss." A
Russian will say, " Paul Petrowitsch," meaning Paul, Peter's
son; or " Maria Nikolajewna," meaning Maria, daughter of
Nicholas.

During the intense cold of the winter season in Moscow foreigners are surprised when strangers stop them on the streets
and, without a word, begin to rub their noses with snow.
When the reason of this seemingly unwarranted action is understood the foreigner is very grateful. He knows that the
Russian perceived his nose was freezing, or was about to drop
off, and rubbed it with snow to save it.

" Pritri, pritri noss samorss " (Rub, rub; your nose is freezing), is the cry one often hears on the streets of Moscow in
winter.

At what are called " Chartschewna " very good dinners are
served for twenty or thirty kopecks — ten or fifteen cents.
Hard-boiled eggs, pickles, salted or smoked fish, and pastry
filled with mushrooms, rice, and meat, form the ordinary bill
of fare in these places. Russians are methodical in their diet.
Each season has its particular dish, particular kind of fruit,
soup, etc. Meats and fruits are in favor about the middle of
August. One thoroughly versed in this feature of Russian
life needs no calendar: a glance at the bill of fare for dinner
would disclose to him the exact month and season.

St. Petersburg is more brilliant than Moscow, but it is not
as interesting. It is too much like other imperial cities. Its
streets are wide, the buildings are modern and handsome, fashionable equipages dash by, the people one meets seem to belong more to the nineteenth century. It has none of that Oriental appearance which characterizes Moscow. An interesting
relic shown in St. Petersburg is the log-cabin of Peter the
Great. The cabin has been incased by a substantial building
of stone, but otherwise it is in the same condition as when in-

habited by its royal occupant. The arrangement of the furniture in his bedroom is the same; and the skiff which Peter made with his own hands, the "Father" of the Russian fleet, is in one end of the room where he left it.

In a journey of two thousand miles in Russia, the first and only tunnel that I saw was at Wilna. All the rest was over monotonous, level plains. Near Wilna there is a monument. The inscription reads:

"IN 1812 RUSSIA WAS INUNDATED BY AN ARMY OF 700,000 MEN. THIS ARMY RECROSSED THE FRONTIER WITH 70,000 MEN."

Brief but expressive.

When at Eduytkuhn we crossed the frontier into Germany, I drew a sigh of relief at being once more out of despotic Russia. My passport,* which had been carefully examined by the police before I was given permission to leave the empire, was no longer needed. I folded it up, with its *visés* in Turkish, Bulgarian, Russian, and other languages, to keep as a souvenir; and after fifty tedious hours in a third-class car, arrived in Berlin from St. Petersburg.

---

* I left home without any passport at all: only with difficulty did I get as far as Vienna. Travel east of Vienna without passports is not only difficult but impossible, and in Vienna, therefore, I was compelled to buy one from the American Minister at a cost of thirteen gold gulden.

CHAPTER XXIV

SOME three years previous to my visit, an acquaintance, a medical student, had gone to Berlin. I had his old address; immediately on my arrival I hunted him up. A stout musician occupied the number my friend had given me. He had been there two years, knew nothing of the previous occupant, and could only advise me to inquire at the nearest police-station. I did so.

"H'm," said the police-sergeant, "you want to know the address of Blank? Just wait a moment," and going to a shelf he took down a large and dusty volume. He thumbed the pages for ten or fifteen minutes.

"Ah, here you are," he said, looking up. "'Blank, born Philadelphia, twenty-six years old, medical student, Protestant religion, father merchant in Philadelphia; arrived in Berlin September 23, 1882, lodged No. —— Leipziger Strasse; 23d September, 1883, removed to No. —— Koenig Strasse; on July 1st removed to Dresden, lodging at No. —— Kleinepackhofgasse.'"

The official paused. There was no further entry in his book regarding Blank.

"If your friend is not at that number on the Kleinepackhofgasse in Dresden," continued the officer, "the authorities there can inform you as to his subsequent movements."

There was no necessity for further inquiry. I wrote to my friend on the Kleinepackhofgasse, and received a reply within two days. It is difficult for a stranger to lose himself in Berlin. If you forget the number of your lodgings, stop the first policeman you meet.

"Pardon, mein Herr," you say to him. "My name is John Smith. Will you be kind enough to tell me where I live?"

The officer telephones to police headquarters, and in five minutes hands you your address; then you go on your way admiring or condemning, according to your taste, a system of espionage so perfect as to produce this almost incredible result.

When I called on an acquaintance in Berlin, an old and wealthy citizen, one put down in the "Address Book" as a "Rentier," that is, one living on his income, I found his household in a state of the utmost confusion. The furniture was scattered about as if a western cyclone had struck it; the table-ware, silver service, and spoons were heaped upon the big dining-table. My acquaintance was in the midst of this confusion, pencil and note-book in hand, his brow covered with perspiration, although the season was winter.

"What on earth does all this mean?" I asked, after the first salutations. "Taking my advice and going to America?"

"Oh no," cheerily answered Herr V. "Merely changing servants."

"Merely changing servants? Does one have to overturn one's house to change servants?"

"To a certain extent, yes. In Germany the Government is paternal; has its finger in every pie, so to speak. When the yearly change of servants is made, it is necessary to take an inventory of every article in your house. If anything is missing it must be found or accounted for, and not until then can you sign the servant's papers required by the police. If all is right the official blanks are filled, a copy is given to the servant, one you keep, and the other is given to the police. This system insures honest servants."

To me it looked as if the main thing insured was an unbearable interference in private affairs. I expressed this opinion to Herr V. He seemed surprised at my inability to see the beauty of the Government's looking after its subjects' household affairs.

Herr V., reading from the official "Address Book," edited by R. Von Leutsch for the Imperial Government, gave the following figures regarding European armies:

Germany's standing army contains 492,614 men; the reserve numbers 1,456,677 men and 35,427 officers. The German fleet comprises 95 ships, with 592 cannon and 17,286 men. The number of horses used by the army in peace is 242,415.

Russia in peace has a standing army (including field army and men in active service) of 800,000 men; this number is swelled in war to, in round numbers, 2,000,000.

France in war can bring an active army of 2,423,164 men in the field. Her full army, that is, including every male capable of bearing arms, is 3,753,164.

Italy is credited with a standing army of 750,765 men. With the reserves the number is 2,119,250.

Monaco has five officers and sixty-three men.

While a part of these armies exists only on paper, still, the number actually in service, and thus drawn away from the number of producers, is enormous. As long as the nations of Europe spend their energies marshalling vast hosts, and glaring at each other over breastworks of fixed bayonets, the masses will inevitably be ground down in the hard mill of poverty— miserable hewers of wood and drawers of water.

In Berlin I assumed considerable style. I occupied a front room on the third floor of a house on the Friederich Strasse— the principal street of the city. The room was carpeted, there were white curtains at the window, the furniture was plain and neat—altogether a very cosey, snug little room. The prettiest sort of a red-cheeked German maid, plump arms, and white cap on her blond head, brought me coffee and buttered rolls, and wished me a good appetite in the morning. For all this I paid one and a half marks per day—thirty-six cents. My dinners usually cost a mark—twenty-four cents. There were cheaper places, but I was becoming extravagant. I dined usually at a restaurant next door to the main post-office. Notwithstanding my fluent command of German, the proprietor guessed at once that I was American.   He had been to England, and was very proud of his knowledge of the language.   For a mark, Jack (that was his name) furnished an excellently cooked dinner, comprising soup, roast-beef, mutton, vegetables, dessert, fruit, and beer or soda-water.   I grew quite fat upon this generous diet after my tough experiences in Russia and the East.

Berlin has no boulevard or avenue to compare with the Ring Strasse of Vienna; but leave out the Ring Strasse, and Berlin is far the handsomer city.   Its most interesting associations are those connected with Frederick the Great.   At Potsdam the palace of Sans-souci ("without care") is kept in precisely the same condition in which its great occupant left it.   His flutes, music, cradle, old clothes—all are there.   The chair in which he died occupies the same place by the window from which the great king took his last look at the trees and flowers, and the sun and the bright, blue skies.   Voltaire's room also remains unchanged.   Its mural decorations—monkeys, parrots, peacocks, etc., which Frederick meant as an allusion to the French philosopher's monkey-like appearance, his talkativeness and vanity —are as fresh in color as if painted yesterday.   Voltaire understood the hint intended by the odd decorations, but he knew when he had a good thing.   It was not until the king resorted to more than mere hints that the great wit stood, not on the order of going, but went at once.

Frederick's tomb is in Potsdam.   It was in this damp, gloomy chamber that the King of Prussia, in 1813, swore eternal war against Napoleon.   Recently (August, 1886), on the occasion of the hundredth anniversary of Frederick's death, the German Kaiser Wilhelm said his prayers in the gloomy tomb at Potsdam, and had the coffin of his great ancestor covered with flowers.   The Kaiser Wilhelm in the long four and a half score years of his life has witnessed remarkable changes.   He was a man in soldier's uniform, when, seventy-three years ago, Prussia's king, defeated and humiliated, swore over the tomb of Frederick to revenge his country's disasters.   He lived to be crowned emperor in Louis XIV.'s palace at Versailles; and he lives to-day, the head of the strongest military power on earth, loved by his people more than ever as he rounds out the full century of his eventful life.

It has been said that a sure way to convert a Socialist is to let him become the owner of ten dollars. That method is uncertain. Herr Bebel was a Socialist twenty years ago when a poor man ; he is now a wealthy manufacturer, and more of a Socialist than ever. He is a member of the Reichstag, and the recognized leader of the Socialist and anti-Bismarck party. The Parliament House, a plain, ordinary-looking building, is passed by many travellers because not " starred " by Baedeker. I found it interesting. Bismarck rarely enters until the members have taken their seats; then the Iron Prince stalks down the aisle as if he owned the building and all the members in it. If disapproval of his speech is in any way manifested, the chancellor storms, declares that he is only a servant of his Majesty, the Emperor, that so are all the members of the Reichstag, and any one disputing that fact either by word or action, such as ridiculing his, Bismarck's speeches, is a traitor.

Day by day the Democrats, or men who do not believe that a bill or measure is above criticism because introduced by an emperor's chancellor, are getting a little more boldness. Even now Bismarck is forced to debate and explain, where a few years ago he would haughtily declare the measure was desired by their master the Emperor, and that that was sufficient. When such changes have occurred in Imperial Germany, lovers of Democratic governments and of freedom have cause to be hopeful. Progress is slow but sure.

The anti-tariff party in Germany are called " Progressionists." They are led by Eugene Richter and Professor Virchow, two able men who are doing their best to teach the people that taxes do *not* make wealth : seemingly a very comprehensible fact, yet the people are slow to grasp it. The Progressionists, in a hopeless minority, occupy seats on the left; back of them are the Socialists ; in the centre are the Catholics ; on the right are the Liberals and Conservatives, the latter divided in several factions.   Very few of the parties, except the Progressionists, seem to know what they want.   They sit like school-boys and listen to Prince Bismarck's scolding lectures.   At the time of my visit one of the members asked for an explanation of the Government's action in expelling the Poles from the eastern provinces.   Bismarck replied in effect that it was none of their business.   Those were not his words, but the meaning and effect were the same.   The audacious member who thought an emperor should explain why he banished a whole people from a province sat down a sadder but not a wiser man.

In the production of light operatic music Vienna excels Berlin; Berlin, however, leads in the production of heavy or classical music.   In Vienna a crowd of composers flood the market with waltz and light operatic music.   Zell and Genee have formed a literary firm for the production of opera librettos.   They turn out librettos to order on any subject, and on the shortest notice.   Milloecker, the composer of "The Beggar Student," frequently obtains his librettos from Zell, Genee & Co.   Strauss bought his "Merry War" libretto from them.   Karl Milloecker was formerly second flutist in a second-rate orchestra.   He has not as much originality as Strauss, yet his operas enjoy greater popularity.   This is due to his superior conception of comedy.   Everything Strauss handles seems to have something of a waltz flavor.   He is the greatest writer of waltzes that ever lived, and it is because his talent runs so exclusively in that line that his success as an opera composer is limited.

The Berlin musical conservatories bear a high reputation.   To their excellence several noted violinists owe much of their success.   Miss Madge Wickham, an American girl, after graduating with honor from the principal conservatory, gave a number of concerts in Berlin and in the provinces.   Everywhere she won the favor both of critics and people.   Miss Maud Powell, of Chicago, is another violinist who has been well received by Berlin audiences.

Cologne, though a provincial city, is able to boast of one of the best musical conservatories in Germany, which is to say, in

Europe. Doctor Wuellner, formerly of Dresden, is now at the head of the Cologne Conservatory. As an instructor in theory and the art of conducting, he has no superior. He receives a salary of twenty-five thousand marks ($6000), a large salary for Germany.

The head of the Paris Conservatory of Music is Ambrose Thomas, the composer of " Mignon." The French Government grants every year a certain number of musical scholarships. The winner of one of these scholarships receives free tuition, first in the Paris Conservatory, and afterwards in the Italian school at Milan. The latter does not now enjoy the reputation it once did. Neither the Milan school nor any other Italian school of music will compare with the German conservatories. But the French Government could not stomach the idea of sending scholars to her ancient enemy across the Rhine. Moreover, since 1870, anything French is looked down upon in Germany. Few French operas succeed nowadays on German boards. Audran's " Grand Mogul " and " Gillette " may be mentioned as two exceptions. Those light and breezy productions, after a long run in Paris, met with almost equal success in Berlin.

Audran used to live on dry bread in a garret. His " Mascotte " had a seven hundred nights' run in Paris, and the lucky composer now has a pocket by no means empty. It is said Audran purposes abandoning the field of light opera, and will enter more lofty and classical regions. It is scarcely probable, however, that the mind which produced the " Mascotte " will ever be able to compose anything in the highly classical and heavy style of Richard Wagner.

CHAPTER XXV.

AMSTERDAM.—A LONG SERMON.—HONORS TO AN ACTRESS.—STORY
OF A DUTCHMAN'S NOSE.

When I landed in Amsterdam one Sunday morning, I saw
hundreds of men and boys flying kites. The city contains a
net-work of canals. Some of the graybeards were so absorbed
with their kite-flying, their eyes were so constantly looking
heavenward, I feared they would tumble backward into the canals. With practice, however, had come skill, and as near as
some of them backed to the water's edge, none fell in.

I intended to stay but one day in Amsterdam. An untoward
incident caused me to stay two days. I had gazed half an hour
at the old men flying kites, and was proceeding to the celebrated
Zoological Gardens, when I passed the open door of a church,
and conceived the unhappy thought of entering.

"I will merely see what a Dutch church is like," I said to
myself, "then I will go on to the Gardens."

I entered, spent five minutes gazing at the dim windows, at
the few ancient and faded paintings, then turned to go. Alas!
it was impossible. The doors were locked. I was forced to
listen to the very end of that Dutch sermon—the longest sermon, I am sure, that any one, Dutch or English, ever preached.
When finally the services ended and the doors opened, it was
too late to go to the Gardens, so I stayed over another day.

In Holland matches are almost as large around as lead-pen-
cils. Match-safes are large in proportion. Cigars are twice as
thick as American cigars. The Dutch wooden shoe is a small
boat. They seem to seek, not grace or beauty, but solidity—
extreme solidity. They attain clumsiness.

Returning Monday morning from the Zoological Gardens, I

found the streets jammed and packed with an immense crowd. Every window was filled with faces, every lamp-post was adorned with two or more urchins. The occasion was evidently something unusual. Many houses were draped in mourning. When at length a funeral cortége approached, preceded by a band playing solemn dirges, and followed by the military and a vast concourse of citizens, I concluded the King or some other high dignitary was dead. I was mistaken. The deceased to whom these honors were being paid was an actress. She had amused the Amsterdam populace for fifty years; the populace was now showing its respect for her services and her genius. In America five hundred years' successful service would not gain an actor or actress such public honors or recognition.

My train did not leave until midnight. I took advantage of the opportunity to call on the Dutch musician, my former fellow-tramp, whose address I found in my note-book. He was sitting in an old arm-chair, the lamp turned down, the room lighted by the cheerful glow of a bright coal fire.

"Ah! welcome, old fellow!" he exclaimed. "Off with your overcoat and draw up to the fire."

I had often pictured to myself the snug, cosey quarters of the German student-class, but never had my wildest fancy painted a room full of pulleys, ropes, Indian clubs, bean-bags, and similar odd machines. After the first salutations I spent fully ten minutes gazing at the various contrivances around me.

"What on earth does it all mean?" I asked.

"Not so fast!" replied the Wagnerian musician. "We have not come to that yet. I will explain presently."

Turning up the light, he pushed a little table between us.

"First supper, then my story," he began, taking up a dish of oatmeal and a pot of boiled prunes. "This, with a glass of hot water, will constitute our supper."

"Prunes and hot water! Excuse me, but I have just dined."

"Ah! then I shall have to sup alone;" and drinking a glass of hot water, he began to slowly eat the oatmeal and prunes.

When he had finished he pushed aside the plates, removed the table, and faced me with the question,

"Do you see anything peculiar about my nose?"

I began to doubt my friend's sanity. There he sat, his tall figure reclining in his easy-chair, an intelligent, handsome head, asking me if I saw anything peculiar about his nose! Was he crazy? I assured him I observed nothing extraordinary about his nasal organ, except that it was an unusually white and finely chiselled specimen; whereupon he continued, with a grave look,

"Six months ago, after parting from you at Munich, I returned to Amsterdam, and shortly afterwards fitted up my gymnasium, got my books of hygiene, gave up beer, and began living on a frugal diet of oatmeal and fruits. From your remark, and from my own observation, I perceive that I have been successful.

"On the return trip from Munich I stopped at Ruedesheim, on the Rhine, to transact some business with an old friend of my father's. Herr Siefert's home was at a country place several miles from the town, and I rode thither on horseback. When within a short distance of my destination I overtook a young lady, also on horseback, and travelling in the same direction as myself. Observing her graceful figure and erect carriage, I mustered courage, spurred my horse, and overtaking the fair stranger, raised my hat and bowed.

"'Can you direct me to Herr Siefert's?' I asked.

"'Certainly'—a beautiful blush suffusing her cheeks. 'You have but to keep this straight road. But may I not ask if this is Herr Mies?'

"'At your service; and you are—'

"'Marie Siefert. Papa has been expecting you for a day or two. I guessed who you were the moment you asked after him.'

"We then rode on together, I feeling as if I were floating in the air, every moment more and more bewitched by my beautiful companion. With clear-cut, regular features, rosy cheeks, sparkling brown eyes, a wealth of nut-brown hair blown loosely by the wind, and a figure as trim and symmetrical as a sylph's, I thought her the handsomest woman I had ever seen. My admiration was but ill concealed, and she wore an amused smile as we cantered along.

"It was near sundown when we reached 'Der Ruh,' Herr Siefert's place. My fair guide, excusing herself, retired, leaving me in charge of her brother, who showed me to my room. There, left to myself half an hour before supper, I sat down to reflect. You will think it absurd, but the matter had actually gone that far—I was plotting and planning how to find an excuse for prolonging my stay. Love at first sight? Perhaps it was, I will not say; but if you had seen her! there never was a lovelier girl. I dreaded the time when my visit would come to an end. The ringing of a bell suddenly interrupted my reflections. A few moments later August Siefert knocked at my door, and we walked in together to the dining room. The family were around the table. Upon my entrance they arose.

"'Herr Mies, I believe,' said Frau Siefert, a motherly old lady; 'your mother and I were old friends. This is my daughter.'

"'I believe I have had the pleasure—' I said, as I turned and beheld my fair guide.

"'What?' she said, opening wide her beautiful eyes. 'Why, I never saw you before in all my life!'

"I was amazed, dumfounded.

"'Surely,' I stammered—'surely, Fraulein, why—er—' I could go no further.

"'You have been dreaming!' said the young lady, with a silvery laugh. 'But come, if we take so much of your time in introductions, you will lose your supper.'

"During the whole meal my thoughts were bent in a vain endeavor to solve Fraulein Siefert's incomprehensible conduct. The rest of the family had not seemed to notice it. After supper I went into Herr Siefert's study to talk over business matters. It was late before we said good-night and retired. When

I entered the breakfast-room the next morning Fraulein Siefert greeted me pleasantly. After breakfast she left the room, returning in a few minutes, however, dressed in her riding-habit.

"'Good-morning, Herr Mies,' she said, seeming to have forgotten that she had already spoken at the table. 'Have you thoroughly recovered from the fatigue of yesterday's ride?'

"'Yes, Fraulein; but I have not recovered from the surprise your reception at the supper-table gave me.'

"'At the supper-table?' and her great brown eyes opened wide, precisely as they had done when I was introduced to her in the dining-room. 'Why, I have not seen you since I came in from my ride.'

"'What!' I exclaimed, 'you did not see me? Truly, this is extraordinary! When I met you last night you did not remember riding with me; now you remember the ride, but forget that you saw me last night. Explain—what does it mean?'

"'Simply—that you are mistaken. On returning from my ride yesterday I went up-stairs to stay with my little brother, who was fretting. I did not come down to supper at all. But *auf wiedersehen*. I am going away to spend a few days at uncle's,' upon which she smiled and flitted out of the room.

"Was I dreaming? I began to think there was some mental affliction, and abandoned any efforts at solving the mystery. At the dinner-table, when we were all seated, in walked my beautiful riddle.

"'How have you passed the morning?' she inquired, with a friendly smile.

"'Quite well; and I am glad to find you back so soon.'

"'Back! I have not been away.'

"'Ah—so you changed your mind?'

"'Indeed, no. Did you imagine I was going away?'

"I could make no coherent reply.

"'Oh no,' I stammered, 'not at all—that is—yes—I—er— thought—thought you *might* go away.'

"Frau Siefert here kindly came to my relief and changed the subject. After that day things went on more smoothly. Fraulein Siefert evinced no more of the puzzling eccentricities which at first had so astonished me. We walked, rode, and read together. The day before I was to leave I asked Herr Siefert for the hand of his daughter. He consented, but she—she refused. My disappointment was stunning. I mounted my horse and galloped down the road. The fresh air seemed to quiet my nerves ; when at last I turned my horse homeward I felt calmer. Returning, I saw Fraulein Siefert approaching on her gray pony. I determined to suppress my feelings, and speak with only the most studied formality.

" ' Why, how do you do, Herr Mies ?' she said, as I came up; ' I am glad to see you again.'

This greeting was so strange, so unexpected, I was speechless. A moment more my surprise gave way to amazement as a living second of my angel rode up and greeted me with a slight bow.

" ' Twins !' I ejaculated.

" ' Did you not know it before ?' said she whom I had first met, with a merry laugh. ' I am Marie, and this is my sister Annie, whom you have seen all the week.'

" The mystery was now clear, and as we rode on together I almost forgot my repulse in recalling the amusing *contretemps* of the first few days of my visit.

" That night I could not sleep. I deserted my room for the grape arbor, which had been a favorite retreat during my visit. As I sat there in the still night air, thinking over my hopeless love, the sound of voices was wafted to my ears. Whose voices were they ? I recognized one as that of my darling's.

" ' Oh, why did you refuse him ?' I heard one of them say. ' He is handsome, and father says he is clever.'

" What was this ? My heart almost stood still as I listened to catch her answer. She seemed to whisper it.

" ' I liked him—I admired him. But, oh, sister, how could I marry a man with such a red nose ?'

" ' Great Heaven,' I groaned, ' and is this the cause ?'

" I rushed to my room, lighted a candle before the glass, and gazed long and intensely at the reflection of my unfortunate nose.

"Yes; she was right. It was a red nose, and I was a fool to imagine a beautiful creature like she could love a red-nosed man.

"'But she shall marry me yet,' I said, gritting my teeth, 'she shall marry me, and this accursed nose shall bleach as the driven snow.'

"I looked back a few years at the time when my nose was white. Why had it become red? It was unnatural. I determined to find the cause, and remedy it if in human power. Within a week I was at the celebrated hygienic home of Dr. Therbideaux, in Paris, where I began my nose-bleaching under the doctor's instructions, drinking gallons of hot water, bathing several times a day, living on prunes and fruit, and parboiling my feet in order to bring the redness down from my nose.

"'Curses on my feet! I did not care if *they* turned red; she wouldn't see *them*.'

"In a few weeks a perceptible improvement had taken place. The redness in my nose abated, while the redness in my feet increased. When I returned to Amsterdam it was with a load of Dr. Therbideaux's books, and my mind stored with his valuable advice and instruction. Since then I have rigidly followed his prescribed course, and in addition have here in my room a gymnasium for exercise, to equalize the system and prevent the blood settling in the nose."

The musician paused. A painful suspicion darted upon my mind. I seized a hand-glass and critically examined my own nose. Had the color of that feature anything to do with my Mary Ann's rejection of me? Were all girls so decidedly opposed to red noses? Casting a furtive glance at Mies, I now perceived his nose was as white as the fairest woman's.

"And this angel—this Venus?" I said. "Where is she? What if she be won while you are preparing for the conquest?"

"Ah, I shall risk that. I have thought for some time my

nose was white enough. You strengthen me in my belief, and I shall soon put the matter to the test."

Three weeks from that night I received news of my friend's "Verlobung" (engagement).

"He deserves his luck," I thought; "any man who will live on prunes and hot water to win a girl is a trump of the first order."

CHAPTER XXVI.

PEASANT LIFE IN BELGIUM.—CURIOUS IDOL IN BRUSSELS. —ITALY
REVISITED. — THE POTENTIALITY OF A FLANNEL SHIRT. — OLD
FRIENDS AND BEGGARS IN NAPLES.—FLOUNDERING IN FRENCH.
—WHY PARIS IS MAGNIFICENT.—THE THIRD NAPOLEON.—PAT-
RONIZING PARIS THEATRES TO AVOID BUYING FUEL.—A FUSSY
ENGLISHMAN.

THE Belgian laborer is as industrious, perhaps, as the laborer
of any other country in the world; two circumstances, however,
operate to lessen the results which his energy and labor should
produce. First, the extreme density of population and con-
sequent great amount of competition; secondly, his habits of
intemperance.

Beer among the Germans, and light wines among the French
and Italians, are consumed almost to the exclusion of other
beverages; but in Belgium the working-man drinks not only
an unwholesome and inferior quality of wine and beer, but,
to a considerable extent, rum and gin also. Rum and gin
drinking are on the increase. Many workmen lose Mondays
through their Saturday night and Sunday dissipations.

In the matter of habitations the standard in Belgium is better
than that in Italy. A moderately thrifty workman will rent a
tenement-house of from two to four rooms, paying therefor
from three to six dollars a month. In rural districts houses are
generally provided with a small plot of ground for gardening.
In the large cities this is wanting. The houses in Antwerp and
Brussels are built solidly together. The hall-ways opening into
the houses are generally dark and narrow, and the stairs leading
to the upper stories exceedingly crooked and steep. Often a rope
is provided to hold to when going up the steps, it being impossible, or at least dangerous, to ascend otherwise.

The system of "Bauerdoerfer"—peasant villages—so universal in Germany and some other European States, does not prevail in Belgium. The peasant's house is usually detached, is one story high, and thatched. In addition to gardening, the peasant generally raises a little poultry, a pig or two, and cows, all these animals being housed either in one of the rooms of the peasant's house, or in small sheds adjoining. The women treat animals under their charge with the greatest care. In cold or rainy weather they are particular to put a rough blanket on the cows; they give them warm food, and in many ways care for small details which in other countries are neglected.

In some of the large glass manufacturing establishments expert glass-blowers earn as high as three dollars a day. Such men must have powerful lungs to blow large vessels. This class frequently own their own homes, or, if not, rent comfortable houses, paying ten to fifteen dollars a month rent. The number, however, who receive the above-mentioned wages bear a small proportion to the whole. Skilled paper-makers, iron-workers, woollen-weavers, and similarly engaged workmen will not average more than fifty to sixty-five cents a day.

Some of the large manufacturers are taking steps towards the betterment of the condition of their operatives, such as founding or encouraging social clubs, reading - rooms, furnishing plain, wholesome dinners at cost price, etc. At Seraing the employés of the "Cockerill Works" enjoy many comforts and conveniences not enjoyed by employés of other places. The hospital erected by the works is maintained at a cost of $10,000 a year. There are savings-banks, sick funds, good elementary schools, and public kitchens and dining-rooms for those who desire to use them. At Seraing the works comprise every branch of industry connected with the manufacture of iron, as coal-mines, iron - stone mines, puddling furnaces, cast-steel works, engine-factories, etc. Women engage in work quite as arduous as men, but their pay is invariably ten to thirty per cent. less. The following table will show the income, condition, and cost of living of a collier's family.

Coal Collier at Liege.*

Condition. — Family of six: parents, daughter aged fifteen, boy aged eleven; two girls, aged nine and eight. The father is a coal collier; mother shovels coal; girl of fifteen carries coal on her back; the two children sweep manure off the streets. Occupy small house with three rooms—dingy, dirty locality, no effort at ornamentation. Family illiterate. Father gets drunk. A poor quality of beer is the ordinary drink, but a considerable amount of gin is also consumed. The mother is coarsened by hard toil, the daughter becoming so; while the two manure-sweepers, living in the slums, rapidly lose whatever refinement of nature they may once have possessed. Father works twelve hours a day—six hours on and six hours off.

Diet.—Breakfast: rye bread and coffee, and occasionally a little cheese. Dinner: soup, beans, bread; sometimes varied by potatoes or rice, cabbage, etc., beer. About once a week bacon or salt pork. Supper: rye bread, coffee or beer.

Cost of Living :	Per Year.
Rent.	$24 00
Bread.	87 60
Meats.	18 25
Coffee, milk, etc.	43 80
Beer and spirituous liquors.	43 80
Groceries.	76 65
Clothing and shoes.	62 00
Fuel and light.	15 50
Total	$371 60

	Per Year.
Earnings of father.	$156 00
Earnings of mother.	87 00
Earnings of daughter.	58 00
Earnings of two children.	72 50
Total yearly earnings of five persons.	$373 50
Expenditures	371 60
Surplus.	$1 90

There is a very curious fountain in Brussels called the "Manikin," which is regarded by the inhabitants somewhat as the Ethiopian regards his idol in the African jungle. When eccentric people die they leave legacies to the Manikin. An old

---

* From my report to U. S. Bureau Labor Statistics, p. 426.

lady not long ago bequeathed him one thousand florins with which to buy clothing. The city authorities pay a man two hundred francs a year to act as his valet. This valet has in his charge a great number of costumes, all of which are worn by the Manikin at one time or another on festive occasions. During the many vicissitudes of the city, the Manikin has always been carefully, if not idolatrously, handled. In 1747, when Louis XV. captured the city, his soldiers dressed the Manikin in the white cockade. In 1789 he was dressed in the Brabant revolution colors, afterwards the French dressed him in their colors; and finally, in 1830, during the Belgian revolution against the Dutch, the little fellow was dressed by the revolutionists in a workman's cap and blouse!

"The celebrated Manikin Fountain," says the guide-book, "is two hundred yards south-west of the Hotel de Ville."

I noted the Hotel de Ville one morning, and set out on a journey of exploration. I went what seemed about two hundred yards, then looked around for the fountain and the Manikin. I explored all the nooks and corners of the neighborhood, my expectation on the *qui vive*. Seeing nothing curious or strange, I began to fear I had taken the wrong direction.

"Pardon, monsieur," I said, stopping a passer-by and pulling out my conversation-book in four languages. "Can you direct me to the Manikin?"

The passer-by shrugged his shoulders and looked surprised. "*That* is the Manikin."

I looked and saw a small, shabby affair that I had passed a dozen times. The famous Brussels Manikin is merely a bronze figure eighteen or twenty inches high. The only thing curious about it is its curious history. It is a mystery how so commonplace a bit of bronze has managed to play a part in the history of a great city.

I went up the Rhine in winter. It was misty and cold. There were few passengers. Those few, as they stood huddled in the prow of the boat trying to gaze through the mist at the hills and castles, looked thoroughly miserable.

"What geese people can make of themselves," I said.
"These poor tourists actually fancy they are having a nice
time."

I did not include myself in this number, for I was not mak-
ing the trip to see the Rhine. Having so recently seen the
Kazan Defile and the stupendous scenery of the lower Danube,
I was not particularly anxious to see the lesser beauties of the
Rhine. I was merely making a leisurely return trip to sunny
Italy.

On the way I stopped at several places that I had before
visited as a tramp; and I had opportunity to estimate the
potentiality of a flannel shirt and shabby appearance. When
I entered my old hotel in Milan dressed in a brand-new suit of
tailor-made clothes, the landlord did not recognize me.

"What is the price of your cheapest room?"

"Due lire cinquante" (half a dollar).

"Are you sure you have none cheaper?"

"Si, si, signore, that is very cheap. I have none cheaper."

"Strange," I said. "I stopped here not a year ago, and I
paid but half a lira—ten cents."

The padrone stared in amazement. Not until I showed him
my name on his register did he realize that I spoke the truth.
He then saw that my being better dressed did not mean that I
was to be cheated. I got my old room at the old price.

From Naples I again made the ascent of Mount Vesuvius,
this time by carriage to the cone, and up the cone by the wire
railway. In Resina a crowd of beggars gathered and formed a
picturesque but dirty escort half way to the cone. One of
them, a ragged, curly - headed, jolly - looking Neapolitan, kept
along-side the carriage on its slow ascent, and begged for a few
soldi "to buy a dish of macaroni." It was impossible to dis-
courage him. To all my rebuffs he smiled, showed his fine
teeth, and said "he knew the signore would give him a plate
of macaroni." I admired his good-natured impudence, and at
length gave a few soldi to get rid of him. After about two
miles on the way, seeing nothing more was to be made, the

cavalcade of beggars, flower-girls, organ-grinders, and guides dispersed, and we were left to finish the journey alone. At the upper station I saw the man with whom I had spent a night a year before. He seemed as glad to see me as though he had never tried to swindle me. He congratulated me on my "fine clothes," and the money which (in his opinion) my improved wardrobe indicated I had fallen heir to.

After a month's pleasant sojourn amid scenes that were partly new, partly familiar, I set out towards Paris. My tongue refused to master the French pronunciation. At Modane, on the French side of the Mont Cenis Tunnel, I found Italian of as little avail as though Italy were in another hemisphere instead of only a few miles away. I wanted a ticket for "Macon." I pronounced it "Mākŏn" in a sensible English way. The ticket-agent stared at me. I tried other pronunciations:

"Mason—Masone—Mahson," etc.

At each pronunciation the agent looked more puzzled than before. But suddenly an inspiration seemed to seize him.

"Ah—je comprens—Mahcong—Minuit."

"Oh, very well," I said, "if that is the way you pronounce 'M-a-c-o-n,' give me a ticket for Minuit."

The Frenchman glared at me, ran his hand through his hair, and slammed his little window down with such violence as almost shattered the glass.

I was in despair. I approached every official I saw with,

"Monsieur, je desire un billet pour Minuit."

They all stared and shrugged their shoulders. Fortunately, I at length came across a man who spoke a little English. Then I learned why the officers shrugged their shoulders when I asked for a ticket to "Minuit." "Minuit" is no station at all; it is the French for "midnight." What the agent tried to convey to me was, that no train started for Macon until "minuit" (midnight).

In Paris it is possible to live very cheaply. There is a restaurant in Cardinal Richelieu's old palace, where an excellent dinner with wine costs only thirty-five cents. It was my custom to dine in the cardinal's palace on Sundays. On week-days I frequented cheaper and less aristocratic quarters. Connected with one of the largest bazaars in Paris is a restaurant, where three thousand people daily dine at a cost not exceeding fifteen cents each. When I first went to this place I took a seat at a table, as one usually does in restaurants, and called for a waiter. None came, for there were none in the establishment. The workmen sitting by laughed. They made me understand by signs that each guest helped himself. I went to the counter, where I was given a piece of bread for one cent, a plate of soup for three cents, meat and potatoes four cents, a dessert of prunes two cents—ten cents for the entire dinner.

The most expensive item in Paris is fuel. I had a cosey little room on the Rue de la Harpe (Bayard Taylor stopped on the same street forty years ago), for which I paid fifteen cents a night. In this room was the tiniest sort of a stove. At most it could not consume more than a dozen sticks of wood a day ; but wood is sold by the pound—five cents for a small stick. On cold winter nights I found it more economical to go to the theatre than to remain in my room. I saw Sara Bernhardt in Sardou's "Theodora" for half a franc—ten cents. Had I remained in my room, it would have required at least twenty cents' worth of wood to have kept me from freezing.

In the theatre I was followed by a woman in a white cap and apron, who demanded "pourboire" (drink-money.) She performs no service other than to smile upon you as you enter the theatre door. This smile she considers worth one cent. She was indignant at me for differing with her, and letting her stand, hand out-stretched, before my seat without giving the customary sou.

The curtains of most French theatres are covered with huge advertising placards. They claim the cards are not only more interesting than landscape paintings, but, what to them is more to the point, they are more profitable. Advertisers pay liberally for space on the curtains of the large theatres.

When I called on a lady friend in Paris I found her in a

state of excitement. She had just rented a flat and paid the rent. A few hours thereafter a brass-buttoned official with a cocked hat entered her flat and began counting the doors and windows. Her astonishment was great. Next day her disgust was greater. Another official appeared, and she had to pay one hundred francs tax on the doors and windows! The fewer doors and windows in one's house in Paris the less are one's taxes. This seems to be putting a premium on darkness and poor ventilation.

One day in the Paris Bourse I occasioned something of a scene. I wore my broad-brimmed sombrero; in my pocket I had a bag of bread and prunes. I took a position in the gallery overlooking the mob of maniacs, and began eating my bread and prunes. For some moments the roaring and wild shouting continued, deafening as the noise of cannon; then of a sudden there was a hush. I looked down—they had caught sight of me; my unconventional appearance and proceeding struck them. The members of the Bourse pointed their fingers at me, threw up their hats, shouted, waved their arms frantically—it was a Pandemonium. I saw they wished to frighten me, and determined to maintain my post until the last prune was eaten. A gendarme put a stop to my heroic design. He interrupted me in the midst of a graceful bow that I was making to the hooting and jeering speculators, and conducted me out of the building.

The magnificence of Paris is not due to the beauty or grandeur of individual edifices; it is the *tout ensemble* that is imposing. When the third Napoleon said to Baron Hausmann, "Baron, a boulevard would look well here, let one be made," Baron Hausmann hastened to obey. After the old buildings had been demolished and the ground cleared for the erection of the new ones, the order would go forth imposing a heavy tax on the builder of a house inferior to a certain standard of height and magnificence. Handsome private buildings secured, Napoleon would then order a public edifice to be erected at each end of the boulevard, and perhaps a column or fountain in the middle.   These boulevards, with arrays of imposing private buildings on each side, at the ends magnificent temples or arches, in the middle fountains or Egyptian obelisks, render Paris the grandest city in the world.

In the Salle Cheminies, in the Louvre, is a painting which goes far to explain the love the French soldiers bore the first Napoleon.   The scene is laid in Jaffa.   His officers stand back, timid, hesitating, muffling their faces to avoid the deadly contagion ; but the Little Corporal, pale, beautiful, fearless, touches his men, speaks to them, soothes the brows of the dying. The painting is one of great excellence.   You forget that it is a mere picture.   For the moment you see the soldiers, hear their dying groans, their cries of " Vive Napoleon !"   In Versailles there are acres of paintings celebrating the exploits of the great emperor, but none tell such a tale as this " In the Pest-house at Jaffa."

When the Germans occupied the Versailles palace they carefully covered the Napoleon paintings, and after the siege left them in as good condition as they had found them.   Should the French ever gain possession of the Rhine, I doubt whether they would show similar moderation towards the " Germania " monument.   That lofty memorial of French defeat and humiliation would not long survive in French hands.

When I took a seat in a second-class compartment in the Paris station there sat opposite me a fussy Englishman.   A friend, who had come to see him off, inquired if he had a nice seat.   " Oh," replied the Englishman, " I have a space with my back to the horses."   (He was riding backward.)   This fussy individual assured me that the Channel was always " nahsty." " You will find it the nahstiest bit of water you ever saw."   I had seen some rough weather on the Pacific; I had been on the Black Sea during an equinoctial storm ; but by the time we landed at Folkestone I quite agreed with the Englishman that the Channel " was the nahstiest bit of water " I had ever seen.

CHAPTER XXVII.

FACTORY LIFE IN ENGLAND.—THE SPINNERS AND WEAVERS OF HAL-
IFAX.—TABLE OF WAGES AND PRICES.—TIMIDITY OF LONDONERS.
— FRIGHTENED BY TIN CANS AND OVERCOATS. — VEGETARIAN
RESTAURANTS. — HOW TO LIVE ON FOUR CENTS A DAY. — AT THE
GRAVE OF GOLDSMITH.—WRETCHED CONDITION OF LONDON DOCK-
YARD LABORERS.

ON landing at Folkestone I proceeded at once to Halifax, and
delivered the letter of introduction I was fortunate enough to
possess addressed to Dr. F. H. Bowman, a Fellow of the Royal
Society, and a scientist of some repute, as well as chief owner
of the largest cotton-mills in Yorkshire. In his great works
fifty to sixty thousand pounds of cotton - yarn are spun per
week, or about five hundred miles of yarn per minute! The
three huge engines which supply the power are fed by mechanical stokers, and consume five thousand tons of coal a year.

"I shall be happy to have you investigate the condition of
our operatives," said Dr. Bowman, "and there will be no better
way than to make you acquainted with some of the men. You
can mix with them, be invited to their houses, see their families,
their homes, and observe their general mode of living," saying
which he touched a bell, and bade an attendant bring one of
the spinners to the office. We continued chatting pleasantly
for about five minutes, when the attendant returned, accompanied by a young man apparently not above thirty years of age.

"Ah, Mr. Sunderland!" said Dr. Bowman. "Mr. Sunderland,
this is Mr. Meriwether, from America. He wishes to mix with
the men—wishes to see how they live. Can't you help him?"

The intelligent-looking workman smiled good-naturedly.

"I'll do what I can, sir," he said, and so, under his wing, I
set about my task.

"The rule," said Mr. Sunderland, "is to pay according to the amount of work done. Every Saturday we knock off at one o'clock, so that a week's work consists of only 56½ hours. In that time a fairly good spinner or 'mule-minder' will earn on an average $7.20. A young woman will earn from $2.40 to $3.60. A young man of the same age (14 to 17 years), $2.88 to $3.60. Children under ten are forbidden by Act of Parliament to work in factories; and between ten and fourteen years of age they may work not more than one half the day, going to school the other half. For a week of 28¼ hours a child earns anywhere from 42 to 84 cents. An 'overlooker,' one who understands machinery, makes $9.60 per week. There are ten overlookers in the Bowman Mills. The superintendent of a mill gets about £3, or $14.58."

"These wages seem fairly good," said I, "but are not the necessaries of life so dear as to counteract the advantage of good wages?"

In response to this question Mr. Sunderland gave me some facts and figures, which I will put into the form of a table.

Table of Prices, Halifax, England, December, 1885.

Flour, No. 1.................per pound	2½ to 3	cents.
Flour, No. 2................. " "	2⅜ " 2½	"
Ham................. " "	16 " 23	"
Beef, best................. " "	20 " 22	"
" second grade................. " "	15 " 18	"
Pork, fresh................. " "	15 " 18	"
" salt................. " "	13 " 16	"
Tea................. " "	40 " 50	"
Coffee................. " "	22 " 35	"
Eggs, in December.................per dozen	24	"
" " summer................. " "	12	"
Coal, retail.................per ton $3 60		"
" wholesale................. " " 1 80		"
Rent of house with two bedrooms 14 × 12 feet, parlor and small kitchen, per week.................	88	"
Gas, per 1000 feet.................	54	"
Sunday suit, woollen clothing................. 6 00 to 9 60		"
Shoes, first class, machine sewed................. 1 92		"

With such figures thirty to thirty-five shillings ($7.20 to
$8.40) per week is not bad. I was, therefore, not altogether
unprepared to find Mr. Sunderland's home neat, clean, and comfortable. There were, in all, four rooms—two bedrooms, a kitch-
en, and a dining-room (also used as a parlor). This room was
carpeted, and the walls hung with pictures. An open fire threw
out a grateful warmth—the general atmosphere was one of
plain, honest comfort. Mrs. Sunderland, a bright, smiling little
woman, formerly a mill operative, but now staying at home attending to her baby, was frank and talkative.

"You should be here of a Saturday," she said, "then the
men have a great time at foot-ball. They stop work at one,
and play from that time almost until night. Clubs come from
other towns—Bradford, Leeds, Manchester; but our Halifax
club can play as well as any of them ; it always holds its own,
doesn't it, Will ?"

Mr. Sunderland good-naturedly corroborated her remarks,
and, turning to me, added,

"But as foot-ball is not much played in America, I fear it
would not interest you. You would probably take more interest in a visit to our club. There is to be an entertainment in
the hall to-night, to which you will be welcome."

Of course I went. The songs and recitations were good, so
was the lecture ; I have rarely spent a more pleasant evening
than that passed with the factory hands and mechanics of the
West Ward Liberal Club, Halifax.

"These clubs," said Mr. Sunderland, "are becoming very popular in the great manufacturing districts. Their influence is
decidedly beneficial. The cost of membership is only one dollar and forty-four cents a year. Instead of loafing on the streets
or at the publican's, the workman passes part of his leisure time
at his club-house, in the reading-room, or in the billiard-room,
or in the lecture-hall, listening to the lectures, musicales, etc.,
which are given at frequent intervals throughout the year."

From figures furnished me, and from my own observations,
I am able to state exactly the income and cost of living of Eng-

lish mill hands. The following table, for the family of a cotton-spinner, will serve as an illustration, not only for that particular class of labor, but for other classes also; the bricklayer, the blacksmith, the carpenter, etc., earns and spends about the same that the spinner does.

English Cotton-spinner.

Family of three: parents and child.

Condition.—Occupy tenement-house containing four rooms. House is comfortably furnished, looks neat and clean. Parlor is carpeted and well lighted, two windows looking on street. Wife was formerly a weaver in carpet-mills, but does not work now; has a brother in the army, and a sister emigrated to New Zealand. Earnings of the father per week, $7.91; per year, $411.32.

Diet.—Breakfast: tea or coffee, bread and butter, sometimes bacon. Dinner: beef or chops, bread, potatoes, occasionally a pudding. Supper: tea, bread and butter; sometimes potatoes or other remnant of dinner warmed over.

Cost of Living:

	Per Day.	Per Year.
Bread and flour	9 cents	$32 95
Meats, salt and fresh	12 "	43 80
Coffee and tea	4 "	14 56
Potatoes and vegetables	7 "	25 55
Milk	6 "	21 90
Fruits, dried and fresh	2 "	7 30
Groceries of all other kinds	41 "	149 65
Total cost of food	81 cents.	$295 71
Clothing		37 60
Gas, and other light		5 51
Fuel		14 25
Club dues		1 44
Rent		45 76
Incidentals		11 96
Total cost of living, three persons		$412 23
Total earnings, one person		411 32
Deficit		91

At the entrance of the British Museum is a warning, part of which reads thus:

" No bags, parcels, or coats carried over the arm allowed in the building until they have been carefully searched by the police."

Fortunately, the day I visited the museum it was raw and cold. I did not carry my overcoat on my arm, and thus escaped being searched by the police. The English manifest in some things a wonderful amount of timidity. They refuse to have a tunnel under the Channel for fear the French will crawl through and eat them; they shiver and call "police" when an Irishman passes with a lunch or a tin can. At the time of my visit London was in an uproar because some crank had thrown a petition into the royal carriage. The imagination of the timid Londoners saw in this a plot against her Majesty's life.

The Guelphs are a prolific race; whenever a son or daughter of the Queen marries, the English people are drained of immense sums to pay the marriage bills and annuities. When I asked an Englishman what benefit the people received in return, he replied that the Prince of Wales was the hardest worker in all England, that he was constantly in demand to open expositions, lay corner-stones, dedicate libraries, etc. There are, doubtless, thousands of Englishmen but a degree removed from starvation, who, if they considered the matter, would bitterly protest against helping to maintain out of their miserable pittance a royal family, and the numerous German princes imported to mate with the daughters of that family. These, however, are outweighed by that larger class who, though ready at a moment's warning to resist interference of the sovereign in affairs of government, yet cling tenaciously to the old system, to the empty husk with all its form and folly.

Twenty odd years ago Dr. T. L. Nichols, an American, originated in London the idea of "vegetarian" restaurants. He began with one small, ill-equipped establishment; there are now dozens of them, and each a bonanza to proprietors and customers. The bill of fare contains ordinarily such dishes as oatmeal or crushed wheat, with sugar and milk; various kinds of vegetable soup; potatoes, lentils, and other vegetables; puddings of rice or bread, stewed fruit, pie, bread, tea, coffee, and milk. For sixpence—twelve cents—any three of these dishes are served; for fourpence, any two. Each course is liberal in quantity. For sixpence, and even for fourpence, a very substantial meal may be had. In London few housewives bake bread. It is otherwise in provincial cities, where a large proportion of workmen's families do their own baking. They seem particularly fond of a light bread or roll called "scone," made with soda, and eaten while hot.

I heard Dr. Nichols give a lecture in the Royal Aquarium on "How to Live on Twopence a Day." The venerable lecturer, a man far in the seventies, but still alert and active, said he had for experiment limited himself to twopence a day, and had actually fattened! If I remember correctly, his main diet was crushed wheat and milk. The economical traveller will do well to remember these vegetarian restaurants. A very good one is that on the Minnories, No. 155.

One bitter December day, when on a ramble through the maze of courts and inner courts of the Temples of Law, I came across a grave on which lay a bunch of fresh roses. The grave was that of Oliver Goldsmith. There was a kind of mournful pleasure in this rencontre. As I stood there, the sleety rain dripping from my umbrella on the fast freezing flowers, I thanked the unknown hands that had paid this tribute to the memory of the unfortunate poet and scholar. Near Goldsmith's grave are the tombs of Knight Templars of the thirteenth and fourteenth centuries.

Returning from Holloway prison, whither I had gone to visit Editor Stead of the *Pall Mall Gazette*, I stopped at Bunhill Cemetery, near Finsbury Circus, and walked through that small graveyard in the heart of London, surrounded by tall buildings and manufactories. I noted the tombs of John Bunyan, Isaac Watts, and "Richard Cromwell, his vault." On the base of a plain shaft is this inscription: "Daniel De Foe, born 1661, died 1731. Author of Robinson Crusoe. This monument is the result of an appeal in the Christian World newspaper to the boys and girls of England for funds to place a suitable memorial upon the grave of Daniel M. De Foe. It represents the united contributions of 1700 persons. September 1870."

An odd epitaph in Bunhill Cemetery reads: "Here lies dame Mary Page, relict of Sir Gregory Page; died 1728 aged 56. In 67 months she was tapped 61 times. Had taken away 240 gallons of water without ever repining at her case or fearing the operation."

On Bunyan's tomb is a recumbent figure. Originally the figure may have resembled the author of "Pilgrim's Progress," but the stone has crumbled and yellowed with years; time and small urchins have destroyed whatever resemblance may once have existed.

I stopped a man on High Holborn Road to inquire the way to Smithfield Market. The man looked like a butcher—fat, red cheeks, and brawny arms. I told him I was an American.

"What!" he exclaimed, "an American? Why, I understand you very well. You speak as good English as I do. Come with me, I will show you the market myself."

He accompanied me on my stroll through the enormous market, and pointed out the huge elevators which receive carloads of meat at a time from the underground roads, and shoot it up to the market, where it is placed on the stalls for sale. The Englishman did not seem to recover from his surprise at my fluent English.

"Blarst my heyes," I heard him mutter as I walked away— "blarst my heyes if them Yankee chaps ain't cute — been in Lunnon only three weeks and can talk as good as I do!"

In London, the modern Babylon, the city of five million inhabitants, there is so much wealth on the one hand and poverty on the other, the searcher after labor facts finds it difficult to make a beginning. Chance favored me. Strolling along the Thames I saw the dock-yard navvies at work. They aroused my interest, and the next week was spent in studying this class, undoubtedly the most wretched and poorly paid class in England.

Though the absolute sum received by the regularly employed navvy is greater than the wage of a laborer or even skilled mechanic in Italy, yet the former has a more trying and inclement climate; his wants, fancied or real, are more numerous; he is less able to maintain health and happiness on eighty cents a day than is done in Italy on half that sum. The condition of the irregularly employed navvy is, of course, even more deplorable.

The docks of London, Liverpool, and the other large seaports are crowded with these miserable men awaiting the uncertain chance of a few hours' employment. Through the fogs and drizzling rains of the long English winters they stand shivering around, and when a vessel arrives to be unloaded, a hundred men apply for work where only ten are needed. In a word, this class of men, though willing, even anxious to work, may be regarded as in a state little short of beggary. Within the last few years charitable societies have turned their attention in some degree towards this large and needy class, and now, at many places, especially at the London Docks, they have established stands where is furnished at a nominal price a plain, nourishing meal consisting ordinarily of hot soup, beef hash, lentils, coffee, and bread. Were it not for this charity it would be difficult to understand how the London and Liverpool and other dockyard navvy succeeds in existing — existing, for that he does not *live* the following table will show:

London Dockyard Laborer.

Family numbers five: parents and three children.

Condition.—Occupy two small rooms, uncomfortable and unclean. Family dress miserably; all drink too much. Father receives ten cents per hour when employed, but does not average above five or six hours per working-day. Wife goes out house-cleaning, scrubbing, etc. The children are for the most part left to care for themselves—are growing up, apparently, to become either beggars or criminals.

	Per Year.
Earnings of the father	$145 00
Earnings of the mother	91 25
Total earnings per year	$236 25

Diet.—Breakfast: bread and coffee. Dinner: bread, potatoes, and occasionally a bit of fat pork or bacon; seldom or never fresh meat. Supper: bread and coffee (chiccory).

Cost of Living:

	Per Day.		Per Year.
Bread and flour......................	21 cents	....	$76 65
Coffee and chiccory...................	3⁴⁄₇ "	....	13 00
Milk.................................	3 "	....	10 95
Meats................................	4 "	....	14 60
Cheese...............................	2³⁄₇ "	....	8 34
Potatoes.............................	3½ "	....	12 72
Other vegetables (lentils, etc.)	2½ "	....	9 12
Groceries............................	11 "	....	40 15
Food costs five people	51 cents...........		$185 53
Rent at two shillings per week...........................			24 96
Beer, gin, and tobacco.................................			22 00
Clothing..			21 90
Fuel, lights, and incidentals............................			17 00
Total cost of living for family of five...............			$271 39

Here, it will be seen, is a family of five persons living on fifty-one cents a day, using in a year only twenty-two dollars' worth of clothing, and practising economy in every way, yet at the end of the year coming out $35.14 in debt.

Is free-trade responsible for this miserably paid class of labor?

"Yes," say Protectionists. "England has free-trade, she also has pauper labor; *ergo*, free-trade causes pauper labor."

This neat and nimble logic is too much for my sluggish reason to grasp. I examined the official statistical reports and learned that if England has paupers now under free-trade, it had many more forty years ago under protection, notwithstanding the population was less then than now. Speaking in round numbers, while the population in 1860 was under 29,000,000, and in 1885 was over 35,000,000, the number of paupers has decreased from 850,000 in 1860 to 780,000 in 1885; the number of criminals convicted in 1860 was 14,000, in 1885 only 11,000. Savings-bank deposits have increased from £40,000,-

000 in 1860 to £90,000,000 in 1885. The national debt in 1860 was £822,000,000, in 1885 only £740,000,000. Exports in 1860 amounted to £165,000,000, in 1885 to £296,000,000. Shipping in 1860 amounted to 4,600,000 tons, in 1885 to 7,400,000 tons.

In other words, with an increase in population of 7,000,000, the national debt has been decreased by £82,000,000, the number of paupers has been decreased by 70,000; exports have increased by £131,000,000; the tonnage of English vessels has been increased by 2,800,000 tons; the prices of all necessaries of life have become lower; wages have risen—and all within the last twenty-five years under a free-trade policy.

CHAPTER XXVIII.

ENGLISH ENGINES AND ROADS.—A SOCIALIST MEETING IN LIVER-
POOL.—ODD ARGUMENTS IN FAVOR OF TEMPERANCE AND IRISH
HOME RULE.—HINTS TO PEDESTRIANS.—SUMMARY AND CONCLU-
SION OF "THE TRAMP TRIP."

THE trains between London and Liverpool are drawn by
huge engines, with driving-wheels six and a half and seven feet
in diameter. The rate of speed ranges between fifty and sixty
miles an hour. In England, and also in some of the European
States, the law of the road is just the reverse of ours. Railway-
trains, carriages, trucks, etc., all go to the left, not to the right.
"Keep to the left (not right) as the law directs," is the sign
one sees on stations and guide-posts.

I attended an open-air meeting in Liverpool. The speaker
was an Irishman. He employed a novel argument in favor of
Irish home rule.

"Give Ireland home rule," he said, from his stand on a bar-
rel top, "and you English workmen will have less competition.
Thousands of Irishmen will return to their own country. Instead of three Irishmen looking for one man's place, there will
be only one Englishman where the employer wants three."

The crowd seemed impressed by this argument, but hooted
when the speaker went into a rhapsody over Ireland, "the land
of morality, of virtue, and piety."

The orator who followed the home rule advocate was a Socialist. He described a visit to the mansion of the Duke of
Westminster at Chester:

"Some of the chairs cost ninety guineas. The ceiling of
one room cost fifteen thousand pounds. Those chairs are
yours. You made them; why do you not keep them? You

get only thirty shillings a week; the duke's income is fifteen thousand pounds a week. Does he earn that money? No; it is yours. Shoemakers work fourteen hours a day making shoes; their own shoes let water in at one end and out at the other. All we want is to keep a fair share of what we ourselves produce. Through all the ages we have built palaces and dwelt in hovels [cries of " Hear, hear !"]. The duke's dogs and horses are better fed than the men who built his palace. I would take away some of the duke's fifteen thousand pounds a week and the Queen's fourteen hundred pounds a day, and add to the four shillings a day of the laborer, the artisan, the mechanic. It is they who earn that money; it is they who should keep it."

The vast crowd that listened to this man's address was composed in great part of hard, honest toilers. They listened attentively, and occasionally cried, " Hear, hear !" in token of approbation. Straws show which way the wind blows. There is an undercurrent in England that in time will come to the surface and sweep away king and dukes and purse-proud employers.

The Socialist speaker had not used tobacco for seventeen years.

" I do not use it," he said, " because I am determined not to help the robbing Government by paying tobacco duty."

He advised workmen to eschew both whiskey and tobacco for the same reason. His advice was good; the reason, however, seemed to me to savor of absurdity.

Perhaps few or none who have accompanied me in these pages on my " Tramp Trip " will care to make such a trip in person. I will nevertheless add a few hints on pedestrianism. The first and most important item is the outfit. Unless that be selected with judgment the trip will seem more like work than pleasure. Two or three pounds more or less are ordinarily of no moment; but when it comes to packing two or three pounds extra on your back five hundred or a thousand miles, it is a matter of considerable moment. If the tour be begun in Italy the outfit should be provided at home. Few tourists walk in Italy, and pedestrian outfits cannot be bought there. The knapsack must be water-proof and limp, so as to permit its being folded when not in use. I tried twenty trunk-stores in New York before finding the right article. There were any number of regular army knapsacks to be had, but they are made on frames always of a certain bulk, empty or filled, and are not desirable.

A knapsack secured, the next thing is to fill it. Absolutely indispensable articles are a compass and map of the country to be visited, a water-proof coat, two suits of underclothing, an extra flannel shirt, and a pocket drinking-cup. This allowance of clothing may seem small, it is, however, enough. In Europe you can give out linen at night to be washed, and receive it again the next day. New articles can always be bought when needed. The map is best obtained abroad. For one dollar I got a map of Italy giving all the national pikes and even small dirt roads. With such a map it is difficult to mistake the way. The rubber-coat is serviceable not only against rain but also cold; for though in sunny Italy, when you climb her hills you will find what Hamlet found at Elsinore—a nipping and an eager air. The ground may be damp, but spread out your rubber-coat, lay your head on your knapsack, and you are independent of chill and dampness. I have often slept thus on the roadside even during a rain. The rubber-coat should be bought in America. I had to pay in Naples four dollars and a half for an indifferent article that in New York would not have cost three dollars.

When the outfit is obtained there remains another essential— a stout pair of legs and a stout will. The first day or two— feet blistered, muscles swollen, limbs stiff and tired—the novice is apt to become disheartened. My second day out from Naples was rainy; the twenty-five-mile walk of the preceding day had made great blisters on my feet. When I limped into a village inn about dark, weary and soaked, I would have taken to the railroad had there been one, and ended my pedestrian trip then and there.   Fortunately, the nearest railroad station was fifteen miles distant.   In two or three days the blisters disappeared, the soreness of the muscles abated, and I felt thoroughly happy.

Only he who has tried it can appreciate the independence of a walking tour.   You make your own time schedule—come when you please and go when you please.   That old castle on the hill to the right looks interesting.   From the train, if seen at all, it is only a glimpse; but the pedestrian sallies gayly forth, ascends the hill at leisure, rummages among the ruins, clambers over the walls, and sees a hundred objects of which the traveller who is hurried from point to point never even dreams.

Once, in the Neapolitan States, as I was walking along, a curious-looking stone pen about three feet high caught my eye.   On investigating, I found, instead of a pen, a singular well thirty or forty feet deep, square in shape, and a kind of stairs in the interior leading down to the bottom.   These stairs or steps consisted merely of stones projecting from the sides of the well, one a foot or so under the other, winding around from side to side until the bottom was reached.   There was no railing, and though the steps were slippery with moss, I ventured to make the descent.   A drink of clear, cold water and a view of the subterranean aqueduct that led from the well rewarded me for my trouble.   This is a sample of the incidents which make a pedestrian trip enjoyable.

Expenses depend upon the willingness of the pedestrian to economize.   A four and a half months' trip through Italy need not cost above a hundred dollars, including steamship passage from and to New York.   The price of a round-trip ticket, steerage, New York to Naples, is fifty dollars; time consumed in making the round trip is six weeks.   On the remaining fifty dollars the pedestrian can, as I have shown, live very comfortably for one hundred days.

Suppose it were desired to make the trip I did, only without any walking, the expense account would stand thus:

New York to Naples, *via* Marseilles—4456 miles............... $25 00
Railroad fare in Italy, taking in Naples, Rome, Florence, Pisa,
   Bologna, Venice, Milan, Como—596 miles.................. 11 11
Railroad fares in Switzerland 7 25
Railroad fares in Germany, taking in Strasbourg, Baden-Baden,
   Heidelberg, Stuttgart, Munich—363 miles.................. 4 30
Railroad and Danube boat fares in Austria, taking in Linz, Vienna,
   Buda-Pesth... 6 65
Buda-Pesth to Constantinople, through Bulgaria............... 12 65
Constantinople to Odessa, Black Sea (steerage) 3 00
Odessa to Berlin, taking in Kijew, Moscow, and St. Petersburg—
   2220 miles 29 36
Berlin to Cologne—364 miles............................... 5 80
Cologne to Paris—306 miles................................ 5 75
Paris to London—255 miles (2d class)....................... 10 00
London to New York....................................... 15 00

Total cost of transportation from New York and back...$135 87

The distance covered is nearly if not quite fourteen thousand miles, seven thousand of which, on steamers, includes subsistence as well as transportation.

A year's subsistence at half a dollar a day amounts to $182.50. Thus the entire cost of a year's trip, embracing every land from Gibraltar to the Bosporus, amounts to $318.37.

I am undecided whether to advise the pedestrian to go alone or to choose a companion. Travelling without a companion is undeniably lonesome; there is, however, this advantage—it compels you to mingle with the people. You learn more about them than if you had a friend to talk with. Although I started alone, I frequently had the company of other travellers. Mr. Arnold Strothotte, of St. Louis, Mr. John Bradley, of Philadelphia, and Mr. George L. Burr, of Ithaca, N. Y. — chance travelling companions—were with me on a portion of my trip. I owe them thanks for lightening a number of what otherwise might have proved very lonesome hours.

After an eleven days' voyage from Liverpool, the steamer *City of Chester* landed at New York, and thus ended my "Tramp Trip."

APPENDIX.

I RECROSSED the ocean in midwinter, and before leaving London had made to order by a fashionable tailor a heavy Melton overcoat. It cost sixteen dollars. In America forty dollars would have been the price.

On arriving in New York, I stood on the platform of a Third Avenue surface car and talked with the driver, a wearied-looking man, his face pinched with cold. His overcoat, like Nanki-Poo, was a "thing of shreds and patches." He looked at my Melton admiringly. Presently he addressed me:

"I would like to ask you, sir," he said, "how much you gave for that coat?"

"Sixteen dollars."

His eyes opened with astonishment.

"Sixteen dollars! Why, this thing of mine cost eighteen. Tell me, where did you get your coat?"

"In London."

The poor fellow turned to his horses sadly disappointed.

Protectionists talk of the horrors of an "inundation" of English goods. As I looked at the shivering car-driver, it seemed a pity he could not be "inundated" by a good warm overcoat. That car-driver works thirteen or fourteen hours a day for two dollars. If his clothing, fuel, and other necessaries were reduced fifty per cent. in price he could live on fifty per cent. less than he now spends; he could afford to work fewer hours and have a little time to pass with his family. But Protectionists oppose such a reduction, on the ground that free-trade means pauper wages, and tariffs mean high wages.

Investigation showed me that that country in Europe with *least* protection pays *most* wages, that free-trade has nothing to do with the poverty of any European State. The *real* cause of poverty in Europe is the great wealth of the few. The masses must always be poor when a few kings and nobles hoard such enormous lion's shares. The Czar of Russia drains his people of $9,125,000 a year, or $25,000 a day. Germany's emperor receives $6,000 a day; the emperor of Austria $10,000. The Sultan of Turkey gets $18,000 a day and five hundred wives to boot. Is it surprising that the people of Turkey are dissatisfied? Is not the costly bauble of monarchy, the oppression of standing armies, the scandalous waste by corrupt officials of the people's money—is not all this in great part responsible for the poverty and suffering of the European masses?

How absurd to attribute the cause to free-trade; free-trade, the very thing which European States have not—the very thing which they know least about! When America has a monarchy and an aristocracy and a royal family alone costing sixty-five million dollars a year—the yearly sum Europe pays directly for royalty—when that day comes, then indeed it may come to pass that the level of American labor will sink to the level of European labor.

England—England with its royalty, its endless red tape, its idle aristocracy, its army of useless officials—England alone of all monarchical forms of governments pays its laboring classes living wages, and England alone has free-trade. America with all its abundance of land, its democratic and comparatively inexpensive government, its sparsity of population—even favored America is pulling behind that little island in the sea; is taking a second place when her natural advantages entitle her to the very foremost seat among the nations. Formerly we had the lion's share of the carrying trade of the world. What have we now? I have been in the ports of almost all the seas on the globe. When I saw an American vessel I stared at it curiously, so great a rarity was it amid the forest of masts of vessels belonging to other countries.

Italy has protective tariffs; skilled Italian mechanics earn only half a dollar a day. England has no tariffs, but English mechanics earn from $1.21 to $1.50 a day.

Germany is heavily protected; a German bricklayer earns sixty cents a day. German weavers and spinners receive sixty cents for a day of twelve to thirteen hours. For a day of only nine to ten hours the unprotected English spinner gets $1.15.

Russia has high tariffs; but the Russian laborer averages one-third less wages than the English laborer.

I have prepared two tables; the one will show at a glance the wages received in protected Italy, Germany, Switzerland, Russia, France, and Belgium as compared with the wages received in free-trade England—the other will show the amount of tariffs imposed upon certain articles by different European States. For the wage-table a claim to only approximate and relative correctness is made; to attempt more in so small a compass would be impossible as well as absurd. Wages differ in the same country, in the same town, in the same shop or factory. It is sufficient to the purpose to give the average, or general figure. For instance, in Berlin bricklayers receive four to five marks a day—ninety-eight cents to one dollar and twenty cents. But, generally speaking, the German brick-layer receives no more than fifty to sixty cents a day; moreover, the cost of living in Berlin is dearer than elsewhere in Germany. I weigh such facts, and in my table state the wages of a German bricklayer as being sixty cents a day.

For Russia the estimates are based upon the time actually en-gaged at work, which is seldom above nine months a year. To de-duct one-fourth from the amount received when actually at work, in order to strike an average for the year, would convey an incor-rect idea, for the Russian *lives* only nine months, the other three he is existing—existing at a cost of from five to six cents a day. Dur-ing the three coldest months of the winter he remains buried in his hovel, making nothing, spending almost nothing—hibernating like the bear. I have for these reasons chosen to regard the Russian year as consisting of but nine months, and the figures in the table are constructed on that basis.

Let the Protectionist read these tables and say why, if protection protects, if tariffs make high wages, the protected States of Europe are in so impoverished a condition. If free-trade causes stagnation and low wages, why is England so far ahead of her protected Euro-pean competitors? so far ahead of her own condition forty years ago, before she had the sense to adopt a free-trade policy?

Until these questions are answered, the thoughtful student can-not but ask himself,

"Does protection protect?"

COMPARATIVE TARIFF TABLE.*

Article.	Tariff in Italy.†	Tariff in Germany.‡	Tariff in Austria.§	Tariff in Switzerland.∣	Tariff in Russia.¶
Woollen shawls	$4.60–$60.00				per lb.........$3.96
Woollen goods		per lb......$ .65	$100.00	$3.86–$9.72	" 1.08
Wall-paper			55.00		
Blankets	22.00		12.50	2.32– 5.80	
Wefs of yarn			$27.50– 60.00		
Leather, tanned	5.00				per pood**....10.80
Carpets	12.00		25.00	3.86– 9.72	" lb. 45
Furs			250.00		
Silks, laces, and fichus	per 2¼ lbs, 1.60		45.00		
Velvet and velvet materials, as buttons, etc			12.50		
Oil-cloth				3.86	
Silk manufactures	per 2¼ lbs, 1.20			7.70–11.58	
Salt meats, canned meats, etc		4.76		.77	per pood, 36.7 lbs,.96
Perfumery				13.51	
Ropes, cords, etc			2.50		per pood 53
Paints				5.79	
Tulle				7.70	per lb....$ .54–2.64
Window-glass				1.54– 4.82	10%, and per pood, 4.00
Mirror-glass				3.08– 7.72	
Wooden-wares				9.65	
Baskets				1.54– 7.72	
Gloves				19.30	
Boots and shoes				6.75–15.44	
Watch materials and watches		each...$ .3⅓–.71	17.50	3.08	
Clocks			37.50	5.79	
Locomotives			37.50	1.93	
Railroad carriages				.08	
Boats				.08	
Iron, forged, rolled, or drawn		per ton, 7.50– 37.50		.11	
Rails				.33	
Wire rope				.25	
Wire, simple, leaded, coppered, etc			3.00	.77	
Sheet iron				.58	
Cast-iron ware, wrought iron, etc		per ton, 7.50– 37.50		.49– 1.15	per pood 60–1.20

Article			
Iron pipes, gas pipes, etc.			1.35– 5.79
Wheat	.72		
Cotton thread	11.42– 16.66	.50	
Laces and embroideries	83.30		11.58
Matches and tapers	2.38	2.50	
Yarns, cords, and spinning materials	5.71		
Ornamental feathers, dressed	214.20		
Horn buttons	23.80		
Ready-made wearing apparel	160.65–285.60	40%	15.44–19.30
Artificial flowers	214.20	200.00	
Linen yarn and goods	11.19– 16.66	17.50	20%
Linen ticking	14.28– 28.56		
Thread lace and embroidered wefts and laces	190.40	125.00	528.00
Precious stones	14.28	15.00	
Cutlery	each....2.38		each....7.72
Axes	2.38	10.00	each....19
Hardware in general, etc.		75.00	
Ivory goods, toys, etc.	per lb.....28	7.00–30.00	per lb....1.16– 3.88 44
Cotton yarns and goods		each 50	5.79–19.30
Hats	each 7.14		12 0–4.38
Oxen			
Embroidered linen goods		125.00	
Rubber goods		7.50– 25.00	
Nails		.50– 3.50	
Umbrellas			7.72–11.58
Pies			per pood.....4.80
Coal			per ton.....1.00

* Tariff is imposed per 220 pounds, except where stated to be otherwise.

† The lira computed at 20 cents.

‡ The mark computed at 24 cents.

§ The gold florin computed at 50 cents.

‖ Franc computed at 20 cents.

¶ The ruble computed at 50 cents.

** The Russian pood is 16.38 kilograms, and equals 36.7 lbs.

N.B.—A blank space opposite the name of an article does not necessarily mean that that article is not taxed; the author was able to obtain only a *partial* list of articles subject to tariff taxation in the several States mentioned.

COMPARATIVE WAGE TABLE.

Daily Wages.

OCCUPATION.	In Italy.	In Germany.	In Switzerland.	In Russia.	In France.	In England.	In Belgium.
Boot-makers	$.40-$.80	$.84-$.96	$.60-$1.00	$.75-$1.20	$.79	$1.21-$1.40	$.90
Brick-burners		.60				1.21	
Laborers	.20-.40	.24-.48	.40-.60	.21-.50	.66	.82	
Bricklayers	.50-.70	.60-.72	.70-.90	.75-1.00		1.81	.55-$.80
Blacksmiths	.60-.75	.60-.72	.75	.87-1.18	.80-$.92	1.42	.70-.90
Carpenters and joiners	.40-.60	.72-.96	1.00	.87-1.32	.90	1.34-1.54	.62-.80
Engineers		.72-.84	.90-1.00	.94-1.32		1.02	.80-.90
Engine-drivers		.96			1.00-1.47	1.50	.93-1.08
Gas-fitters		.51-				1.50	
Glaziers		.48-.72			.80-1.00	1.15	.65
Painters and paper-hangers	.76	.65-.72	.90-1.20	.81	.80-1.00	1.17-1.50	.68-1.00
Plumbers	.60-.65	.60		.91	.80-1.20	1.27	.40
Weavers, women	.20-.40	.37½	.40		.50-.60	.69	.60
" men	.25-.50	.60	.66		.80-1.00	1.20-1.42	
Carders and spinners, men		.48-.84		.40	.40-.60	1.20-1.80	.40
" " women		.43		.33¾	.50-.70	.90	
Spinners, women		.37½	.40	.25	.60-.80	.90	.60
" men		.60-.72	.66	.36		1.15	
Coat-makers, men		.96-1.92			.80-1.20	1.33-3.33	
" cutters		.96-1.92			.80-.90	2.00-5.00	
Pantaloon-makers, men		.72-.84				1.41-4.10	
" women		.60-.72	1.00-1.15			1.30-2.66	
Machinists	.50-.80	.51-.84				1.50-2.30	
Firemen		.60-.72		.30-.50		.81-1.20	
Section hands		.60	.50-.60	.36-.50		1.00-1.30	.30-.55
Paper-mill hands		.36-.42	.46-.60	.50		.61-.96	.60-1.90
" skilled		.52-.78	.44-.80		.92	.81-1.24	.55
Bakers	.65	.60	1.00	.50-1.00	.80	1.08-1.16	.60-.75
Printers	.50-.76	.80	.80	.30-.50		1.00-1.50	2.00-3.00
Glass-blowers, skilled	.80-1.50	.36-.60	.90-1.00	1.00		1.00-1.68	.55-.70
" factory hands	.50-.60	.60-.84	1.20-1.50				.85
Tailors	.70-1.00	.48-.96	.60-1.20		.70-1.20	1.37	
Mechanics, skilled	.50-.80	.36-.72			1.00-1.60	.87-.96	
" ordinary	.40-.60				.80-1.20		
Shepherds	.02-.07	.48-.96	.60-1.50	1.00			
Watch-makers		.61	.60-.70	.33¾	.73-1.10		
Tinsmiths	.60					1.00-1.21	

VALUABLE AND INTERESTING WORKS

FOR

PUBLIC & PRIVATE LIBRARIES,

PUBLISHED BY HARPER & BROTHERS, NEW YORK.

MACAULAY'S ENGLAND. The History of England from the Accession of James II. By THOMAS BABINGTON MACAULAY. New Edition, from New Electrotype Plates. 5 vols., in a Box, 8vo, Cloth, with Paper Labels, Uncut Edges and Gilt Tops, $10 00; Sheep, $12 50; Half Calf, $21 25. Sold only in Sets. Cheap Edition, 5 vols., 12mo, Cloth, $2 50.

MACAULAY'S MISCELLANEOUS WORKS. The Miscellaneous Works of Lord Macaulay. From New Electrotype Plates. 5 vols., in a Box, 8vo, Cloth, with Paper Labels, Uncut Edges and Gilt Tops, $10 00; Sheep, $12 50; Half Calf, $21 25. Sold only in Sets.

HUME'S ENGLAND. History of England, from the Invasion of Julius Cæsar to the Abdication of James II., 1688. By DAVID HUME. New and Elegant Library Edition, from New Electrotype Plates. 6 vols., in a Box, 8vo, Cloth, with Paper Labels, Uncut Edges and Gilt Tops, $12 00; Sheep, $15 00; Half Calf, $25 50. Sold only in Sets. Popular Edition, 6 vols., in a Box, 12mo, Cloth, $3 00.

GIBBON'S ROME. The History of the Decline and Fall of the Roman Empire. By EDWARD GIBBON. With Notes by Dean MILMAN, M. GUIZOT, and Dr. WILLIAM SMITH. New Edition, from New Electrotype Plates. 6 vols., 8vo, Cloth, with Paper Labels, Uncut Edges and Gilt Tops, $12 00; Sheep, $15 00; Half Calf, $25 50. Sold only in Sets. Popular Edition, 6 vols., in a Box, 12mo, Cloth, $3 00; Sheep, $6 00.

GOLDSMITH'S WORKS. The Works of Oliver Goldsmith. Edited by Peter Cunningham, F.S.A. From New Electrotype Plates. 4 vols., 8vo, Cloth, Paper Labels, Uncut Edges and Gilt Tops, $8 00; Sheep, $10 00; Half Calf, $17 00.

MOTLEY'S LETTERS. The Correspondence of John Lothrop Motley, D.C.L., Author of "The United Netherlands," "John of Barneveld," "The Rise of the Dutch Republic," etc. Edited by George William Curtis. With Portrait. Two Volumes, 8vo, Cloth, $7 00.

MOTLEY'S DUTCH REPUBLIC. The Rise of the Dutch Republic. A History. By John Lothrop Motley, LL.D., D.C.L. With a Portrait of William of Orange. Cheap Edition, 3 vols., in a Box. 8vo, Cloth, with Paper Labels, Uncut Edges and Gilt Tops, $6 00; Sheep, $7 50; Half Calf, $12 75. Sold only in Sets. Library Edition, 3 vols., 8vo, Cloth, $10 50.

MOTLEY'S UNITED NETHERLANDS. History of the United Netherlands: From the Death of William the Silent to the Twelve Years' Truce — 1584–1609. With a full View of the English-Dutch Struggle against Spain, and of the Origin and Destruction of the Spanish Armada. By John Lothrop Motley, LL.D., D.C.L. Portraits. Cheap Edition, 4 vols., in a Box, 8vo, Cloth, with Paper Labels, Uncut Edges and Gilt Tops, $8 00; Sheep, $10 00; Half Calf, $17 00. Sold only in Sets. Original Library Edition, 4 vols., 8vo, Cloth, $14 00.

MOTLEY'S JOHN OF BARNEVELD. The Life and Death of John of Barneveld, Advocate of Holland. With a View of the Primary Causes and Movements of the "Thirty Years' War." By John Lothrop Motley, LL.D., D.C.L. Illustrated. Cheap Edition, 2 vols., in a Box, 8vo, Cloth, with Paper Labels, Uncut Edges and Gilt Tops, $4 00; Sheep, $5 00; Half Calf, $8 50. Sold only in Sets. Original Library Edition, 2 vols., 8vo, Cloth, $7 00.

HILDRETH'S UNITED STATES. History of the United States. First Series: From the Discovery of the Continent to the Organization of the Government under the Federal Constitution. Second Series: From the Adoption of the Federal Constitution to the End of the Sixteenth Congress. By Richard Hildreth. Popular Edition, 6 vols., in a Box, 8vo, Cloth, with Paper Labels, Uncut Edges and Gilt Tops, $12 00; Sheep, $15 00; Half Calf, $25 50. Sold only in Sets.

STORMONTH'S ENGLISH DICTIONARY. A Dictionary of the English Language, Pronouncing, Etymological, and Explanatory: embracing Scientific and other Terms, Numerous Familiar Terms, and a Copious Selection of Old English Words. By the Rev. JAMES STORMONTH. The Pronunciation Revised by the Rev. P. H. PHELP, M.A. Imperial 8vo, Cloth, $6 00; Half Roan, $7 00; Full Sheep, $7 50. (New Edition.)

PARTON'S CARICATURE. Caricature and Other Comic Art, in All Times and Many Lands. By JAMES PARTON. 203 Illustrations. 8vo, Cloth, Uncut Edges and Gilt Tops, $5 00; Half Calf, $7 25.

DU CHAILLU'S LAND OF THE MIDNIGHT SUN. Summer and Winter Journeys in Sweden, Norway, Lapland, and Northern Finland. By PAUL B. DU CHAILLU. Illustrated. 2 vols., 8vo, Cloth, $7 50; Half Calf, $12 00.

LOSSING'S CYCLOPÆDIA OF UNITED STATES HISTORY. From the Aboriginal Period to 1876. By B. J. Lossing, LL.D. Illustrated by 2 Steel Portraits and over 1000 Engravings. 2 vols., Royal 8vo, Cloth, $10 00; Sheep, $12 00; Half Morocco, $15 00. (*Sold by Subscription only.*)

LOSSING'S FIELD-BOOK OF THE REVOLUTION. Pictorial Field-Book of the Revolution; or, Illustrations by Pen and Pencil of the History, Biography, Scenery, Relics, and Traditions of the War for Independence. By BENSON J. LOSSING. 2 vols., 8vo, Cloth, $14 00; Sheep or Roan, $15 00; Half Calf, $18 00.

LOSSING'S FIELD-BOOK OF THE WAR OF 1812. Pictorial Field-Book of the War of 1812; or, Illustrations by Pen and Pencil of the History, Biography, Scenery, Relics, and Traditions of the last War for American Independence. By BENSON J. LOSSING. With several hundred Engravings. 1088 pages, 8vo, Cloth, $7 00; Sheep or Roan, $8 50; Half Calf, $10 00.

MÜLLER'S POLITICAL HISTORY OF RECENT TIMES (1816–1875). With Special Reference to Germany. By WILLIAM MÜLLER. Translated, with an Appendix covering the Period from 1876 to 1881, by the Rev. JOHN P. PETERS, Ph.D. 12mo, Cloth, $3 00.

TREVELYAN'S LIFE OF MACAULAY. The Life and Letters of Lord Macaulay. By his Nephew, G. Otto Trevelyan, M.P. With Portrait on Steel. 2 vols., 8vo, Cloth, Uncut Edges and Gilt Tops, $5 00; Sheep, $6 00; Half Calf, $9 50. Popular Edition, 2 vols. in one, 12mo, Cloth, $1 75.

TREVELYAN'S LIFE OF FOX. The Early History of Charles James Fox. By George Otto Trevelyan. 8vo, Cloth, Uncut Edges and Gilt Tops, $2 50; Half Calf, $4 75.

WRITINGS AND SPEECHES OF SAMUEL J. TILDEN. Edited by John Bigelow. 2 vols., 8vo, Cloth, Gilt Tops and Uncut Edges, $6 00 per set.

GENERAL DIX'S MEMOIRS. Memoirs of John Adams Dix. Compiled by his Son, Morgan Dix. With Five Steel-plate Portraits. 2 vols., 8vo, Cloth, Gilt Tops and Uncut Edges, $5 00.

HUNT'S MEMOIR OF MRS. LIVINGSTON. A Memoir of Mrs. Edward Livingston. With Letters hitherto Unpublished. By Louise Livingston Hunt. 12mo, Cloth, $1 25.

GEORGE ELIOT'S LIFE. George Eliot's Life, Related in her Letters and Journals. Arranged and Edited by her Husband, J. W. Cross. Portraits and Illustrations. In Three Volumes. 12mo, Cloth, $3 75. New Edition, with Fresh Matter. (Uniform with "Harper's Library Edition" of George Eliot's Works.)

PEARS'S FALL OF CONSTANTINOPLE. The Fall of Constantinople. Being the Story of the Fourth Crusade. By Edwin Pears, LL.B. 8vo, Cloth, $2 50.

RANKE'S UNIVERSAL HISTORY. The Oldest Historical Group of Nations and the Greeks. By Leopold von Ranke. Edited by G. W. Prothero, Fellow and Tutor of King's College, Cambridge. Vol. I. 8vo, Cloth, $2 50.

LIFE AND TIMES OF THE REV. SYDNEY SMITH. A Sketch of the Life and Times of the Rev. Sydney Smith. Based on Family Documents and the Recollections of Personal Friends. By Stuart J. Reid. With Steel-plate Portrait and Illustrations. 8vo, Cloth, $3 00.

STANLEY'S THROUGH THE DARK CONTINENT. Through the Dark Continent; or, The Sources of the Nile, Around the Great Lakes of Equatorial Africa, and Down the Livingstone River to the Atlantic Ocean. 149 Illustrations and 10 Maps. By H. M. STANLEY. 2 vols., 8vo, Cloth, $10 00; Sheep, $12 00; Half Morocco, $15 00.

STANLEY'S CONGO. The Congo and the Founding of its Free State, a Story of Work and Exploration. With over One Hundred Full-page and smaller Illustrations, Two Large Maps, and several smaller ones. By H. M. STANLEY. 2 vols., 8vo, Cloth, $10 00; Sheep, $12 00; Half Morocco, $15 00.

GREEN'S ENGLISH PEOPLE. History of the English People. By JOHN RICHARD GREEN, M.A. With Maps. 4 vols., 8vo, Cloth, $10 00; Sheep, $12 00; Half Calf, $19 00.

GREEN'S MAKING OF ENGLAND. The Making of England. By JOHN RICHARD GREEN. With Maps. 8vo, Cloth, $2 50; Sheep, $3 00; Half Calf, $3 75.

GREEN'S CONQUEST OF ENGLAND. The Conquest of England. By JOHN RICHARD GREEN. With Maps. 8vo, Cloth, $2 50; Sheep, $3 00; Half Calf, $3 75.

BAKER'S ISMAÏLIA: a Narrative of the Expedition to Central Africa for the Suppression of the Slave-trade, organized by Ismaïl, Khedive of Egypt. By Sir SAMUEL W. BAKER. With Maps, Portraits, and Illustrations. 8vo, Cloth, $5 00; Half Calf, $7 25.

ENGLISH MEN OF LETTERS. Edited by JOHN MORLEY.
The following volumes are now ready. Others will follow:

JOHNSON. By L. Stephen.—GIBBON. By J. C. Morison.—SCOTT. By R. H. Hutton.—SHELLEY. By J. A. Symonds.—GOLDSMITH. By W. Black.—HUME. By Professor Huxley.—DEFOE. By W. Minto.—BURNS. By Principal Shairp.—SPENSER. By R. W. Church.—THACKERAY. By A. Trollope.—BURKE. By J. Morley.—MILTON. By M. Pattison.—SOUTHEY. By E. Dowden.—CHAUCER. By A. W. Ward.—BUNYAN. By J. A. Froude.—COWPER. By G. Smith.—POPE. By L. Stephen.—BYRON. By J. Nichols.—LOCKE. By T. Fowler.—WORDSWORTH. By F. W. H. Myers.—HAWTHORNE. By Henry James, Jr.—DRYDEN. By G. Saintsbury.—LANDOR. By S. Colvin.—DE QUINCEY. By D. Masson.—LAMB. By A. Ainger.—BENTLEY. By R. C. Jebb.—DICKENS. By A. W. Ward.—GRAY. By E. W. Gosse.—SWIFT. By L. Stephen.—STERNE. By H. D. Traill.—MACAULAY. By J. C. Morison.—FIELDING. By A. Dobson.—SHERIDAN. By Mrs. Oliphant.—ADDISON. By W. J. Courthope.—BACON. By R. W. Church.—COLERIDGE. By H. D. Traill.—SIR PHILIP SIDNEY. By J. A. Symonds.—KEATS. By S. Colvin. 12mo, Cloth, 75 cents per volume.

POPULAR EDITION. 36 volumes in 12, $12 00.

COLERIDGE'S WORKS. The Complete Works of Samuel Taylor Coleridge. With an Introductory Essay upon his Philosophical and Theological Opinions. Edited by Professor W. G. T. SHEDD. With Steel Portrait, and an Index. 7 vols., 12mo, Cloth, $2 00 per volume; $12 00 per set; Half Calf, $24 25.

REBER'S MEDIÆVAL ART. History of Mediæval Art. By Dr. FRANZ VON REBER. Translated and Augmented by Joseph Thacher Clarke. With 422 Illustrations, and a Glossary of Technical Terms. 8vo, Cloth, $5 00.

REBER'S HISTORY OF ANCIENT ART. History of Ancient Art. By Dr. FRANZ VON REBER. Revised by the Author. Translated and Augmented by Joseph Thacher Clarke. With 310 Illustrations and a Glossary of Technical Terms. 8vo, Cloth, $3 50.

NEWCOMB'S ASTRONOMY. Popular Astronomy. By SIMON NEWCOMB, LL.D. With 112 Engravings, and 5 Maps of the Stars. 8vo, Cloth, $2 50; School Edition, 12mo, Cloth, $1 30.

DAVIS'S INTERNATIONAL LAW. Outlines of International Law, with an Account of its Origin and Sources, and of its Historical Development. By GEO. B. DAVIS, U.S.A., Assistant Professor of Law at the United States Military Academy. Crown 8vo, Cloth, $2 00.

CESNOLA'S CYPRUS. Cyprus: its Ancient Cities, Tombs, and Temples. A Narrative of Researches and Excavations during Ten Years' Residence in that Island. By L. P. DI CESNOLA. With Portrait, Maps, and 400 Illustrations. 8vo, Cloth, Extra, Uncut Edges and Gilt Tops, $7 50.

TENNYSON'S COMPLETE POEMS. The Complete Poetical Works of Alfred, Lord Tennyson. With an Introductory Sketch by Anne Thackeray Ritchie. With Portraits and Illustrations. 8vo, Extra Cloth, Bevelled, Gilt Edges, $2 50.

LEA'S HISTORY OF THE INQUISITION. History of the Inquisition of the Middle Ages. By HENRY CHARLES LEA. Three Volumes. 8vo, Cloth, Uncut Edges and Gilt Tops, $3 00 per vol.

FLAMMARION'S ATMOSPHERE. Translated from the French of CAMILLE FLAMMARION. With 10 Chromo-Lithographs and 86 Wood-cuts. 8vo, Cloth, $6 00; Half Calf, $8 25.

CHARNAY'S ANCIENT CITIES OF THE NEW WORLD. The Ancient Cities of the New World: Being Voyages and Explorations in Mexico and Central America, from 1857 to 1882. By DÉSIRÉ CHARNAY. Translated by J. Gonino and Helen S. Conant. Illustrations and Map. Royal 8vo, Ornamental Cloth, Uncut Edges, Gilt Tops, $6 00.

GROTE'S HISTORY OF GREECE. 12 vols., 12mo, Cloth, $18 00; Sheep, $22 80; Half Calf, $39 00.

"THE FRIENDLY EDITION" of Shakespeare's Works. Edited by W. J. ROLFE. In 20 vols. Illustrated. 16mo, Gilt Tops and Uncut Edges. Sheets, $27 00; Cloth, $30 00; Half Calf, $60 00 per Set.

GIESELER'S ECCLESIASTICAL HISTORY. A Text-Book of Church History. By Dr. JOHN C. L. GIESELER. Translated from the Fourth Revised German Edition. Revised and Edited by Rev. HENRY B. SMITH, D.D. Vols. I., II., III., and IV., 8vo, Cloth, $2 25 each; Vol. V., 8vo, Cloth, $3 00. Complete Sets, 5 vols., Sheep, $14 50; Half Calf, $23 25.

LIVINGSTONE'S ZAMBESI. Narrative of an Expedition to the Zambesi and its Tributaries, and of the Discovery of the Lakes Shirwa and Nyassa, 1858 to 1864. By DAVID and CHARLES LIVINGSTONE. Illustrated. 8vo, Cloth, $5 00; Sheep, $5 50; Half Calf, $7 25.

LIVINGSTONE'S LAST JOURNALS. The Last Journals of David Livingstone, in Central Africa, from 1865 to his Death. Continued by a Narrative of his Last Moments, obtained from his Faithful Servants Chuma and Susi. By HORACE WALLER. With Portrait, Maps, and Illustrations. 8vo, Cloth, $5 00; Sheep, $6 00.

CURTIS'S LIFE OF BUCHANAN. Life of James Buchanan, Fifteenth President of the United States. By GEORGE TICKNOR CURTIS. With Two Steel-Plate Portraits. 2 vols., 8vo, Cloth, Uncut Edges and Gilt Tops, $6 00.

GRIFFIS'S JAPAN. The Mikado's Empire: Book I. History of Japan, from 660 B.C. to 1872 A.D. Book II. Personal Experiences, Observations, and Studies in Japan, from 1870 to 1874. With Two Supplementary Chapters: Japan in 1883, and Japan in 1886. By W. E. GRIFFIS. Copiously Illustrated. 8vo, Cloth, $4 00; Half Calf, $6 25.

THE POETS AND POETRY OF SCOTLAND: From the Earliest to the Present Time. Comprising Characteristic Selections from the Works of the more Noteworthy Scottish Poets, with Biographical and Critical Notices. By James Grant Wilson. With Portraits on Steel. 2 vols., 8vo, Cloth, $10 00; Gilt Edges, $11 00.

SCHLIEMANN'S ILIOS. Ilios, the City and Country of the Trojans. A Narrative of the Most Recent Discoveries and Researches made on the Plain of Troy. By Dr. Henry Schliemann. Maps, Plans, and Illustrations. Imperial 8vo, Illuminated Cloth, $12 00; Half Morocco, $15 00.

SCHLIEMANN'S TROJA. Troja. Results of the Latest Researches and Discoveries on the Site of Homer's Troy, and in the Heroic Tumuli and other Sites, made in the Year 1882, and a Narrative of a Journey in the Troad in 1881. By Dr. Henry Schliemann. Preface by Professor A. H. Sayce. With Wood-cuts, Maps, and Plans. 8vo, Cloth, $7 50; Half Morocco, $10 00.

SCHWEINFURTH'S HEART OF AFRICA. Three Years' Travels and Adventures in the Unexplored Regions of the Centre of Africa — from 1868 to 1871. By Georg Schweinfurth. Translated by Ellen E. Frewer. Illustrated. 2 vols., 8vo, Cloth, $8 00.

SMILES'S HISTORY OF THE HUGUENOTS. The Huguenots: their Settlements, Churches, and Industries in England and Ireland. By Samuel Smiles. With an Appendix relating to the Huguenots in America. Crown, 8vo, Cloth, $2 00.

SMILES'S HUGUENOTS AFTER THE REVOCATION. The Huguenots in France after the Revocation of the Edict of Nantes; with a Visit to the Country of the Vaudois. By Samuel Smiles. Crown 8vo, Cloth, $2 00.

SMILES'S LIFE OF THE STEPHENSONS. The Life of George Stephenson, and of his Son, Robert Stephenson; comprising, also, a History of the Invention and Introduction of the Railway Locomotive. By Samuel Smiles. Illustrated. 8vo, Cloth, $3 00.